STUDIES IN HISTORY, ECONOMICS AND PUBLIC LAW

Edited by the
**FACULTY OF POLITICAL SCIENCE
OF COLUMBIA UNIVERSITY**

Number 574

JUDICIAL REVIEW OF LEGISLATION IN NEW YORK
1906–1938

BY

FRANKLIN A. SMITH

JUDICIAL REVIEW OF LEGISLATION IN NEW YORK
1906-1938

BY

FRANKLIN A. SMITH

AMS PRESS
NEW YORK

COLUMBIA UNIVERSITY
STUDIES IN THE
SOCIAL SCIENCES

574

The Series was formerly known as
Studies in History, Economics and Public Law.

Reprinted with the permission of Columbia University Press
From the edition of 1952, New York
First AMS EDITION published 1968
Manufactured in the United States of America

Library of Congress Catalogue Card Number: 71-76658

AMS PRESS, INC.
NEW YORK, N. Y. 10003

TO MY PARENTS

ACKNOWLEDGMENTS

I WISH to thank Professor Edward S. Corwin of Princeton who graciously took the time to read the manuscript of this book. Dean John A. Krout and Professor Dumas Malone also read the copy and made helpful suggestions, as did Professors Robert Lynd, Arthur MacMahon, Allan Nevins, and Karl Polanyi.

Assistance was given me as well by Professors Henry Steele Commager, Oliver P. Field, William Anderson, and by Louis B. Boudin. To the librarians, especially Miss Margaret Hall, who rendered valuable service, I express my appreciation.

Baker, Voorhis and Company have kindly granted permission to quote from *The Powers of the New York Court of Appeals* by Henry Cohen.

To all the others who in any way contributed help, I am indeed grateful.

FRANKLIN ABBOTT SMITH.

FOREWORD

THE need for a study such as this becomes apparent after a survey of the reasons for embarking upon it.

In 1944 Professor Oliver P. Field, after completing a project of his own covering certain aspects of judicial review, commented as follows:

> The historical and theoretical phases of judicial review of legislation have been discussed by Professor Charles G. Haines in his *The American Doctrine of Judicial Supremacy,* and the legal effects of holding a statute invalid, in so far as that affects the disposition of pending cases or subsequent cases under the invalidated statutes, have been discussed in my *The Effect of an Unconstitutional Statute.* Numerous other authors have discussed various phases of judicial review, but with the exception of Judge Edgerton, then Professor of Law at Cornell University, who made a detailed study of the cases and statutes involved in the Supreme Court's review of Congressional statutes in the *Cornell Law Quarterly,* 1937 vol. 22, pp. 299-348, no intensive study has been made of state or federal legislation to ascertain the operative facts with respect to its application. This is not because such a study was not thought of, but probably because it involved such an enormous amount of work and outlay of money that few individuals could have undertaken the task on their own initiative.[1]

Over a century has elapsed in which the constitutionality of thousands of laws has been passed upon by the state and federal courts. These decisions, especially the more controversial, have been followed by periods of excitement, in which sweeping and dogmatic generalizations of the most contradictory nature have been made with reference both to the theory and practice of the celebrated institution known briefly as judicial review. The basis in known fact for many of these generalizations has been slim indeed. Until relatively recent

[1] Field, Oliver P., *Judicial Review of Legislation in Ten Selected States* (Bloomington, Indiana, 1943), pp. 8-9.

times the gathering of facts concerning the institution itself, as distinguished from the general constitutional history of which it forms so large a part, has been largely in the hands of those who had axes to grind. Nevertheless much valuable factual material has been gathered, particularly since 1886, when George Bancroft started the long line of modern works on this subject. The names of Coxe and Meigs, of Warren and Boudin, of Beard and Dougherty, of Davis and Roe and Ransom attest to the interests and industry of students of the subject since that date. Systematic and scholarly studies have come from the pens of Professors Haines and Field mentioned above, of Professors Edward S. Corwin, Andrew C. McLaughlin, Benjamin F. Wright and Robert K. Carr, to mention some of the most prominent.[2]

2 Bancroft's pamphlet, *A Plea for the Constitution of the United States of America Wounded in the House of Its Guardians* (New York, 1886), was provoked by the decision in the last of the Legal Tender cases, Juilliard *v.* Greenman (1883) 110 U. S. 421. The names of the more important works by the authors listed in the text are:

    Coxe, Brinton. *An Essay on Judicial power and Unconstitutional Legislation; being a commentary on parts of the Constitution of the United States* (Philadelphia, 1893).

    Meigs, William M. " The Relation of the Judiciary to the Constitution." *American Law Review*, 19: 174-203 (March-April, 1885).

    The Relation of the Judiciary to the Constitution (New York, 1919).

    Warren, Charles. *The Supreme Court in United States History* (Boston, 1922). Three volumes.

    Boudin, Louis B. " Government by Judiciary," *Political Science Quarterly*, 26: 238-270 (June, 1911).

    Government by Judiciary (New York, 1931). Two volumes.

    Beard, Charles A. " The Supreme Court: Usurper or Grantee? ", *Political Science Quarterly*, 27: 1-35 (March, 1912).

    The Supreme Court and the Constitution (New York, 1912).

    Dougherty, John Hampden. *Power of Federal Judiciary over Legislation: its origin; the power to set aside laws; boundaries of the power; judicial independence; existing evils and remedies* (New York and London, 1912).

    Davis, Horace A. *The Judicial Veto* (Boston and New York, 1914).

    Roe, Gilbert E. *Our Judicial Oligarchy* (New York, 1912).

    Ransom, William L. *Majority Rule and the Judiciary; an examination of current proposals for constitutional change affecting the relation of the courts to legislation* (New York, 1912).

These studies have generally concentrated upon the operations of the Supreme Court. In the search for state precedents for federal judicial review, and in the consideration of the Supreme Court's review of state acts, it is true that cases have necessarily been studied. A number of the outstanding state cases have also been examined because of their general importance, such as the Ives case in New York. However, only two full length studies of judicial review in the states are known to exist. One of these is the unpublished master's thesis of Joseph H. Hixson, which is a study of court decisions holding acts unconstitutional in Ohio prior to 1922.[3] The other is Margaret Nelson's dissertation on judicial review in Virginia, which treats both decisions sustaining and voiding state acts up to 1928.[4]

Since the material for this study had of necessity to be restricted to a part of the whole, it may be asked why New York was chosen and why for these particular years. The answer lies in the importance of New York both culturally and politically.

Haines, Charles Grove. *The American Doctrine of Judicial Supremacy* (New York, 1914), Second edition (Berkeley, California, 1932).

Field, Oliver P. *The Effect of an Unconstitutional Statute* (Minneapolis, 1935).

Corwin, Edward S. "The Establishment of Judicial Review." *Michigan Law Review*, 9: 102-125, 283-316 (December, 1910 and February, 1911).
"The Basic Doctrine of American Constitutional Law," *Michigan Law Review*, 12: 247-276 (February, 1914).
The Doctrine of Judicial Review (Princeton, 1914).
Court over Constitution: a Study of Judicial Review as an Instrument of Popular Government (Princeton, 1938).

McLaughlin, Andrew C. *The Courts, the Constitution and Parties; studies in constitutional history and politics* (Chicago, 1912).

Wright, Benjamin F. *The Growth of American Constitutional Law* (Boston, 1942).

Carr, Robert K. *The Supreme Court and Judicial Review* (New York, 1942).

3 Joseph H. Hixson, "The Judicial Veto in Ohio," thesis (M. S.) (Ohio State University, 1922).

4 Margaret V. Nelson, *A Study of Judicial Review in Virginia* (New York, 1947).

Ever since the census of 1820, New York State has led the Union in population. It has, furthermore, been preëminent in commerce and in certain lines of industry, as well as in the arts. It has been a key state politically, containing within its borders the most populous city in the land, and what is referred to as upstate New York, with its agricultural, particularly dairying, interest. The decisions of its courts have been highly respected since the days of Chancellor Kent by other judicial bodies, including the United States Supreme Court, and its contributions to the bar, the bench and to American political life in general, from Alexander Hamilton to Thomas E. Dewey, are well known. It therefore seems of great interest and significance to examine the operation of judicial review in so important a state. The importance of New York, however, is matched by the number of cases arising in its courts in which judicial review has been involved. A study dealing with all of these cases in detail would demand the issuance of a tome or tomes of mammoth proportions. Consequently it appeared desirable to concentrate on a limited period of time. In 1917 a most useful article appeared by Professor Corwin on " The Establishment of Judicial Review in New York." [5] This was based upon the five volume *Constitutional History of New York* by Charles Z. Lincoln published in 1906,[6] Volume IV of which contained the Constitution of 1894, as amended to 1905, with each article annotated to that date. All the cases cited in Lincoln and in the Corwin article, which had reference to the constitutionality of acts of the state legislature, have been examined. The only treatment known of judicial review since 1905 is Chapter V of Volume VII of the series issued in 1938 by the New York State Constitutional Convention Committee, for the guidance and instruction of the delegates to the convention assembled in New York in that year. This chapter covered very summarily those decisions holding acts unconstitutional from 1914

[5] *Michigan Law Review*, 15: 281-306 (February, 1917).

[6] Charles Z. Lincoln, *Constitutional History of New York*, Volumes 1-5 (New York, 1906).

to 1937. Though its value is not to be discounted, it is unfortunately marred by minor inaccuracies and omissions, which indicate carelessness of a seemingly avoidable nature.[7] The examination made by this writer was not based primarily on that list of cases.

1906, then, seemed a good year to begin the study. 1938, in which a constitutional convention was last held, has been chosen as the most suitable landmark for a terminus. The generation between saw notable changes in New York State. The Constitution drawn up by the Convention of 1915 was rejected by the voters, but a number of amendments similar to proposals in that document, dealing with such topics as Home Rule, Administrative Reorganization and the Executive Budget, were later adopted. In the intervening period New York grew from a population of less than nine million to over twelve million. A substantial portion of this increase was contributed by immigrants who came to this country in large numbers before the Federal Act of Restriction was passed in 1924. The industrial production of the state increased correspondingly, though not without fluctuations, as a few figures cited here will indicate.

	Number of Establishments	Value of Production	Cost of Materials
1904	37,194	$2,488,345,579.	$1,348,603,286.
1919	49,330	$8,867,004,906.	$4,943,213,919.
1929	39,273	$9,892,763,168.	$4,935,505,313.
1937	29,749	$7,314,446,524.	$3,998,266,070.

	Number of Wage Earners	Wages in the Year
1904	856,947	$430,014,851.
1919	1,228,130	$1,458,206,804.
1929	1,104,335	$1,648,379,433.
1937	995,658	$1,236,048,186.[8]

[7] New York State Constitutional Convention Committee, Vol. VII, *Problems Relating to Legislative Organization and Powers* (Albany, 1938).

[8] United States Bureau of the Census, quoted in the World Almanac and Book of Facts, 1941 (New York, 1941). The results of a study made in 1923, showing New York's stature as the leading industrial state, may be found in National Industrial Conference Board, *Industrial Progress and Regulatory Legislation in New York State* (New York, 1927), pp. 9 ff.

Other developments of great importance, such as the inventions which contributed to the increase in wealth already mentioned, affected the daily life of the people. The automobile and radio are two prominent examples of such technological progress. Events of national moment such as the first World War and the Russian revolutions of 1917 and their aftermath, constitutional amendments, such as prohibition and woman suffrage, and the depression of 1929, all made themselves felt in the province of the legislator and the judge. At the same time certain factors remained constant throughout this period. The major outline of the judicial system as it had emerged after 1846, when, among other transformations, it had been made elective, remained the same as did most of the features of the general structure of government of the state. It is of interest to note how far and to what degree the currents of life external to the courts were reflected in the decisions and opinions.

Politically, the state in 1906 was under conservative Republican domination at Albany. The progressive wave which appeared in other states was soon to show itself in the administration of Charles E. Hughes (1906-1910). The current of progressivism continued to manifest itself in the victories of Democratic candidates for governor in 1910 and 1912. Though Charles S. Whitman, who had been a crusading District Attorney, was the relatively conservative governor of the state from 1915-1918, he was succeeded by the liberal Democrat Alfred E. Smith in 1919. From the latter year through 1938, with the exception of the two year period 1921-1922, when the Republican Nathan L. Miller, elected in the Harding landslide of 1920, was in office, the state was under three governors, Alfred E. Smith, Franklin D. Roosevelt, and Herbert H. Lehman, all of them Democratic and all of them more or less committed to the principle of state intervention in the life of the community on the behalf of what was deemed to be the social welfare. The same tendency reflected in the line of governors is discernible in the activities of the state legislature. Because of the fact which will be brought out in Chapter XII that the legislative apportionment of the state has favored the Republican party, we find that the Democrats controlled both houses of the state legislature only three times in the whole period 1906-1938, namely—1911, 1913, 1935. This did not mean, however, that the legislature failed to enact what might be referred to as social welfare legislation. Notwithstanding the differences between them, the Democratic governors and the Republican legislatures were responsible for the enactment of laws regulating various facets of the life of the state, as will be brought out in succeeding chapters. Here of course we have a situation which makes the attitude of the courts toward such laws of interest. We have a wealthy and influential state in which there is a sizable body of legislation placed on the books during the period selected for study.

The major source for this book has been the court reports which have generally given the information desired, though the practice of the courts, in a number of instances, of handing down extremely brief opinions has contributed some difficulty in the determination of the nature of the constitutional point at issue. The three series of court reports which form the primary source for the cases discussed are the New York Reports (abbreviated as N. Y.), which contain the decisions of the Court of Appeals, the highest appellate court in the state; the Appellate Division Reports (abbreviated as A.D.), in which are found the decisions of the second highest ranking state tribunal; and the Miscellaneous Reports (abbreviated as Misc.), which include the decisions of the Supreme Court, the Surrogate's Court, and other courts of record.

A check list of the materials used by Professor Field for his study, which is deposited in manuscript form at the University of Minnesota, was kindly provided by Professor William Anderson of that institution. The materials themselves were unfortunately of such nature that further transmission was impracticable. This list, too, was found incomplete though of great aid. The various digests, such as Abbott's New York Digest, also were of value in finding the type of case sought. It is hoped that all cases in which acts have been held unconstitutional by the New York courts have been found. It is more difficult to determine whether an act has been held *constitutional* by implication in a particular case, because of the judicial canon that a statute is not to be held unconstitutional unless it is necessary for the decision of the case. It is believed that, with the exception of some disputable decisions, all the cases in which the appellate courts have ruled that acts were constitutional during these years have likewise been scrutinized.

This treatise is concerned with the attitude of the state courts to state statutes, that is, the attitude of one branch of the government toward a coördinate branch. This was the same problem examined by Professor Edgerton in the article cited above. Confusion has been found in the discussions of judicial review, owing to the failure of certain writers on the subject to distinguish between the attitude of a court to a coördinate legislature and to a subordinate law-making body. The famous declaration of Justice Holmes that " The United States would not come to an end if we lost our power to declare an act of Congress void " was not extended to apply to the power of the Supreme Court to decide on the validity of state laws.[9] Just as there has been disapproval of the former practice with approval of the latter, because of the necessity of preventing state governments from encroaching upon the sphere of the federal government, so, similarly, state court rulings on municipal ordinances and local laws are logically in a different category than those on enactments of the state legislature. Although there is an interconnection in such matters as Home Rule, it has been decided to omit treatment of cases involving the validity of municipal ordinances and local laws, as well as of administrative decisions, because of the lengthy treatment needed to cover such subjects, in addition to the logical difference between the two types of cases.

[9] Robert Eugene Cushman, *Leading Constitutional Decisions*, Eighth edition (New York, 1946), p. 214.

The material has been presented with a view to contributing toward the answering of certain questions frequently posed. Among these may be mentioned: Which clauses of the Constitution are most often interpreted by the courts? Has the possession of the power to hold acts unconstitutional been necessary to prevent inroads on the judicial branch of the government? Have the courts protected civil liberties from attacks by the legislature? What has been the attitude of the courts toward legislation dealing with the various social, economic and cultural issues during these years? It is hoped that some light may have been shed on these and other queries.

For the purpose of examining the conglomeration of decisions which was handed down in these years, the cases in which restrictions on the powers of the legislature were involved have been dealt with first. Decisions on acts passed under powers either granted directly by the Constitution or universally understood to be possessed by the legislature, such as the police power, have then been covered. Since there has been more general acceptance on the part of many observers of the necessity of judicial review as a defense for the judicial branch of the government, and as a protection for civil liberties, than as a safeguard for other constitutional restrictions, the former topics have been taken up at the outset. Those who would accept judicial review as a rampart for civil liberties or the courts themselves, are frequently found to be opposed to this institution as a protection to the rights of contract or of property, and contrariwise. To be sure, as many have pointed out, there is no absolute line of demarcation between the various groups of cases discussed and the attitudes taken toward them. Other methods for examining them might well have been adopted. The writer hopes, however, that the exposition will prove serviceable to those interested in the subject.[10]

10 The standard general history of New York is Alexander C. Flick, *History of the State of New York* (New York, 1935) 10 Volumes, Volumes VII-X of which deal with the period covered.

TABLE OF CONTENTS

	PAGE
FOREWORD	7

CHAPTER I
The Judicial System of the State of New York 19

CHAPTER II
Regulation of the Courts 40

CHAPTER III
Civil Liberties 57

CHAPTER IV
Commerce, Privileges and Contracts 78

CHAPTER V
Just Compensation 98

CHAPTER VI
Titles 107

CHAPTER VII
Home Rule 115

CHAPTER VIII
Local and Special Acts 136

CHAPTER IX
Due Process, Equal Protection and Freedom of Contract 145

CHAPTER X
Police Power 163

CHAPTER XI
Education, Civil Service and Conservation 184

CHAPTER XII
Taxation 194

CHAPTER XIII
The Legislature as a Branch of Government 215

SUMMARY AND CONCLUSIONS 221

CHAPTER I

THE JUDICIAL SYSTEM OF THE STATE OF NEW YORK 1906-1938

A. The Structure and Function of the Courts

THE highest court in New York State is the Court of Appeals. It consists of seven judges, one chief and six associates, elected at large for fourteen year terms. The governor is allowed by the Constitution to appoint not more than four justices of the Supreme Court to serve as associate judges of the Court of Appeals whenever the latter certifies that the number of causes pending in the court prevents the disposal of such causes with reasonable speed. Since 1920 it has not been found necessary for such extra appointments to be made. In case of the temporary absence or inability to act of any of its members, the court itself has had the power since 1925 to designate any justice of the Supreme Court to serve during such period of inability to act. However, no more than seven judges may sit in any case. Five members constitute a quorum, with the concurrence of four necessary to a decision. The Constitution of 1894 limited the jurisdiction of the court to the review of questions of law, except where the judgment was of death. Except in this latter contingency, appeals were allowed to be taken as of right "only from judgments or orders entered upon decisions of the Appellate Division of the Supreme Court, finally determining actions or special proceedings, and from orders granting new trials on exceptions, where the appellants stipulate that upon affirmance judgment absolute shall be rendered against them."[1] The Appellate Division might "allow an appeal upon any question of law which in its opinion ought to be reviewed by the Court of Appeals."[2] The legislature was given

[1] New York State Constitutional Convention Committee, Vol. I, *New York State Constitution Annotated* (New York, 1938), Part 2, p. 134.
[2] *Ibid.*

the power to further restrict the jurisdiction of the court and the right of appeal to it, with the exception that the right of appeal should not depend upon the amount involved.

In 1925, when several important amendments concerning the judiciary were adopted, the jurisdiction of the Court of Appeals was widened. It was allowed to review cases " where the Appellate Division, on reversing or modifying a final judgment in an action of a final order in a special proceeding, makes new findings of fact and renders final judgment or a final order thereon." [3] In addition appeals were allowed to the court directly from a court of original jurisdiction where the judgment was of death, and in other criminal cases from an Appellate Division or as the legislature might provide. In civil cases appeals were allowed under five conditions, the most important of which for the purpose of this dissertation were numbers one and three. Number one allowed appeals " as of right, from a judgment or order entered upon the decision of an appellate division of the Supreme Court which finally determines an action or special proceeding wherein is directly involved the construction of the constitution of the state or of the United States, or where one or more of the justices of the Appellate Division dissents from the decision of the court, or where the judgment or order is one of reversal or modification." [4] Number three allowed appeals " as of right, from a judgment or order of a court of record of original jurisdiction which finally determined an action or special proceeding where the only question involved on the appeal is the validity of a statutory provision of the state or of the United States under the constitution of the state or of the United States; and on any such appeal only the constitutional question shall be considered and determined by the court." [5] In other cases the Appellate Division

[3] New York State Constitutional Convention Committee, Vol. II, *Amendments Proposed to New York Constitution 1895-1937* (New York, 1938), p. 476. Hereinafter referred to as Amendments Proposed.

[4] *Ibid.*, pp. 476-77.

[5] *Ibid.*, p. 477.

might certify that one or more questions of law had arisen which ought to be reviewed by the Court of Appeals.[6]

Ranking next to the Court of Appeals is the Appellate Division of the Supreme Court. Up to 1925 it consisted of seven justices in the First Department and five in each of the other three, thus comprising the four departments into which the legislature was directed to divide the state. The First Department was to consist of the county of New York while the others were to " be bounded by county lines and be compact and equal in population as nearly as may be." [7] The legislature could not increase the number of departments but might alter them once every ten years. No more than five justices were to sit in any case, four to constitute a quorum, with the concurrence of three necessary to a decision. The governor was to appoint the members from among all the justices elected to the Supreme Court, choosing a Presiding Justice who was to act in that capacity during his term of office and reside in his department. The other justices were to serve for five year terms, or for the unexpired portions of their terms of office (as Supreme Court justices), if less than five years. A majority of the members were to reside in the department in which they served. It was also prescribed that " No justice of the Appellate Division shall exercise any of the powers of a Justice of the Supreme Court, other than those of a Justice out of court, and those pertaining to the Appellate Division or to the hearing and decision of motions submitted by consent of counsel." [8]

In 1899 the governor was given the power to make temporary designations in case the Presiding Justice should certify that one or more members were needed for the speedy disposi-

[6] *Ibid.*, pp. 477-78. The above account is based on the section of the Constitution dealing with the court's jurisdiction which was Article 6, Section 9 in the 1894 Constitution and was changed to Article 6, Section 7 by the general amendment of 1925.

[7] Article 6, Section 2, Constitution of 1894. New York State Constitution Annotated, *op. cit.*, Part 2, p. 130.

[8] *Ibid.*, p. 131.

tion of business.[9] In 1905 an amendment allowed a justice of the Appellate Division who had been previously forbidden to, to hold any term of the Supreme Court and exercise any of the powers of a Supreme Court justice in any other department than that in which he served, when not engaged in performing his duties as a member of the Appellate Division.[10]

In 1925 the number of justices in the Second Department, which comprised Kings County, as well as the rest of Long Island and Staten Island, and had grown greatly in population, was increased to seven. The prescription was laid down that the departments should be bounded by the lines of judicial districts (explained hereafter) instead of by county lines. In place of the presiding justice, the Appellate Division was to certify the need for additional temporary appointments, and was also to certify when such need no longer existed, whereupon the service of the appointee was to cease. In order to prevent the waste of time incurred by a rehearing, a justice of the Appellate Division was allowed to decide causes or proceedings submitted before his becoming a member. Finally the power given to the Appellate Division in each department to fix the time and places for holding trial terms as well as special terms therein, omitted in the amendment of 1905, was restored.[11]

In the first and second departments, the appellate divisions were given the power in 1925 to establish appellate terms of the Supreme Court. These were to consist of not less than three nor more than five Supreme Court justices appointed from time to time by the Appellate Division and residents of the department. No more than three were to sit in any case, two to constitute a quorum and the concurrence of the same number was needed for a decision. These appellate terms could be discontinued and reestablished as the Appellate Division might

---

[9] Amendments Proposed, *op. cit.*, p. 383. He already possessed such power in case of absence or inability to act.

[10] *Ibid.*, p. 389.

[11] *Ibid.*, pp. 467-69. See p. 390 for omission in 1905 amendment.

determine and that body might also revoke any designation to serve therein. These terms were to "have jurisdiction to hear and determine all appeals now or hereafter authorized by law to be taken to the Supreme Court or to the Appellate Division other than appeals from the Supreme Court, a Surrogate's Court, or the Court of General Sessions of the city of New York, as may from time to time be directed by the Appellate Division establishing such appellate term." [12] Appeals might be allowed to the Appellate Division by either the appellate term or the Appellate Division which established it, whenever it was felt that a question of law or fact ought to be reviewed.

The first section of the judiciary article in the 1894 Constitution continued the Supreme Court as the court having general jurisdiction in law and equity. The members of this court were chosen by the electors of each of nine districts for fourteen year terms. The legislature was given the power to alter these districts once after every enumeration of the inhabitants of the state under the Constitution and reapportion the justices. The number of justices was to consist of those in office at the time of the adoption of the Constitution (January 1, 1895) plus those transferred to the court by Article 6, Section 5, which abolished the superior courts of New York City and Buffalo, the New York City Court of Common Pleas and the City Court of Brooklyn, transferring their members to the Supreme Court after January 1, 1896. In addition twelve new members were added, three in the first district, three in the second and one in each of the others. In 1905, the legislature was authorized to increase the number of justices, the number not to exceed one for each 80,000 or fraction over 40,000 of the population in the first and second districts, nor to exceed one for each 60,000 or fraction over 35,000 in each of the others. The legis-

---

[12] Amendments Proposed, *op. cit.*, p. 470. Article 6, Section 3 added in 1925.

lature was also allowed to erect another judicial district ont of the second district.[13]

In 1925, the legislature was allowed to alter the district once after every federal census, as well as each state enumeration, with the districts to be bounded by county lines. The population requirements were made uniform for all districts, the limit being set at one justice for each 60,000 or fraction over 35,000 of the population of each district. A justice might " perform the duties of his office or hold court in any county " except as might be otherwise provided in the article.[14]

Below the Supreme Court are a variety of courts, some mentioned in the Constitution such as the county courts, the Surrogate's courts, the New York County Court of General Sessions, the New York City Court and the justices of the peace.[15] In addition, the legislature may establish inferior local courts of civil and criminal jurisdiction but no court so created was to be a court of record, nor have " any equity jurisdiction, or any greater jurisdiction in other respects than is conferred upon County Courts by or under this article.[16] The power to establish children's courts and courts of domestic relations was

[13] Article 6, Section 1 as amended in 1905. Amendments Proposed, *op. cit.*, pp. 376-77; Article 6, Section 4 prescribing terms of judges, *ibid.*, p. 400; Article 6, Section 5, *ibid.*, pp. 402-403.

[14] Article 6, Section 1 as amended in 1925, *ibid.*, pp. 464-65.

[15] County Courts, Article 6, Section 14 Constitution of 1894, *ibid.*, pp. 436-37; amended 1913 to allow increase in number, *ibid.*, pp. 448-49; after 1925 Article 6, Section 11, *ibid.*, 484-86; Surrogates' Courts, Article 6, Section 15, Constitution of 1894, *ibid.*, p. 451; after 1925 Article 6, Section 13, *ibid.*, pp. 497-98; New York County Court of General Sessions incorporated in Constitution in 1925, Article 6, Section 14, *ibid.*, pp. 498-99; New York City Court incorporated in Constitution in 1925 Article 6, Section 15, *ibid.*, pp. 499-502; Justices of the peace Article 6, Section 17 in Constitution of 1894 providing for election, *ibid.*, p. 454; amended in 1925 to include Municipal Court justices of New York City and other inferior local courts, *ibid.*, p. 519; further amended in 1929, *ibid.*, p. 520.

[16] Article 6, Section 18 Constitution of 1894, *ibid.*, p. 455; after 1925, *ibid.*, pp. 523-24.

specifically granted to the legislature in 1921.[17] It is not felt necessary to go into detail concerning these lower courts, for reasons to be discussed hereafter.

The court for the trial of impeachments consists of the President of the Senate, the senators and the judges of the Court of Appeals. In 1925, as an aftermath of the impeachment and conviction of Governor William Sulzer, it was provided that on the trial of an impeachment against the governor or lieutenant-governor, the temporary president of the senate was not to act as a member of the court, a restriction previously applicable to the lieutenant-governor. The assembly may impeach by a majority vote of all the members elected, a conviction requiring the concurrence of two-thirds of the members of the court present. It was also provided in 1925 that removal from office after impeachment should disqualify the person from holding and enjoying any public office of honor, trust or profit under the state, the word *public* being added.[18]

Vacancies in both the Court of Appeals and the Supreme Court are to be filled at the next general election happening not less than three months after such vacancy occurs, the governor to fill the vacancy by appointment, with the advice and consent of the Senate if that body is in session. The appointment so made continues until the last day of December after the election to fill the vacancy.[19]

Judges and justices cannot serve in office after the last day of December of the year in which they reach the age of sev-

17 *Ibid.*, pp. 457-8, Article 6, Section 18; unchanged after amendment of 1925, Article 6, Section 18, *ibid.*, pp. 523-24.

18 Article 6, Section 13, 1894 Constitution, *ibid.*, p. 435; after 1925 Article 6, Section 10, *ibid.*, pp. 482-83.

19 For Supreme Court justices Article 6, Section 4, 1894 Constitution, *ibid.*, p. 400; with change of one word continued after 1925, *ibid.*, p. 471; for Court of Appeals Article 6, Section 8, 1894 Constitution, *ibid.*, pp. 414-15; after 1925, Article 6, Section 6, *ibid.*, pp. 474-75.

enty.[20] It was also provided that judges of the Court of Appeals were not to hold any other office or public trust, and that votes for any of them, whether by the legislature or the people for other than a judicial office, were to be void.[21] To hold the office of judge of the Court of Appeals, justice of the Supreme Court, surrogate or judge of any other court of record except in Hamilton County, as to the office of county judge or surrogate, it is required to be an attorney and counsellor of the state.[22]

A special procedure was provided for the removal of judges. For those who were members of the Court of Appeals and the Supreme Court a two-thirds vote of all the members elected in each house of the legislature for a concurrent resolution was required. For all other judicial offices, except justices of the peace and judges or justices of inferior courts not of record, a two-thirds vote of all the members elected to the Senate, on a message from the governor recommending removal, was required.[23] The judges just mentioned as excepted, such as justices of the peace, might be removed for cause after notice and hearing by such courts as might be prescribed by law.[24] The cause of removal must be entered on the journals.

[20] Article 6, Section 12, 1894 Constitution, *ibid.*, p. 429; unchanged by amendment of 1909, *ibid.*, pp. 430-31; after 1925 extended to office of surrogate Article 6, Section 19, *ibid.*, pp. 529-30.

[21] Article 6, Section 10, 1894 Constitution, *ibid.*, p. 427; after 1925 extended to allow service as members of a Constitutional Convention Article 6, Section 19, *ibid.*, pp. 429-30.

[22] In 1894 this provision only applied to the Court of Appeals, Supreme Court, county judges and surrogates, with the exception of Hamilton County as noted above. Article 6, Section 20, 1894 Constitution, *ibid.*, p. 460; after 1925 amendment Article 6, Section 19, *ibid.*, pp. 529-30. Hamilton County has the smallest population of any county in the state.

[23] Article 6, Section 11, 1894 Constitution, *ibid.*, p. 427; extended in 1925 to except Municipal Court Justices along with justices of the peace from requirement of two-thirds vote of Senate. Article 6, Section 9, *ibid.*, pp. 481-82.

[24] Article 6, Section 17, 1894 Constitution, *ibid.*, p. 454; extended in 1925 to include New York City Municipal Court justices, *ibid.*, p. 519; unchanged by 1929 amendment, *ibid.*, p. 520.

In the case of legislative removals notice and hearing must be provided and the yeas and nays are to be entered on the journal.[25]

In 1894, the Constitution had provided that judges and justices should receive a compensation established by law, which was not to be increased or diminished during their terms of office.[26] It was also provided that except for justices of the peace, no judicial officer should receive any fees or perquisites of office and that members of the Court of Appeals, of the Supreme Court and county judges or surrogates elected in counties with a population of over 120,000 should not practice as attorney in any court of record in the state or act as referee. The legislature might impose the same prohibition upon other county judges and surrogates as well.[27]

In 1909, an amendment established the salary of Supreme Court justices at $10,000 a year. Members of the Appellate Division were to receive $2,000 more, except for the presiding justices, who were to receive $2,500 added to their $10,000. Those in the first and second departments were to receive the compensation that they were then receiving. In addition, ten dollars a day was granted to a justice in the third or fourth departments assigned to hold trial or special terms in a district outside the one in which he was elected, for expenses while actually engaged in holding these terms.[28] In 1925, the provision that compensation should not be increased or diminished during the judicial term of office, which had been omitted in 1909, was restored in somewhat different form. It then read "All judges, justices and surrogates shall receive for their services such compensation as is now or may hereafter be established by law, provided only that such compensation shall

[25] Article 6, Section 11, 1894 Constitution, *ibid.*, p. 427; unchanged by amendment of 1925 Article 6, Section 9, *ibid.*, pp. 481-82.

[26] Article 6, Section 12, *ibid.*, p. 429.

[27] Article 6, Section 20, *ibid.*, p. 460; continued with slight change after amendment of 1925 Article 6, Section 19, *ibid.*, pp. 529-30.

[28] Article 6, Section 12, *ibid.*, pp. 430-31.

not be diminished during their respective terms of office." [29] The legislature could now increase salaries during the judge's term of office. The provisions for specific figures as just given by the 1909 amendment were eliminated.

Although the salaries of the judges are not given in the Constitution, they are and have been generous in comparison with those of other judges both state and Federal. In 1905 the Chief Judge of the Court of Appeals received $10,500 a year and the Associate Judges $10,000. The Supreme Court Justices were paid $7,200. In 1912, $3,700 extra were granted the judges of the highest court for expenses, while the Supreme Court Justices were then paid as mentioned above. In 1925 the salaries of the members of the Court of Appeals were raised to $22,500 for the Chief Judge and $20,000 for the Associates. The following year the salaries of the Supreme Court Justices were raised to $15,000. By 1938, the justices in the first, second and ninth districts, which comprise New York City and the surrounding counties, were receiving $10,000 a year in addition to this last figure, the other salaries remaining the same.[30]

B. The Courts and the Question of Constitutionality

From the standpoint of strict logic, any court in the state, or for that matter in the nation, has the right to declare any law presented to it in an issue unconstitutional. According to the theory of judicial review, as propounded by Marshall, in Marbury v. Madison, and the host of others who have repeated his arguments, the courts decide the issues presented by reference to the law that applies. Since the Constitution, Federal or State, as the case may be, is the supreme law, any other law, whether statute or ordinance, which conflicts with the Constitution is ipso facto null and void. In keeping with this

---

29 *Ibid.*, p. 529, Article 6, Section 19.

30 *The New York Red Book, An Illustrated State Manual* (Albany, 1905), pp. 541, 544; *ibid.* (1913), pp. 565, 567; *ibid.* (1926), pp. 160, 166; *ibid.* (1927), p. 223; *ibid.* (1938), p. 196.

theory, the courts in no sense veto laws, but apply the supreme law to the matter before them. Thus no court, whether it be that of a justice of the peace, a city magistrate or the highest court in the land, could avoid holding any statute which seemed in its opinion to conflict with the Constitution to be no law at all, if the issue were presented for decision.[31]

In actual practice, however, confusion might easily result and indeed has done so in the past. A court in one locality will differ with that in another as to whether a statute is unconstitutional. In the course of time, such differences will generally be resolved by an appellate court to which the conflicting decisions will be brought. The fact that confusion may result has led the lower courts to be restrained in declaring an act of the legislature unconstitutional. An expression which typifies such an attitude is the following excerpt from an opinion of Surrogate Fowler in 1911 :

> " But the transcendent power of declaring an act of the Legislature unconstitutional should never, in my opinion, be assumed by a court of first instance, except possibly in rare cases involving life or liberty, and where the invalidity of the legislative act is apparent on its face. The exercise of a judicial power to declare acts of the Legislature void should, I think, be reserved to the graver courts of the State, in solemn session in banc, or held for the final review of such great questions. Otherwise the processes of the government may be disorganized by the actions of a single judicial officer possessed of a little brief authority. Such an individual exercise of power tends to bring into contempt with the people an historic jurisdiction, approved by the wisdom of the greatest of mankind— a jurisdiction of fundamental importance to constitutional government when well exercised, and of most evil import when lightly exercised by a single judge animated, perhaps, by some

---

31 See Louis B. Boudin, *Government by Judiciary* (New York, 1932), Volume 1, Chapter 19, "On the Eve of the Crisis," pp. 464-483 for a discussion of this point. The Wisconsin Supreme Court held in the Booth cases that it had the right of judging for itself the constitutionality of general laws passed by the United States Congress and declared the Fugitive Slave Act of 1850 unconstitutional. *Ibid.*, p. 478.

theory squaring with his own conceptions of government or polity. Doubtless the ultimate power to test the validity of legislative enactments by a solemn comparison with delegated constitutional powers is of supreme importance and the keystone of our political fabric. But the power and the exercise of the power are distinct. . . . The due exercise of so fundamental a principle of American government—one so vital to national existence—should not, I think, be invaded rashly, so degraded by an immoderate use in a court of first instance. For these reasons the surrogate would regard it as a breach of decorum for him to undertake to pass upon the validity of Chapter 676, Laws of 1910. In this court the constitutionality of an act of the Legislature must be presumed for the sake of propriety if for no other reason." [32]

On the other hand, some judges have felt it their duty to hold an act invalid if such was their opinion. In 1912, for example, Justice Benedict gave voice to his beliefs on this subject:

"I deem it proper at this point to say that I wholly disagree with the inference or contention in the brief of the learned attorney-general which is based upon the statement that it is well settled that, where there is a right of appeal, no court should declare in the first instance a statute unconstitutional, but should leave the determination of that question to an appellate court. Such a rule is not sound in law. It is just as much the duty of the court of first instance to declare invalid and prevent clear violations of the Constitution by Legislative enactment as it is the like duty of the court of last resort upon appeal, and the duty should not be evaded by the trial judge by casting the responsibility upon appellate tribunals. And equally is it true that, if the case be doubtful neither the trial court nor courts of review should annul by judicial sentence as repugnant to the Constitution what has been enacted by the law-making power." [33]

[32] Matter of New York County, 72 Misc. 620, pp. 621-22.

[33] People ex rel. Wogan v. Rafferty, 77 Misc. 258 Supreme Court Kings Trial Term, at 263.

It will be found in the subsequent chapters that most of the decisions holding laws unconstitutional have been handed down in the appellate courts. It is important then to know under what conditions questions of constitutionality will be decided on in these courts.

The sections of the Constitution relevant to the bringing of such questions to the Court of Appeals have already been cited.[34] These provisions make it relatively certain that, except for cases originating in the Federal courts, all actions involving the declaration that a state statute is unconstitutional, will eventually reach the Court of Appeals, if one of the parties to the suit desires it to go up from the lower courts. Of course the Court of Appeals, in common with other American courts, has at various times repeated the dictum that no act will be declared unconstitutional unless beyond reasonable doubt and unless necessary to the decision of the case.[35] The particular circumstance that in New York the Court of Appeals has no original jurisdiction makes it necessary to examine the question of constitutionality arising on appeal. Benjamin N. Cardozo, later Chief Judge of the Court of Appeals, writing in

[34] Article 6, Section 7, particularly paragraphs numbered 1, 3 and 4 quoted above, pp. 20-21. Paragraphs 1 and 3 were originally enacted as statutes in 1917 forming Section 588 Code of Civil Procedure.

[35] This has been a principle of jurisprudence in New York since 1812. In that year Justice Smith Thompson of the State Supreme Court, later on the United States Supreme Court, expressing doubts of the power to declare acts unconstitutional, stated:

"But admitting such a power in the judiciary, it ought to be exercised with great caution and circumspection and in extreme cases only. It certainly affords a strong and powerful argument in favor of the constitutionality of a law, that it has passed not only that branch of the legislature which constitutes the greater portion of our court of dernier resort, but also the council of revision which is composed of the governor and the two highest judicial tribunals of the state (next to this court,) and whose peculiar province it is to examine and make constitutional objections to bills, before they become laws ... with such a weight of prima facie evidence in favor of the constitutionality of these laws, I should not have boldness enough to pronounce them void, without the most clear, satisfactory and unanswerable reasons." Quoted in Livingston v. VanIngen, 9 Johnson 506 at 564.

the first decade of this century, stated that the court would not pass on constitutional issues which had not been raised in the lower courts, unless the issue were one of public importance.[36] Henry Cohen, secretary to Associate Judge Irving Lehman of the same court, writing in 1934, said that the court had since abandoned this latter exception. In surveying the cases up to that time he found that on a number of points there seemed to be a conflict of rulings. His conclusions were: 1. That the doctrine had been firmly fixed in construing the section of the Constitution allowing appeals " wherein is directly involved the construction of the constitution of the state or of the United States," that the appeal did not lie if the constitutional question had not been raised for decision in the courts below. 2. The issue must be a substantial one. 3. Most controversial of all, if the appellate division in taking a nonconstitutional ground of decision did so in order to avoid a constitutional issue and the intention to avoid might be inferred as a fact, then the Court of Appeals would hold that the constitutional issue was directly involved.

> " But where the decision is put on the non-constitutional ground, not for the purpose of avoiding a more serious issue, but because that is the issue on which the appellate division would normally decide the case in the absence of a constitutional question, then appeal does not lie to the Court of Appeals as of right. Admittedly, this distinction is not a sharp one; nor is it one which may be applied with mechanical results but if it is not the true distinction then the decisions do not seem possible of logical reconciliation." [37]

36 Cardozo, Benjamin N., *The Jurisdiction of the Court of Appeals of the State of New York*, Second edition (Albany, N. Y. 1909).
" But though a constitutional question may not be raised for the first time on appeal where only private rights are involved (Dodge v. Cornelius, 168 N. Y. 241), the rule, it seems, is otherwise where public interests would suffer if the question were ignored. (Mass. Nat. Bank v. Shinn, 163 N. Y. 360)," p. 47.

37 Cohen, Henry, *The Powers of the Court of Appeals* (New York, 1934), Chapter V, pp. 156-172, quoted at 172.

It would seem highly unlikely then that in any case where a lower court declared an act unconstitutional, and one of the parties desired further appeal, that the case could not go higher. On the other hand, if a lawyer had not been foresighted enough to advance the argument that an act affecting his client's interests was unconstitutional in the lower courts, or if the objection were to be regarded as either frivolous or unnecessary for the determination of the case, the result would be a decision and opinion in which, without access to the briefs and other unpublished records, one would be unable to determine that such objections had been voiced. It is thus much more difficult to state how many acts have been explicitly or implicitly held constitutional than to determine the number in which acts have been invalidated.

It is of interest here to note the attitude toward this power of the courts as reflected in proposed amendments to the Constitution during this period. The proposal to vest the judicial power of the state in the courts, as recommended by the Judiciary Convention of 1921, just as the legislative power had been specifically vested in the Senate and Assembly and the executive power in the governor, failed of final adoption. It passed the Senate and Assembly in 1922 and the Assembly in 1923 but was not reported in the Senate in the latter year. Since it was aimed at the orders of administrative bodies rather than at legislative enactments, its passage would not have meant the definite incorporation in the Constitution of the power of judicial review of legislation.[38]

On the other hand, all the proposals to restrict the power of the courts have failed, both in the legislature and in the Constitutional Convention of 1915. In fact, some of them were not even reported out of committee. Since the courts have refused to render advisory opinions upon the constitutionality of

[38] Amendments Proposed, *op. cit.*, pp. 380-381, 937; New York State Constitutional Convention Committee, Vol. IX, *Problems Relating to Judicial Administration and Organization* (New York, 1938), pp. 18, 428-732. Hereinafter cited as Judicial Problems.

legislation, proposals have been made to make such opinions possible. In 1907 and 1908 it was proposed to add to the then Article 6, Section 9 the following sentence: " Each branch of the legislature and the governor to require the opinion of the Court of Appeals upon important questions of law." [39] In 1912 and 1913 the new section to be added would have read: " The governor or either branch of the legislature shall have authority to require the opinions of the judges of the Court of Appeals upon important questions of law and upon solemn occasions." [40] In the Convention of 1915 one proposed amendment would have allowed the Court of Appeals to render advisory opinions upon the request of either the legislature or the governor.[41] Another would have allowed the court to render such opinions upon the request of the legislature only in those instances where the constitutionality of a proposed statute was involved.[42] In 1923 the identical amendment of 1912 and 1913 was again introduced.[43] In 1928 and 1929 Senator Hastings proposed that " The Court of Appeals shall give its written opinions upon any question of law, whenever requested by the governor, or by the acting governor, under his hand and the seal of the state, or by resolution of either branch of the legislature, assented to by a majority of the members elected to the body, passing such resolution." [44]

Somewhat different was the addition suggested in 1914 of a section empowering supreme court justices to report at any time to the chief judge of the Court of Appeals " defects, omissions, inaccuracies or ambiguities in the Constitution or statute law " with suggestions and recommendations to be con-

[39] Amendments Proposed, *op. cit.*, p. 424.

[40] *Ibid.*, p. 425.

[41] Judicial Problems, *op. cit.*, p. 170(9).

[42] *Ibid.*, (10).

[43] *Ibid.*, p. 182; Amendments Proposed, *op. cit.*, p. 425.

[44] Judicial Problems, *op. cit.*, 182-3; Amendments Proposed, *op. cit.*, p. 480.

sidered by the Court of Appeals. The chief judge of that court was to make known to the presiding officers of the senate and assembly in writing on or before January 15th of each year any such defect, existing in the opinion of the court or any judge thereof, with remedial suggestions and recommendations which were to be reported to the senate and assembly.[45]

Although these proposals were not adopted, it might be pointed out that in other states where the courts do possess the right to give advisory opinions, they have generally held that such opinions will not bind them in the future when and if concrete cases arise under the statutes concerned.[46] Hence the restrictions on the power of the courts if such proposals had been adopted would not, in all likelihood, have been too strong legally, though the moral force might have been of importance.

Another type of curb on the power of the courts is the suggested requirement of an extraordinary majority for the invalidation of laws. Two amendments of this kind were referred to the judiciary committee in the 1915 Convention. Under the first, cases involving constitutional questions were to be appealable to the Court of Appeals as of right. The concurrence of all but one judge would have been necessary to declare any statute unconstitutional, but where unconstitutionality was affirmed, two judges could dissent.[47] The second would have required the concurrence of all the judges to declare any statute invalid. A presumption was to exist in favor of the validity of legislative acts, and no act was to be held unconstitutional unless it was clearly so beyond a reasonable doubt.[48] As some of the most important decisions holding acts unconstitutional have been unanimous, there would still have been room for

[45] Amendments Proposed, *op. cit.*, p. 425; proposed in the senate.

[46] MacDonald, Austin F., *American State Government and Administration*, Third edition (New York, 1946), p. 252.

[47] Judicial Problems, *op. cit.*, p. 170 (3). The text is incorrectly given in Judicial Problems. It may be found in Proposed Amendments to the Constitutional Convention of the State of N. Y., Vol. I (Albany, 1915), No. 147.

[48] *Ibid.*, (5).

controversy over the basic principles of judicial review even if such an amendment had been adopted.

Plans have been presented for having court decisions voiding acts reviewed by some other body. There is no record of a proposal in New York during these years of having the legislature itself be empowered to repass such an act by an extraordinary majority, as has been proposed on the national level by Senator Borah and others. A proposal, similar to the one which Theodore Roosevelt had endorsed, partly because of the Ives and other decisions in New York, to allow acts considered by the courts to be violative of the due process clause only, to be voted on by the people, was introduced in both houses in 1913 and in the Assembly in 1914.[49] In order for such a law to be placed on the ballot, it was required that two thousand electors in each of five counties of the state should petition for the submission of the question at the next general election to be held not less than six months after the decision of the Court of Appeals, and not less than sixty days after the filing of the petition. If a majority of those voting were to decide that the act should become law, it would take effect thirty days after the election and, although subject to amendment and repeal the same as other laws, was not to be construed void under the Constitution. In 1915 a variation of this idea was introduced in the Constitutional Convention. Under this scheme, the constitutionality of a statute could be questioned only upon the express consent of the legislature, and upon such conditions as it might prescribe. On demand of either governor or such number of electors as the legislature might prescribe, the question of constitutionality should be submitted to the electors at a general or special election. If it were then affirmed, it was to be deemed operative from its inception; if denied, it was to be considered repealed as of the date of submission.[50]

In 1929, 1930, 1931 and 1932 Assemblyman Cuvillier proposed the creation of a judicial council, to consist of five mem-

[49] Amendments Proposed, *op. cit.*, p. 24.
[50] Judicial Problems, *op. cit.*, p. 170(4).

JUDICIAL SYSTEM OF STATE OF N. Y. 37

bers, to be appointed by the governor with the advice and consent of the senate for five-year terms, with power to review decisions of the Court of Appeals or any other state courts on legislative acts held contrary to either the United States or New York Constitutions. In addition the governor might receive advice on legal matters affecting the legislature, pardons, reprieves, commutations or any other matters pertaining to his office and duties.[51]

Attempts have also been made to prevent the lower courts from invalidating laws. The proposed amendment by Senator Hastings authorizing advisory opinions, referred to above, also including two sections providing that only the Court of Appeals could declare a state law, a municipal ordinance of a city with a population of over 50,000 or any provision of a city charter unconstitutional. The court was to have original jurisdiction in such proceedings and only the court or a member of it could enjoin the operation of any of the foregoing acts.[52] In 1929 Assemblyman Cuvillier proposed that only the Court of Appeals could rule on the constitutionality of legislative acts, but that its decision should be subject to review by the judicial council, which he was proposing to establish by the amendment discussed above.[53]

General proposals for the recall of elective officers, applicable to but not specifically aimed at the judges, were made in 1911,[54]

51 *Ibid.*, p. 183; Amendments Proposed, *op. cit.*, p. 1206.

52 Judicial Problems, *op. cit.*, pp. 182-3; Amendments Proposed, *op. cit.*, pp. 480-81.

53 Judicial Problems, *op. cit.*, p. 183; Amendments Proposed, *op. cit.*, pp. 465-6. See note 51 *supra*.

54 *Ibid.*, pp. 816-17. Number equal to fifty per cent of electors voting in district at preceding election for governor required to file petition.

1912 and 1914,[55] 1918,[56] and 1934.[57] In 1909 a general amendment making possible the initiative, referendum and recall was proposed. One section provided that no act approved by direct vote of the people should be held unconstitutional and any judge doing so should forfeit his office which should then be deemed vacant and be filled by a general election in not less than sixty days.[58]

The most drastic proposals were those taking the power of judicial review completely away from the courts. In 1912 it was proposed that no act be declared unconstitutional except in so far as the judge or judges were "of the opinion that such enactment conflicts with the provisions of the federal constitution."[59] In 1915, the New York State Federation of Labor requested that the Constitutional Convention abolish the power of the courts to declare laws unconstitutional.[60] A proposal was made in the Convention to abolish the power of the Court of Appeals to pass upon the constitutionality of legislation.[61] In 1918 Assemblyman Whitehorn made two proposals along these lines. The first was to add the following sentence to Article 6, Section 1: "Nothing hereinabove shall be deemed to vest in the courts or any judicial officer the power to pass

[55] *Ibid.*, pp. 817-18. Same requirement as stated in note 54 above, but reduced to twenty-five per cent.

[56] *Ibid.*, p. 1239. Number equal to ten per cent of voters at last preceding general election for all candidates for office involved required for petition. Statement of grounds for demand for recall of not more than two hundred words required also.

[57] *Ibid.*, p. 1199. Identical requirement as stated in note 56 above.

[58] Proposed Article III, Section 1-f, *ibid.*, p. 1162; a number equal to twenty-five per cent of vote for governor in particular territory from which officer elected, required for petition. *Ibid.*, p. 1167. Whole amendment, *ibid.*, pp. 1157-74.

[59] *Ibid.*, p. 379.

[60] "Memorial of the New York State Federation of Labor," Documents of the Constitutional Convention of the State of New York (Albany, 1915) Document Number 17.

[61] Judicial Problems, *op. cit.*, p. 170(6).

upon the constitutionality of a statute or declare any statute unconstitutional."[62] The second was to add the following new section as Article 1, Section 20: "Constitutionality of statutes not to be passed upon by court or judicial officer. No court or judicial officer shall pass upon the constitutionality of a statute, or declare any statute unconstitutional."[63]

The conclusion to be drawn from the evidence available is that the institution of judicial review as applied to legislative acts, though criticized during these years, was in no serious danger of being uprooted completely, and except at the height of the Progressive movement, was not menaced by an attempt to curb it severely. Yet it must be kept in mind that the anger and dissatisfaction at decisions of the courts had other channels for actual or potential expression. Amendment of the Constitution, which in New York requires a majority vote of two successive legislatures and the consent of the electorate,[64] has been utilized on occasion. It is also possible to replace the judge or judges delivering an unpopular decision, though the relatively long terms and the fact that the judges are not elected in the same year, did not make such a method very effective, unless the popular discontent continued over a period of years. The opinion of Associate Judge Werner of the Court of Appeals in the Ives case, for example, has been held responsible for his defeat when running later for Chief Judge. Lastly, the limitations of the practice of judicial review itself, such as the refusal of the judges to consider political questions, or to pass upon constitutional questions in the abstract, and the general rule, which judges have often been accused of violating, of regarding acts of the legislature as valid, unless unconstitutional beyond a reasonable doubt, have all served to forestall an outburst against the judiciary. Further explanations of these points may be reserved until the cases themselves have been examined.

62 Amendments Proposed, *op. cit.*, p. 380.
63 *Ibid.*, p. 1184.
64 Article 14, Section 1.

CHAPTER II
REGULATION OF THE COURTS

ONE aspect of judicial review, on which there has been virtual unanimity among those who have admitted the principle at all, is that the courts should have the power to defend themselves. As early as 1794, James Kent, later Chief Justice of the Supreme Court and Chancellor, and author of the famed commentaries, said:

> But the judicial power is the weakest of all, and as it is equally necessary to be preserved entire, it ought not in sound theory to be left naked without any constitutional means of defense. . . . The right of expounding the Constitution as well as laws, will however be found in general to be the most fit, if not only effectual weapon, by which the courts of justice are enabled to repel assaults, and to guard against encroachments on their chartered authorities.[1]

In the years that have intervened, the courts have had occasion to examine many alleged infringements of the judicial prerogative, sustaining most, while voiding some. Although there have been various types of cases, several distinct categories may be discerned. Controversies have arisen over the jurisdiction of the different courts. Another source of litigation consisted of those instances where non-judicial or extra-judicial functions had been assigned to the courts. A third group involved the authority given the Court of Claims to make awards based on morality and justice, but having no foundation in law other than the legislative acts dealing with the particular claims. As with most attempts to classify an assortment of diverse cases arising from sundry situations, there is a miscellany not falling into any of these categories.

[1] "Kent's Introductory Lecture" in *Columbia Law Review*, Vol. III, No. 5, May, 1903, p. 337. This is a reprint of "An Introductory Lecture to a Course of Law Lectures Delivered Nov. 17, 1794 by James Kent, Esq., Professor of Law in Columbia College. Published at the request of the trustees. New York. Printed by Francis Childs 1794."

As far as the functions and duties assigned to the courts by the legislature were concerned, the courts were sometimes willing to accept new powers, and sometimes anxious to reject added burdens. In 1907 the Court of Appeals held unconstitutional a law which provided for the judicial recount and canvass of the votes in the 1905 mayoralty election, in all cities of the first class in which ballots had been preserved. This referred primarily to the election in New York City, where William Randolph Hearst, running as an independent, had come within 5,000 votes of defeating Mayor McClellan, the Democratic candidate, according to the official returns. Charges had been made in the Hearst newspapers that ballot boxes had been dumped into the East River. The recount would indeed have been an embarrassing task for the courts to perform in such tense circumstances. At any rate, the gist of the decision was that if this recount was viewed as a recanvass, then it had to be done by a bi-partisan board. If, on the other hand, it was looked upon as a judicial determination, Article 1, Section 2 required a trial by jury in a quo warranto action.[2] A section of the Public Officers' Law attempted to make a Supreme Court justice the delegate of the Governor in proceedings for the removal of a public officer. This, too, was held void by the Court of Appeals as a violation of Article 6, Section 19, by adding to the duties of the justices.[3] Section 249a of the Town Law, which authorized an application to a county judge for an order permitting the construction of a sewer outlet in a village, was declared invalid in 1930.[4]

On the other hand, Section 115 of the Military Law (Consolidated Laws, Chapter 36) which authorized a Supreme Court justice, in case of riot, to call upon National Guard commanders for aid, was held to be consistent with Article 4, Section 4, which made the Governor the commander-in-chief of

---

[2] Metz v. Maddox (1907) 189 N. Y. 460. Ch. 538, L. 1907.

[3] Richardson v. Scudder (1928) 247 N. Y. 401. Section 34 Public Officers' Law (Cons. Laws Ch. 47) amended by Ch. 15, L. 1928.

[4] Matter of Jordan v. Smith (1930), 254 N. Y. 585.

the military and naval forces of the state, and with Article 6, Section 10, prohibiting the judges from accepting other offices.[5] Likewise, Section 1534 of the New York City Charter, empowering Supreme Court justices in the first or second judicial departments to order a summary public examination of certain public officers and heads of departments, as to the alleged wrongful diversion or misapplication of moneys, and other charges of delinquency and neglect of duty, with the authority to punish witnesses as for a contempt of court, was upheld.[6] A provision for proceedings in the Supreme Court for the legalizing of municipal bonds, or for their issuance, was not considered a delegation of legislative functions to the judiciary.[7] A conflict of powers between the Supreme Court justices and the County Clerk over the appointment of a person to perform clerical duties in the court in the absence of the latter official, was settled in favor of the former when the Court of Appeals sustained Chapter 21, Laws of 1878, allowing them to make the appointment.[8]

A case, involving the reverse question of judicial powers being conferred on non-judicial officers, was Matter of Hertle, in which Section 119 of the Revised Greater New York Charter, under which commissioners were appointed by the mayor to examine the accounts of a city public officer, (Borough President Ahearn of Manhattan) and to take testimony under oath, was held constitutional by the Appellate Division.[9] A Supreme Court justice declared in 1933 that a sec-

[5] People ex rel. Welch v. Bard (1913) 209 N. Y. 304.

[6] Matter of Mitchel v. Cropsey (1917) 177 A. D. 663, 2nd Dept. The court rejected the theory that the act imposed nonjudicial functions upon a judicial branch of the state government. These proceedings were considered of a judicial nature involving the exercise of judicial functions.

[7] Matter of Common Council of Lackawanna (1913) 158 A. D. 263 4th Dept. Article 2A of the General Municipal Law (Cons. Laws Ch. 24) L. 1909, Ch. 29 added by L. 1911, Ch. 769.

[8] Matter of Rogers v. Craig (1921) 231 N. Y. 186.

[9] (1907) 120 A. D. 717 1st Dept. Ch. 466, L. 1901. This was not held to be a judicial function as the commissioners were only empowered to report the results of the investigation to the mayor.

tion of law forbidding the assignment of any part of the salary of an employee of a municipal corporation to a creditor, unless approved in writing by the head of the department in which such employee was employed, to the extent that it attempted to clothe a ministerial officer with judicial powers by authorizing the head of department to give a qualified approval to an assignment of ten per cent of a policeman's salary instead of the whole amount, was invalid. However, in this case Justice Bonynge, who wrote the decision, did not believe that the act authorized such a procedure on the part of a head of department.[10]

The flow of litigation and the resulting creation of tribunals to handle it contributed a share of constitutional problems. The power of the Governor to appoint an extraordinary trial term of the Supreme Court was twice approved by the courts.[11] Another innovation, the authorization of an official referee to do that which a justice at special term might do at any proceeding, was not viewed as impairing the jurisdiction of the Supreme Court, but as being the creation of a new agency to supplement the machinery of the latter court in the exercise of that jurisdiction.[12] The provision of an Appellate Term to hear appeals from the Municipal and City Courts, the members of which were to be appointed by the Appellate Divisions of the First and Second Departments, was another institution upheld

[10] Matter of Neubert v. Butler (1933) 146 Misc. 467 Supreme Court Nassau County Section 86-a General Municipal Law.

[11] People v. Neff (1907) 122 A. D. 135 4th Dept. Section 234 Code of Civil Procedure L. 1895, Ch. 746; People ex rel. Saranac Land and Timber Company v. The Extraordinary Term of the Supreme Court (1917) 220 N. Y. 487 Section 153 Judiciary Law (Cons. Laws Ch. 30). There was no conflict with Article 6, Section 2 and the Governor might appoint such a term whenever the public interest so required.

[12] Matter of Brock (1935) 245 A. D. 5 2nd Dept. Sections 115 and 116 of the Judiciary Law (new sections 116, 117 added by L. 1935, Ch. 854).

by the courts.[13] The division, however, of towns in Suffolk County into police districts, for the purpose of establishing police courts, was declared unconstitutional in 1918.[14]

The question of jurisdiction, as has been stated, was the cause of several controversies settled by the courts. An amendment to the Code of Civil Procedure in 1911, raising the amount for which the City Court of New York City should render judgment from $2000 to $5000, was declared unconstitutional by the Court of Appeals in Lewkowicz v. Queen Aeroplane Company.[15] This case received attention when it was selected in 1913 by the New York State Bar Association's Committee on the Duty of the Courts to Refuse Execution of Statutes in Contravention of the Constitution, as one example of the necessity for the courts to possess the power of judicial review. Mr. Boudin has criticized the committee's argument by pointing to the fact that the act had been sustained in the lower courts, and that Justices Samuel Seabury and Irving Lehman, both of whom later served on the Court of Appeals, had written opinions in favor of the constitutionality of the law. The former, Boudin notes, was " somewhat of a specialist on the subject of the City Court, having written a very learned work about that court of which he was himself at one time a member." [16] In an earlier case a City Court justice had ruled that the legislature might restrict or enlarge that court's juris-

[13] Leach v. Anwell (1912) 154 A. D. 170 2nd Dept. Section 310 Municipal Court Act Ch. 538, L. 1910; Gersman v. Levy (1908) 126 A. D. 83 1st Dept.; in Sakolski v. Schenkel (1906) a provision for the rotation of Municipal Court justices, among the districts of the borough in which they were elected, was found to be within the legislative power. Ch. 598, L. 1904, Supr. Ct., App. Term.

[14] People v. Parve (1918) 181 A. D. 499, 2nd Dept. Ch. 583, L. 1909 as amended by Ch. 294, L. 1910.

[15] 207 N. Y. 290 (1913) Amendment to Section 315 of Code of Civil Procedure by Ch. 569, L. 1911.

[16] Boudin, *op. cit.*, I, 18. See pp. 14-21 for an extended discussion of the report of the New York State Bar Association. The report may be found in New York State Bar Association, *Reports* for 1913, 1914, 1915.

diction with respect to subject matter, amount and persons.[17]

In American Historical Society v. Glenn, an act, which provided that all the process and mandates of the City Court of New York might be executed in any part of the state, was held to violate Article 6, Section 15.[18] Attempts to extend the jurisdiction of the City Court of Binghamton beyond the limits of that city, and to vest in the police justice of the town of Saugerties exclusive jurisdiction to hear and determine all criminal cases in the town, were both forestalled by court action.[19] The Children's Court Act was held to violate Article 6, Section 18, in so far as it conferred on the Children's Court the right to try offenses committed by adults against children, irrespective of the relation of such offense to the " delinquency, neglect or dependency " of any child.[20] A provision in the Municipal Court

---

[17] Kline v. Imperial Coal and Coke Co. (1910) 66 Misc. 616 City Court of New York Trial Term. The court was passing on the jurisdiction given the City Court by Sections 315 and 1780 Code of Civil Procedure over the suit of a non-resident against a foreign corporation, upon a check payable in this state, upon which check payment had been refused.

[18] 248 N. Y. 445 (1928) Court of Appeals. New York City Court Act L. 1926, Ch. 539. The Constitutional provision, enacted in 1925, provided, among other things, that the City Court should have " original jurisdiction concurrent with the Supreme Court."

[19] Darling v. White (1910) 67 Misc. 366 County Court Broome County L. 1902, Ch. 532 Amendment to Section 8 Ch. 537, L. 1899 the act creating the City Council of Binghamton and Section 349 of the Revised Charter of that city L. 1907, Ch. 751; in Gehagin v. Fairbanks (1933) 147 Misc. 685 the Binghamton City Court held that under a later act the legislature had intended to confer jurisdiction on itself over non-resident defendants served with process in Broome County, and that this was valid. Binghamton City Court Act L. 1931, Ch. 482 Section 17 Subd. 1; People ex rel. Slade v. Boice (1909) 63 Misc. 357 County Court Ulster County, Ch. 31, L. 1861 creating the office of police justice of the town of Saugerties.

[20] People v. Hopkins (1924) 208 A. D. 438, 3rd Dept. Ch. 547, L. 1922. In Matter of Walsh v. Walsh (1933) 146 Misc. 604, it was held that a provision that the Children's Court should " subject to limitations herein have ... jurisdiction to determine the question of the rightful custody of children whose custody is subject to controversy, as related to their immediate care " must be read with Article 6, Section 18, under which the court was without power to determine the custody of children not falling within the class of delinquent, neglected or dependent minors. Subd. 1, Section 6 Children's Court Act (L. 1930, Ch. 393).

Code, for service on non-resident defendants by registered mail of a copy of a summons, warrant of attachment and inventory, was considered in conflict with the due process clause as it failed to afford reasonable time and opportunity to defend.[21]

Acts, affecting the jurisdiction of the courts, which were sustained did the following: granted the city judge of Corning the same jurisdiction and authority as the justice of the peace in bastardy proceedings under the law of New York State;[22] gave the City Court of Buffalo the same power to fine or imprison within its jurisdiction as the Erie County Court could do in like cases;[23] authorized the City Courts of Albany and Rochester to have summonses served in any towns adjoining the respective cities;[24] allowed the Municipal Court of New York City to set aside verdicts;[25] created the same Municipal Court a court of record;[26] permitted the Court of Special Sessions to impose indeterminate sentences up to a maximum of three years[27] and to try a charge of criminal contempt of

[21] Arbetter Inc. v. Isabel Inc. (1933) 147 Misc. 54 Municipal Court of New York, Borough of Manhattan, 1st District, Section 48 Municipal Court Code as amended by L. 1931, Ch. 576; Clarke v. Carlisle Foundry Co. (1934) 150 Misc. 710 Municipal Court of New York, Borough of Manhattan, 5th District; Pennington Furniture Co. v. Miller Furniture Co. (1934) 153 Misc. 669 Supreme Court, Appellate Term, 1st Dept.

[22] People ex rel. Heminway v. Bostleman (1913) 82 Misc. 629 Charter of Corning L. 1905, Ch. 142 Supreme Court Steuben Special Term. The judge was not to be required to associate another magistrate with himself in such proceedings.

[23] People ex rel. Borowick v. Hunt (1913) 157 A. D. 818 4th Dept. L. 1909, Ch. 570 Section 70 as amended by L. 1910, Ch. 228.

[24] Failing v. Grounds (1914) 160 A. D. 71 Section 9 City Court Act of Albany Ch. 603, L. 1910; Rochester Exposition Association v. Bogorad (1932) 149 Misc. 200 County Court Monroe County Ch. 413, L. 1921, pursuant to Article 6, Section 18.

[25] Bradstreet's Collection Bureau v. Dayler's Brass Works (1917) 188 A. D. 511 1st Dept. Section 6 and Section 129 of New York City Municipal Court Code L. 1915, Ch. 279.

[26] Matter of Levy (1920) 192 A. D. 550 1st Dept. Ch. 279, L. 1915.

[27] People ex rel. Kipnis v. McCann (1921) 199 A. D. 30 1st Dept. Parole Commission Act L. 1915, Ch. 579.

REGULATION OF THE COURTS

another court;[28] gave the Children's Court exclusive original jurisdiction to determine the liability of any person who wilfully failed or refused to provide for the maintenance of his wife or child, to examine into the ability of any such person adjudged liable to pay for such maintenance, and to order weekly payments to be made;[29] allowed the Supreme Court to entertain an action on a contract made by an assignee for the benefit of his creditors, where the County Court of another county was vested with supervision and control over the assignee;[30] and granted to a family court the right to hear

[28] People ex rel. Frank v. McCann (1930) Subd. 4 Section 31 Ch. 659, L. 1910, 253 N. Y. 221.

[29] La Rocca v. La Rocca (1932) 144 Misc. 737 Children's Court Westchester County Subd. 6 Children's Court Act State of New York; in Matter of Thompson v. Elliott (1934) 152 Misc. 188, Subd. 3 Section 6 of the Children's Court Act (L. 1922, Ch. 547) as construed to confer on the court exclusive jurisdiction to hear and determine prior to birth cases of children born out of wedlock, in accordance with the provisions of the Domestic Relations Law for "the support and education of the child," was considered in harmony with Article 6, Section 18. Justice Smyth, sitting in the Children's Court of Westchester County, pointed out that the law had been acted on for ten years; in Zambrotto v. Jeannette (1936) 160 Misc. 558 a subdivision of the Domestic Relations Court Act giving that court jurisdiction, whenever issues involving a delinquent child were before the court, to try summarily any offense less than a felony against any person alleged to have contributed to the child's delinquency, was sustained. Domestic Relations Court of the City of New York, Queens County Subd. 2, Section 61 Domestic Relations Court Act (L. 1936, Ch. 346); nor was it considered unconstitutional to compel a person liable for the support of a child to furnish support where the child was living with a mother and stepfather. People ex rel. Wagstaff v. Matthews (1938) 168 Misc. 188 Supreme Court Nassau Co. Subd. 2 Section 6 Children's Court Act L. 1930, Ch. 393.

[30] Johnson v. Lasser (1936) 159 Misc. 340 Supreme Court Special Term Albany County. This was the court's interpretation of Article 2, of the Debtor and Creditor Law; two other laws affecting the Supreme Court were construed to prevent their invalidation. The first, Section 879 of the Civil Practice Act, required that an injunction order to restrain state officers should not be granted except by the Supreme Court at a term thereof, sitting in the department where the officers were located. Justice Cotillo held that though the law was mandatory in form, it would nevertheless be construed as directory, for otherwise it would be a restraint upon the chancery jurisdiction of some Supreme Court justices, while conferring it upon others.

cases involving non-resident defendants served with process within the territorial limits of its jurisdiction.[31]

A section of the Municipal Court Code, allowing the deposition of a party to an action in the New York City Municipal Court, about to be brought in that court, to be taken at any time, before or during the trial, in the same manner as such depositions were taken in like cases in the Supreme Court, was not viewed as conferring any equity jurisdiction on the Municipal Court in violation of Article 6, Section 18.[32] The surrogate was given power on the judicial settlement of the accounts of an executor, by a section of the Code of Civil Procedure, to ascertain the title to any legacy, and to try the validity of an assignment of a legacy.[33] Another method of reducing the burden on the courts is the elimination or restriction of the right of appeal from administrative agencies and lower tribunals. The courts sustained three acts affecting appeals: one, preventing persons convicted of a violation of the liquor tax law by the Court of Special Sessions, whose sentences had been suspended, from appealing to the Supreme Court;[34] a second, permitting appeals to the State Commis-

---

Dairy Sealed Inc. v. TenEyck (1936) 159 Misc. 716 Supreme Court New York County. The second, Subdivision 1, Paragraph (f), Clause (5), Section 876-a Civil Practice Act, stated that no item of injunctive relief should prohibit publicity or communication of information regarding the facts involved in any dispute, whether by speaking, picketing or by any other method not involving fraud, violence or breach of the peace. This was interpreted by the same justice as not withdrawing from the court its constitutional power to issue an injunction. Busch Jewelry Co. v. United Retail Employees' Union, Local 830 (1938) 168 Misc. 224 Supreme Court Special Term New York County.

31 Matter of Buoneto v. Buoneto (1938) 278 N. Y. 284 L. 1933, Ch. 482 Section 103 Court of Appeals.

32 Lotz v. Standard Vulcanite Pan Co. (1917) 102 Misc. 68 Supreme Court Appellate Term 2nd Dept. Section 27 (4) of the Municipal Court Code, added by Ch. 610, L. 1916.

33 Matter of Thornburgh (1911) 72 Misc. 619 Surrogate's Court, New York County.

34 Dornhoefer v. Farley (1914) 161 A. D. 600 2nd Dept. Section 2 Liquor Tax Law.

REGULATION OF THE COURTS

sioner of Education from decisions of District Superintendents to dissolve and consolidate school districts, but barring appeals to the courts;[35] and a third, making an award of damages by the New York City Board of Revision of Assessments final and conclusive.[36] On the other hand, the Court of Appeals declared unconstitutional a provision of the Civil Practice Act, which permitted an appeal to the Court of Appeals, as of right, from a judgment or order of an Appellate Division finally determining an action for a specific proceeding, where one or more of the justices, who had sat in the case, refrained from participating in the decision.[37] The Appellate Division sustained a provision of the Agricultural Law, which empowered the Supreme Court, in an action to recover a penalty or forfeiture for a violation of the act, to issue an injunction restraining the defendant from a further violation. It concluded that issuing the injunction was not mandatory, and that there was no intention of invading the equity province of the court in order to take away the discretion vested in it by the Constitution.[38] A part of the Code of Civil Procedure, which gave preference on court calendars to civil actions brought by the People, was construed by the Supreme Court as not depriving the courts of the power to adjourn.[39]

Assaults on the courts might be expected to be aimed either at the salaries or at the tenure of the judges. In 1916 the Court of Appeals upheld an act giving the town boards of towns,

[35] Bullock v. Cooley (1919) 225 N. Y. 566 Court of Appeals Education Law (Cons. Laws. Ch. 16 Section 129).

[36] People ex rel. Crane v. Hablo (1920) 228 N. Y. 309 L. 1901, Ch. 466 amended L. 1918, Ch. 619. This was a provision of the New York City Charter.

[37] Sommer v. Lorsch and Co. (1930) 254 N. Y. 146 Court of Appeals Subd. 1 Section 588 of the Civil Practice Act. This was considered a violation of Article 6, Section 7 Subd. 1.

[38] People v. Clark (1910) 139 A. D. 687, 2nd Dept. Section 20 of Agriculture Law L. 1909, Ch. 1.

[39] People v. McClellan (1907) 56 Misc. 123 Supreme Court New York Trial Term, Sections 791, 793 Code of Civil Procedure.

with a population of 20,000 or over, the power to fix the salaries of justices of the peace at a salary not over $1500, and in the following year sustained another, depriving the Surrogate of Queens County of additional compensation for his services in drawing a jury.[40] In 1931 the authority given the Appellate Division to remove justices of inferior courts, to investigate those courts and the justices thereof, and to designate a Supreme Court justice or a referee to conduct the investigation, was held harmonious with Article 6, Section 17 by the Supreme Court.[41] In 1934 this same court saved an act reducing the salaries of municipal officers, by holding that it did not apply to justices of New York City Special Sessions who were protected from reduction by Article 6, Section 19.[42]

Questions arising as to the selection and removal of judges were decided in another group of cases during this period. Five lawsuits settled in the same year, 1927, upheld a statute providing that if the full term of persons elected to fill a Municipal Court vacancy would expire with an even-numbered year, then their terms should end with the year prior thereto.[43] An act of 1929, authorizing the temporary appointment of justices of the Municipal Court in place of disabled incumbents, was sustained by the Court of Appeals.[44] However, the court declared invalid and severable a provision that the appointee should be

[40] People ex rel. Luyster v. Cooke (1916) 219 N. Y. 628 Affirming 172 A. D. 737 Ch. 11, L. 1915 adding Section 107A to the Town Law; People ex rel. Noble v. Mitchel (1917) 220 N. Y. 86 L. 1914, Ch. 443 Section 26 of the Judiciary Law.

[41] Matter of Handler v. Berry 138 Misc. 584 Supreme Court New York County Ch. 500, L. 1930 amending Section 132 Code of Criminal Procedure.

[42] Matter of Gresser v. O'Brien (1934) 263 N. Y. 622 Ch. 636, 637, L. 1932.

[43] Matter of Carey v. Cruise (1927) 246 N. Y. 237; Matter of Wolff v. Cruise 246 N. Y. 537; Matter of O'Neill v. Cruise 244 N. Y. 528; Matter of Capozolli v. Cruise, 244 N. Y. 529; Matter of Troy v. Cruise, 244 N. Y. 529 Ch. 829, L. 1920. Article 6, Section 17 applying to the election of justices in towns was held not to apply.

[44] Schieffelin v. Goldsmith (1930) 253 N. Y. 243 Ch. 430, L. 1929.

of the same political party as the man he replaced. Carrying on a business by justices of the Court of Special Sessions was forbidden, and made grounds for removal by another act sanctioned by the Appellate Division.[45] It was not considered valid though to give the Mayor of Long Beach the power to revoke the appointment to office of an acting city judge, a procedure requiring a hearing before a court.[46] No objection was found to a law obliging a judge of a court of record to file a certificate with the Secretary of State, giving the judge's age and the date of the conclusion of the term for which he was elected.[47]

The history of claims against the state is a long and checkered one. Its course has led in the past to the creation and abolition of various tribunals to handle this type of case. In 1875 the legislature was forbidden by a constitutional amendment from auditing or allowing any private claim or account against the state, but was permitted to pay such claims as should have been audited and allowed according to law.[48] Since then an alternation has taken place between boards and courts with the matter becoming a political football as one legislature would abolish the existing Board of Claims and establish a Court of Claims, with the process being reversed a few years later. In addition the terms of the judges were changed. In spite of agitation to place the Court of Claims beyond the power of such legislative changes, the Judiciary Article of 1925 (Article 6, Section 23) specifically gave the legislature the unabridged authority to make alterations. The result, however, has been that the Court of Claims, as created in 1915, has not been a political issue since.[49]

[45] Matter of Deuel (1906) 112 A. D. 99 Ch. 601, L. 1905.

[46] Hanower v. Candide (1935) 269 N. Y. 593 Section 191 of Long Beach Charter, L. 1922, Ch. 625.

[47] Johnson v. Flynn (1936) 248 A. D. 649 3rd Dept. Section 23 Judiciary Law.

[48] Article 3, Section 19 (now Article 6, Section 23).

[49] Judicial Problems, *op. cit.*, pp. 390-400.

In 1912 the Court of Appeals decided that the legislature, in abolishing the previously existing Court of Claims the year before and re-establishing the Board of Claims, had not violated Article 6, Section 11 requiring a two-thirds vote of the Senate, on the Governor's recommendation, to remove all other judicial officers, except judges of the Court of Appeals, justices of the Supreme Court, justices of the peace, judges and justices of inferior courts not of record, as the Court of Claims was held to be only an auditing board or quasi-judicial body.[50]

Article 8, Section 9 of the 1894 Constitution provided that:

> Neither the credit nor the money shall be given or loaned to or in aid of any association, corporation, or private undertaking.

Article 7, Section 6 provided that:

> Neither the legislature, canal board nor any person acting in behalf of the state, shall audit, allow, or pay any claim which, as between citizens of the state, would be barred by lapse of time. This provision shall not be construed to repeal any statute fixing the time within which claims shall be presented or allowed, nor shall it extend to any claims duly presented within the time allowed by law, and prosecuted with due diligence from the time of such presentment. But if the claimant shall be under legal disability, the claim may be presented within two years after such disability is removed.[51]

The courts soon evolved a standard in passing upon the acts of the legislature authorizing the Court of Claims to hear, audit and determine the diverse demands against the state. If the claims were morally justified, then the acts were constitutional. If not, they conflicted with the above articles. In the years under discussion six such acts were held invalid, while nine were found satisfactory.

50 People ex rel. Carmody v. Luce (1912) 204 N. Y. 478 L. 1911, Ch. 856.
51 Lincoln, *op. cit.*, Vol. IV, *passim*.

REGULATION OF THE COURTS

These six included attempts to authorize payment of damages to a widow and child of a member of the National Guard whose death had been caused by his own negligence,[52] payment of the expenses of an assemblyman in defending a libel suit,[53] the award of costs for successful defense by a General Sessions judge of an action brought by reason of any act arising out of his judicial duties since 1920,[54] giving of additional recompense to a claimant who had already secured a judgment in the Appellate Division for a sum of $25,000 to which the legislature allowed an addition of $13,000 by the Court of Claims,[55] reimbursing a magistrate for a successful defense of a libel suit,[56] and compensating a company which had built a road for its own purposes.[57]

The acts sustained by the courts legitimized claims arising from the following situations: cancellation of letters patent to a claimant,[58] injuries to an electrician inflicted by an inmate at King's Park State Hospital,[59] an accident at a fair in Syracuse,[60] the fall of an engineer while working for the state,[61] failure of a state-sponsored improvement for which bonds

[52] Lewis v. State (1921) 234 N. Y. 587 Memo. affirming 197 A. D. 712 (1921) 3rd Dept. Ch. 611, L. 1918.

[53] Cuvillier v. State of New York (1920) 250 N. Y. 258 Ch. 711, L. 1927.

[54] Rosalsky v. State of New York (1930) 254 N. Y. 117 Ch. 72, L. 1928. The award was to be "for such sum as shall be just and equitable" not exceeding a stated amount. This was considered too broad and not limited to claims rooted in morality and conscience.

[55] Mendelson v. State (1930) 254 N. Y. 530 Memo. affirming 136 Misc. 242 (1930) Court of Claims.

[56] Corrigan v. State (1932) 260 N. Y. 645 Ch. 475, L. 1929.

[57] Ausable Chasm Co. v. State (1935) 266 N. Y. 326 Ch. 36, L. 1933.

[58] Wheeler v. State (1907) 190 N. Y. 406 Ch. 767, L. 1900.

[59] Munro v. State (1918) 223 N. Y. 208 Ch. 658, L. 1915.

[60] Rosa v. State (1919) 186 A. D. 156 3rd Dept. Ch. 657, L. 1915.

[61] Babcock v. State (1919) 190 A. D. 147 3rd Dept. Ch. 608, L. 1918. Affirmed without reference to constitutionality 231 N. Y. 560 (1921).

had been issued,[62] the reinstatement of an illegally dismissed postal employee,[63] the assumption of liability by the state for torts of its officers and employees,[64] the damages from a flood caused by a defective sluiceway,[65] losses to contractors due to delays in the construction of the state office building at Albany,[66] failure to furnish a proper site for a building foundation,[67] the furnishing by a heating contractor of extra heat when a general contractor needed more time to finish the building of a state hospital,[68] and injuries suffered by a student of a State Normal School while escaping from the building during a fire on a Saturday morning.[69]

Article 3, Section 28 of the Constitution of 1894 provided that:

> The legislature shall not, nor shall the common council of any city, nor any board of supervisors, grant any extra compensation to any public officer, servant, agent, or contractor.[70]

The subject matter and dates of passage of acts declared in violation of this article were: 1918—giving New York City

[62] Williamsburgh Savings Bank v. State (1926) 243 N. Y. 231 Ch. 830, L. 1923.

[63] Farrington v. State (1928) 248 N. Y. 112 Ch. 716, L. 1927.

[64] Jackson v. State (1933) 261 N. Y. 134 Section 2-a Court of Claims Act L. 1920, Ch. 922 amended L. 1929, Ch. 467. This act was retrospective.

[65] Bull v. State (1931) 231 A. D. 313 4th Dept. Ch. 469, L. 1929.

[66] Seglin Construction Co. v. State (1937) 249 A. D. 476 3rd Dept. Ch. 692, L. 1931. The state had compelled cessation of work while the original plans were altered.

[67] Cauldwell-Wingate Co. v. State (1937) 249 A. D. 892 3rd Dept. Ch. 735, L. 1931.

[68] Cascade Automatic Sprinkler Corporation v. State (1938) 277 N. Y. 612 Ch. 694, L. 1931 affirming 248 A. D. 922 (1938) 1st Dept.

[69] Agnew v. State (1938) 166 Misc. 602 L. 1934, Ch. 780. The act relieved the claimants from the burden of showing that the infant was present in the school by invitation or license.

[70] Lincoln, *op. cit.*, Vol. IV.

the privilege of canceling existing contracts, and remaking them on new terms, and 1921—conferring a right of action upon contractors who had relied upon a promise to pay certain claims against the city for delays as a result of the city's act;[71] 1919—authorizing the termination of state highway contracts entered into before April 6, 1917, and conferring jurisdiction upon the Court of Claims to make awards for increased cost incurred in the completion of such contracts;[72] 1923—empowering the Court of Claims to order recompense for the increased cost of performing a construction contract, caused by the delay of another contractor;[73] and 1931—making the state liable for damages to contractors arising from a natural mistake as to the nature of the material to be removed in the construction of a highway, where the contract had barred a plea of misunderstanding or deception, if construed to grant extra compensation.[74]

Two other cases which bore a relationship to the subject of the courts different from those already discussed were Sprintz v. Sexton and People ex rel. Wogan v. Rafferty. In the first of these, an act of 1904, providing that the sale of a portion of a stock of merchandise other than in the ordinary course of trade should be presumed fraudulent and void, was sustained as merely creating a rule of evidence.[75] In the second, an amendment to the Consolidated Laws of 1911, which had prevented the incoming county clerk from appointing a new

[71] McGovern v. City of New York (1923) 234 N. Y. 377 Ch. 586, L. 1918 and Ch. 911, L. 1921.

[72] Gordon v. State (1922) 233 N. Y. 1 Ch. 459, L. 1919.

[73] Barr and Co. v. State (1926) 127 Misc. 75 Court of Claims Ch. 821, L. 1923. A clause in the contract between the claimant and the state recited that no charges were to be made by the contractor for delays from any cause during the progress of the work.

[74] Weston v. State (1933) 262 N. Y. 46 Section 1 Ch. 752, L. 1931.

[75] (1908) 126 A. D. 421 2nd Dept. Ch. 569, L. 1904. A previous act making such bulk sales illegal had been declared unconstitutional in Wright v. Hart (1905).

chief clerk of the county court of Kings County, and vesting the chief clerk with the powers of fulfilling the county clerk's duties at any sitting of the county court, was held to violate Article 6, Section 19 which read " Clerks of the several counties shall be clerks of the Supreme Court, with such powers and duties as shall be prescribed by law. . . ." [76]

Omitting the cases dealing with claims, the net result shows forty-two cases in which the acts involved were held constitutional, sometimes by process of construction, and thirteen in which the acts were ruled invalid. In one case the judge thought the act did not apply to the particular case, but that if it did, it was invalid. Of the cases concerned with claims, twelve acts were sustained and ten invalidated.

In attempting to answer the questions set forth earlier, it would appear that no conscious endeavor was made by the legislature to undermine the courts, but that the judiciary was ever alert to any move to place undesirable burdens upon their shoulders, or to affect their powers or jurisdiction unfavorably. As for claims, the courts stopped several efforts to benefit certain individuals whom the judges considered unworthy of financial recompense, but agreed with the legislature in more instances than those in which they disagreed. On the whole, the more important legislation affecting these subjects was not overturned by the courts and no serious clash on this topic occurred during these years.

[76] (1913) 208 N. Y. 451 Ch. 30, Section 195 Cons. Laws as amended by L. 1911, Ch. 826; Sections 282, 283 as amended by L. 1911, Ch. 640.

CHAPTER III
CIVIL LIBERTIES

A POWERFUL argument advanced in support of judicial review is the need for defending the precious heritage of freedom, the product of centuries of struggle, against legislative onslaughts. Fears of the uncontrolled passions of uncurbed majorities have often been expressed. These fears have led many lawyers, historians and publicists to look to the courts as the guardians of the bill of rights. Since the judges serve for longer terms than the legislators, and are presumably more immune from passing emotional tempests, the feeling has grown that these rights may most safely be entrusted to them.

Furthermore, it is contended that those who were responsible for the inclusion of these bills of rights in our constitutions intended that the courts should have the final say in these matters, very much as in the case of litigation concerning the judicial department of the government.

Two questions will occur to the investigator as worthy of examination: 1. How far has the legislature shown an inclination to invade, suppress or destroy these basic rights? 2. To what extent have the courts fulfilled the role in which they have been cast by a defense of these rights against such legislative attacks? For the purposes of this study, the cases to be examined may be placed in three categories. The first consists of those dealing with freedom of speech, press, religion, assembly and closely related topics. The second includes those which have to do with the indictment and trial of persons accused of violations of the law. The third group comprises those in which the right to vote and questions of the franchise and the ballot were involved.

The provisions of the State Constitution of most relevance for a discussion of the first category of cases mentioned above were:

Article 1

Section 1

Section 1. No member of this State shall be disfranchised, or deprived of any of the rights or privileges secured to any citizen thereof, unless by the law of the land, or the judgment of his peers.

Section 2

Section 2. The trial by jury in all cases in which it has been heretofore used shall remain inviolate forever; but a jury trial may be waived by the parties in all civil cases in the manner to be prescribed by law.

In 1935 the following sentence was added:

The legislature may provide, however, by law, that a verdict may be rendered by not less than five-sixths of the jurymen constituting a jury in any civil case.

In 1937, after the word " waived " was added:

In the manner to be prescribed by law.

In 1937, after the words " by the parties in all civil cases " the phrase " in the manner to be prescribed by law " was omitted, and the following clause added:

and by the defendant in all criminal cases, except those in which the crime charged may be punishable by death.

Section 3

Section 3. The free exercise and enjoyment of religious profession and worship, without discrimination or preference, shall forever be allowed in this State to all mankind; and no person shall be rendered incompetent to be a witness on account of his opinions on matters of religious belief; but the liberty of conscience hereby secured shall not be so construed as to excuse acts of licentiousness, or justify practices inconsistent with the peace or safety of this State.

Section 4

Section 4. The privilege of the writ of habeas corpus shall not be suspended, unless when, in cases of rebellion or invasion, the public safety may require its suspension.

SECTION 5

Section 5. Excessive bail shall not be required nor excessive fines imposed, nor shall cruel and unusual punishments be inflicted, nor shall witnesses be unreasonably detained.

SECTION 6

Section 6. No person shall be held to answer for a capital or otherwise infamous crime (except in cases of impeachment, and in cases of militia when in actual service, and the land and naval forces in time of war, or which this State may keep with the consent of Congress in time of peace, and in cases of petit larceny, under the regulation of the Legislature), unless on presentment or indictment of a grand jury, and in any trial in any court whatever the party accused shall be allowed to appear and defend in person and with counsel as in civil actions. No person shall be subject to be twice put in jeopardy for the same offense; nor shall he be compelled in any criminal case to be a witness against himself; nor be deprived of life, liberty or property without due process of law; nor shall private property be taken for public use without just compensation.

SECTION 8

Section 8. Every citizen may freely speak, write, and publish his sentiments on all subjects, being responsible for the abuse of that right; and no law shall be passed to restrain or abridge the liberty of speech or of the press. In all criminal prosecutions or indictments for libels, the truth may be given in evidence to the jury; and if it shall appear to the jury that the matter charged as libelous is true, and was published with good motives and for justifiable ends, the party shall be acquitted; and the jury shall have the right to determine the law and the fact.

SECTION 9

Section 9. No law shall be passed abridging the right of the people peaceably to assemble and to petition the government, or any department thereof; nor shall any divorce be granted otherwise than by due judicial proceedings; nor shall any lottery or the sale of lottery tickets, pool-selling, book making, or any other kind of gambling hereafter be authorized or allowed within this State; and the Legislature shall pass appropriate laws to prevent offenses against any of the provisions of this section.

SECTION 10

Section 10. The people of this State, in their right of sovereignty, are deemed to possess the original and ultimate property in and to all lands within the jurisdiction of the State; and all lands the title to which shall fail, from a defect of heirs, shall revert or escheat to the people.[1]

The most celebrated case was that of People v. Gitlow, in which the defendant had published an article entitled "The Left Wing Manifesto" in a periodical called *The Revolutionary Age*. The temper of this manifesto may be indicated by a few excerpts:

> The old machinery of the state cannot be used by the revolutionary proletariat. It must be destroyed. . . . The revolutionary epoch of the final struggle of Capitalism may last for years and tens of years; but the Communist International offers a policy and program immediate and ultimate in scope, that provides for the immediate class struggle against Capitalism in its revolutionary implications, and for the final act for the conquest of power. The old order is in decay. Civilization is in collapse. The proletarian revolution and the Communist reconstruction of society—the struggle for these—is now indispensable. This is the message for the Communist International to the workers of the world. The Communist International calls the proletariat of the world to the final struggle.

For this manifesto Gitlow was arrested, charged with violating Sections 160 and 161 of the Penal Laws of 1902, sometimes known as the Criminal Anarchy Law, which forbade the advocation, advising or teaching of the duty, necessity or propriety of overthrowing organized government by force or violence.

[1] Amendments Proposed, *op. cit.*, pp. 1, 9, 10, 11, 39, 40, 44.

The law was sustained by the Appellate Division and by the Court of Appeals. The latter divided four to three, with Judges Cardozo and Cuthbert Pound dissenting on the ground that Gitlow was protected by the Constitution in his use of free speech, and that the provisions of the law were applicable to anarchists, but not to the defendant. The case was appealed to the United States Supreme Court, the law being challenged under the due process clause. Again both law and conviction were sustained, with Justices Holmes and Brandeis dissenting. Justice Holmes enunciated his famous "clear and present danger" doctrine, holding that whether Gitlow's views were considered as an expression of opinion or an incitement to action should not be the determining factor, but that "the question in every case is whether the words used are used in such circumstances and are of such a nature as to create a clear and present danger that they would bring about the substantive evils that (the State) has a right to prevent." He added the qualification that the danger need not be demonstrated, if the attempt were made to cause the forbidden result "at once and not at some indefinite time in the future." This he thought was not the case with Gitlow's manifesto. It is significant that in neither the Court of Appeals nor the United States Supreme Court did the dissenting judges intimate that the sections of the Penal Law, under which the defendant had been arrested, were unconstitutional. Their opinions were based on interpretations of the law itself, read in conjunction with the Constitution. In order to safeguard freedom of speech, no one suggested that these sections be held invalid. However, the opinion of the United States Supreme Court showed now that it regarded the due process clause of the Fourteenth Amendment as applying to protect the customary civil liberties within the states.[2]

[2] People v. Gitlow (1922) 234 N. Y. 132. Court of Appeals, affirmed as Gitlow v. New York (1925) 268 U. S. 652. Judge Pound thought that Gitlow's advocacy of the Soviet system was not criminal under the act of 1902 which he considered applicable only to those believing in no organized form of government. If Gitlow had attempted to implement his views, he would have broken the laws, but otherwise he had not violated this particular act. 234 N. Y. 155. Justice Holmes' opinion may be found at 268 U. S. 672.

Five other noteworthy cases were People v. Crane (1915), People v. Sanger (1918), People ex rel. Doyle v. Atwell (1921), People v. American Socialist Society (1922) and People ex rel. Bryant v. Zimmerman (1928). In the first of these, the requirement that only citizens were to be employed in public works was sustained.[3] In the second, a section of the Penal Law which made it a misdemeanor to sell, advertise, or give information for the prevention of conception, was sustained and in the third, a portion of the Charter of Mount Vernon under which the common council of that city was empowered to prohibit assembling upon streets or congregating upon street corners, and to make ordinances deemed expedient for good government was not found violative of any clause in the Constitution.[4] A prohibition against schools giving instruction without a license from the University of the State of New York, and a stipulation that no license should be granted where doctrines advocating the overthrow of government by force were taught, were upheld by the Appellate Division in 1922.[5] The rise of the Ku Klux Klan led the legislature to require that unincorporated secret societies of twenty or more people, whose members were bound by oath, should file their membership rosters and other information with the Secretary of State. Certain exceptions were made, such as labor unions and fraternities. Both the Court of Appeals and the United States Supreme Court sustained the law as not conflicting

[3] People v. Crane, 214 N. Y. 154, Section 14 Labor Law L. 1909, Ch. 36 (Cons. Laws, Ch. 31). In Gould v. Bennett (1934) 153 Misc. 818 a provision that, in construction of public works by the state or by a municipality, preference should be given to citizens of the state who had been residents for six months prior to employment was not thought to violate the Fourteenth Amendment. Section 222 Labor Law as amended by Ch. 556, L. 1933 Supreme Court New York County.

[4] 222 N. Y. 192 Section 1142 Penal Law; 232 N. Y. 96 L. 1896 Ch. 182 Section 166 Subds. 5, 60.

[5] People v. American Socialist Society 202 A. D. 640 1st Dept. Ch. 667, L. 1921. Section 79 Education Law.

with the clause requiring equal protection in the Fourteenth Amendment.[6]

In Pathe Exchange Inc. v. Cobb (1923), the laws which created a "motion picture commission" with the power to regulate the exhibition of motion pictures were viewed as consistent with Article 1, Section 8 of the State Constitution, and with the Fourteenth Amendment.[7] A law which made one who pretended to tell fortunes a disorderly person was challenged as a violation of religious freedom, but was upheld in People v. Ashley (1918).[8] The state, said the court, might prohibit acts and practices deemed to be detrimental to the community. A provision that the State Commissioner of Education should prepare a program providing for a salute to the flag for the use of the public schools did not violate a person's constitutional right to religious liberty and to freedom of worship in the view of the New York courts.[9]

In only one case was a statute challenged as violating any of what are considered the fundamental freedoms, and declared unconstitutional by the state courts in these years. This was in the case of People v. Altman (1933) where the Appellate Division, by a three to two vote, without opinion, freed a defendant who had been accused of violating an act prohibiting the display of a red flag as an emblem in political activity, on the basis of the United States Supreme Court's decision in Stromberg v. California (1931), in which a similar California law had been held unconstitutional.[10]

[6] People ex rel. Bryant v. Zimmerman (1926) 241 N. Y. 405 Article 5-A Civil Rights Law Section 56 L. 1923, Ch. 664 (Cons. Laws, Ch. 6) Affirmed in 278 U. S. 63 (1928).

[7] 236 N. Y. 539 Ch. 715, L. 1921.

[8] 184 A. D. 520 2nd Dept. Subd. 3 Section 899 of Code of Criminal Procedure.

[9] People ex rel. Fish v. Sandstrom (1938) 167 Misc. 436 Subd. 1, Section 712 Education Law County Court Suffolk County.

[10] People v. Altman 241 A. D. 858. The content of the law (Section 2095-a Penal Law) may be found in the fuller treatment given in 280 N. Y. Supp. 248; Stromberg v. California 283 U. S. 359.

Prohibiting the sale of any property on Sunday, except food and other specified articles, was considered a reasonable restraint within the police power, as advancing the physical and moral well-being of the public by prescribing a day of general rest from labor, and was not an invalid interference with religious liberty.[11]

Since 1821 a provision protecting the writ of habeas corpus has been incorporated in the New York Constitution. As Article 1, Section 4 it has been given above. Attempts have been made to regulate, but not to suspend this writ in New York. One such attempt, limiting applications for the writ to the Appellate Division only " where the person is detained within the judicial district within which the term is held," was declared void in People ex rel. Patrick v. Frost (1909).[12] Two other acts, though, one of which authorized an appeal by the People from an order discharging a prisoner on habeas corpus, and the other of which gave the sole right to hear writs from persons detained in the county jail upon criminal charges to the Supreme Court during its sessions in a county, were sustained.[13]

Article 1, Section 6 of the New York Constitution was held to bar a section of the Code of Criminal Procedure authorizing a trial upon the filing of an information in People ex rel. Battista v. Christian (1928).[14] It was deemed permissible,

[11] Silberberg Bros. v. Douglas (1909) 62 Misc. 340 Supreme Court Erie Special Term Section 267 Penal Code. This provision did not deny equal protection of the laws because of the exception mentioned above. Sunday closing laws had been sustained before 1905. A well-known example is the case of Lindenmuller v. the People (1861).

[12] 133 A. D. 179 2nd Dept. Section 2017 Code of Civil Procedure.

[13] People ex rel. Hubert v. Kaiser (1912) 150 A. D. 541 1st Dept. Section 2058 Code of Civil Procedure. In this same case Section 2032, which required the court on habeas corpus to remand the prisoner if he were detained " by virtue of the final judgment or decree of a competent tribunal of civil or criminal jurisdiction," was also upheld; People ex rel. Whitman v. Woodward (1912) 150 A. D. 770 2nd Dept. Section 25 Code of Criminal Procedure.

[14] 249 N. Y. 314 Section 222 Code of Criminal Procedure. No waiver of the constitutional provision was permitted.

though, to use a fictitious name for the defendant in the subpoena issued by the District Attorney before a grand jury and to omit the subject about which the witness was to be examined.[15] Furthermore, a provision that an indictment for bigamy might be found in the county in which the defendant was arrested was found unobjectionable.[16]

In addition to the provisions relating to trial by jury contained in Article 1, Section 2, Article 6, Section 18 allowed the legislature to create courts of special sessions and inferior local courts and authorize them to try offenses without a jury, and Article 3, Section 18 contained in its list of prohibitions against the passage of private or local bills those having to do with "selecting, drawing, summoning or impaneling grand or petit jurors." [17] These provisions have been the subject of much litigation, not all of which is relevant to the present discussion.

A section of the New York City Charter which dispensed with jury trials in cases of petit larceny in the Court of Special Sessions,[18] and a section of the Code of Civil Procedure providing

[15] Matter of Osborne (1909) 62 Misc. 575 Court of General Sessions of New York County Section 612 Code of Criminal Procedure.

[16] People ex rel. Mayo v. Hanley (1919) 108 Misc. 591 Supreme Court New York Special Term Section 342 Penal Law.

[17] In addition to Lincoln, *op. cit.*, vol. IV, volume VI in the series issued by the New York State Constitutional Convention Committee in 1938 entitled *Problems Relating to Bill of Rights and General Welfare* has been consulted. See pp. 8-9 in particular.

[18] People ex rel. Burns v. Flaherty (1907) 119 A. D. 462 2nd Dept. Section 1410 Charter of New York, L. 1901 following People v. Stein 80 A. D. 457. In People ex rel. Enright v. Meyers (1911) 71 Misc. 77 Section 1458 Consolidation Act of the City of New York (L. 1882, Ch. 410) continued by the Inferior Criminal Courts Act (L. 1910, Ch. 659) defining the offense of disorderly conduct tending to a breach of the peace, which is triable without a jury, was sustained. Court of General Sessions of New York County. An allowable distinction was made between such conduct in cities and in villages, as greater damage, mischief and inconvenience might be caused in the former. Under the act a magistrate might sentence a defendant to six months in the workhouse. In People v. Lipschitz (1923) 120 Misc. 633 Sections 1458, 1459 and 1461, authorizing magistrates to deal with the offense of disorderly conduct upon complaint of a witness, before any police justice in New York City, were sustained. Supreme Court New York County L. 1882, Ch. 410.

for the appointment of a committee for an insane person, appointed by the court on the petition of a state officer, and allowing trial by jury to be waived, were not found in conflict with this article.[19] In People ex rel. Lemon v. Elmore sections of the Public Health Law empowering the District Attorney to bring action, and directing courts of equity to close a building where a house of prostitution was maintained, were sustained as enlarging the scope of the remedy of injunction, but another section directing the imposition of a penalty tax against the person maintaining the nuisance was held unconstitutional.[20] A court is allowed to order one or more issues in a civil action separately tried prior to the trial of other issues on the authority of Smith v. The Western Railway Company (1911)[21] while on the other hand, a defendant may be placed on trial where the indictment includes ninety separate counts according to People ex rel. Luciano v. Murphy (1937).[22] Two innovations of recent years which have obtained judicial sanction are the provision for alternate jurors who serve during the trial and are prepared to substitute in the event of the incapacitation of one of the regular members,[23] and the granting of jury trial in contempt cases, a change partly brought about by the criticism of labor unions and others who viewed the use of the injunc-

[19] Sporza v. The German Savings Bank (1908) 192 N. Y. 8 Section 2323a of Code of Civil Procedure; Section 140 of the Insanity Law, providing that any inmate, held in a criminal proceeding, who, in the opinion of the medical superintendent, was a mental defective and did not show evidence of insanity, might be transferred to a state institution on the application of the superintendent, accompanied by a certificate of mental defect executed by two qualified examiners, was upheld in People ex rel. Sanford v. Thayer (1923) 120 Misc. 571 County Court Ulster County.

[20] (1931) 256 N. Y. 489 Article 17-A of Public Health Law (Cons. Laws, Ch. 45) Section 343-b, Section 343-q constitutional; Section 343-w enacted by Ch. 670, L. 1927 unconstitutional.

[21] 203 N. Y. 499 Section 973 Code of Civil Procedure.

[22] 249 A. D. 879 3rd Dept. affirming 160 Misc. 573 (1936) amendment to Section 279 Code of Criminal Procedure L. 1936, Ch. 328.

[23] People v. Mitchell (1934) 266 N. Y. 15 Section 358-a Code of Criminal Procedure as added by L. 1933, Ch. 588.

tion and commitments for contempt in labor disputes as a threat to civil liberties.[24]

The courts have also been called upon to settle questions arising out of the procedure governing trials, including such problems as the admissibility of evidence. A joint trial could be provided for defendants in a trial for murder in the first degree, despite the fact that it would deprive each defendant of thirty peremptory challenges.[25] Article 1, Section 6, providing that " no person shall . . . be compelled in any criminal case to be a witness against himself," was the basis for a decision of the Court of Appeals in 1910 that the provisions authorizing the comptroller to secure evidence from private books and papers of transfers of stock in violation of the tax law were invalid.[26] Acts requiring a witness to answer questions in civil actions showing that " a thing in action has been bought, sold or received contrary to law " without being excused on the ground that his testimony might convict him of crime,[27] and providing

[24] Kronowitz v. Schlansky (1935) 156 Misc. 717 Supreme Court Kings County Ch. 299, L. 1935. Section 753-a Judiciary Law.

[25] People v. Kassis (1931) 145 Misc. 493 Section 391 Code of Criminal Procedure which provided, in the discretion of the court, for a separate or joint trial of defendants jointly indicted. The defendant, according to the decision, had no constitutional right to any peremptory challenge, though having such a right with challenges for cause. Supreme Court Oneida County.

[26] People ex rel. Ferguson v. Reardon 197 N. Y. 236, Ch. 241, L. 1905 then Article 12 of Tax Laws (Cons. Laws, Ch. 60).

[27] Chappell v. Chappell (1906) 116 A. D. 573 4th Dept. Section 837 Code of Civil Procedure. The court decided, however, that the legislature meant by " crime " certain particular crimes mentioned in the statute, and that the witness in the particular case could not be compelled to answer the question asked if he asserted the answer would tend to accuse him of a crime. In Matter of Birdsall (1906) 49 Misc. 53 a provision of the Forest, Fish and Game Law that " No person shall be excused from testifying in any civil or criminal action or proceeding taken or had under this act upon the ground that his testimony might tend to convict him of a crime " was held not to include a defendant put upon the witness stand by the people, but did apply to persons giving evidence against other persons. L. 1900, Ch. 20, Section 193, as amended L. 1903, Ch. 353 County Court St. Lawrence. A similar result to the Chappell case was reached in Matter of General Footwear Corporation (1931) 140 Misc. 791 in which Section 16 of the Debtor and

that persons refusing to answer legal and pertinent questions by officers or bodies, such as legislative investigating committees, might be committed for contempt, were sustained.[28] It was constitutional to provide that the fact that a defendant was engaged in an illegal occupation, or bore an evil reputation and had been found consorting with persons of like reputation, should be *prima facie* evidence that the consorting was for an unlawful purpose.[29] A requirement that a defendant in a criminal case furnish a bill of particulars setting forth in detail the place or places where he claimed to have been at the time of the commission of the crime, together with the names, addresses, residences and places of employment of the witnesses upon whom he intended to rely to establish his presence elsewhere than at the scene of the crime at the time of its commis-

---

Creditor Law, providing that on an examination conducted thereunder, no witness should be excused from answering on grounds of possible self-incrimination, but that the answers should not be used against him in any criminal action or proceeding, failed to grant the full constitutional protection. Supreme Court New York County.

[28] Matter of Barnes (1912) 204 N. Y. 108. Section 856 Code of Civil Procedure. In Matter of Fenton (1908) 58 Misc. 303, a portion of Section 32 of the Agricultural Law empowering the Commissioner of Agriculture to subpoena witnesses, providing for oaths and making false statements perjury, was sustained. The power to compel the attendance of witnesses and the giving of testimony was not considered distinctively judicial, as the Commissioner of Agriculture reported to the legislature. Supreme Court Erie Special Term. In Matter of Board of Aldermen (1910) 68 Misc. 478, Section 31 of the Charter of Buffalo, giving the chairmen of committees of the Board of Aldermen the power to subpoena witnesses who would be punished for refusal to be sworn or to answer any proper question, was sustained. Supreme Court Erie Special Term. On the other hand, in Matter of Doyle (1931) the Court of Appeals held that a joint resolution of the legislature, passed in 1933, providing that no witness who had claimed privilege and had been directed by a legislative committee to answer should be subject to prosecution or to any penalty or forfeiture for or on account of the transactions concerning which he might testify, did not grant sufficient protection against self-incrimination as a statute was needed. 257 N. Y. 244.

[29] People v. Arcidiaco (1935) 156 Misc. 461 Court of Special Sessions City of New York, Appellate Part, 1st Dept. Subd. 11, Section 722 Penal Law; People v. Berman (1935) 156 Misc. 463 Court of Special Sessions City of New York, Appellate Part, 2nd Dept.

sion, was also held valid.[30] Other laws upheld required a person to obey the subpoena of the State Superintendent of Elections in metropolitan districts, and to testify under oath as to the genuineness of registered voters,[31] declared the voluntary possession of certain dangerous weapons a crime without proof of other criminal intent,[32] and compelled the operators of motor vehicles to supply their names in case of accident.[33] An attempt to make "the presence in an automobile ... of ... a pistol" presumptive evidence of its illegal possession by all the persons found in such automobile at the time the weapon was found, was declared unconstitutional.[34] In People v. Reiss (1938) it was held that a person was not to be excused from testifying in an inquiry where the alleged offenses of others were being examined into, though the others might be co-conspirators with the witness. The witness could not be prosecuted for any transaction to which he testified, and no testimony was to be receivable against him though it could be used as evidence for a charge of perjury.[35] In an earlier case it had been held that any statute which, while compelling a witness to tesify, protected him if he disclosed the circumstances of his offense complied with the constitutional requirements.[36]

The validity of enactments permitting the reading of a deposition of a deceased person, taken by an official stenographer at a hearing before a magistrate, where the defendant or his

[30] People v. Schade (1936) 161 Misc. 212 Section 295-l Code of Criminal Procedure, as added by L. 1935, Ch. 506 County Court Queens County.

[31] People v. Cahill (1908) 126 A. D. 391 2nd Dept. The right to refuse to answer was not taken away. Disobedience of the subpoena constituted a misdemeanor, and false testimony, a felony.

[32] People v. Persce (1912) 204 N. Y. 397 Section 1897 Penal Law 1907.

[33] People v. Rosenheimer (1913) 209 N. Y. 115. See Ch. 10, note 91.

[34] People ex rel. Dixon v. Lewis (1937) 249 A. D. 464 Section 1898-a Penal Law as added by Ch. 390, L. 1936.

[35] 255 A. D. 509 1st Dept. Sections 584 and 1631 of Penal Law (added by L. 1910, Ch. 395; amended by L. 1931, Ch. 774.)

[36] People ex rel. Hunt v. Lane (1909) 132 A. D. 406 2nd Dept. Title 5 Section 41q Penal Code.

70 JUDICIAL REVIEW OF LEGISLATION IN N. Y.

attorney had had an opportunity to cross-examine, and which allowed such depositions to be entered as evidence if the witness were unable to testify because of insanity or because he could not be found within the state, were upheld in two cases in 1914.[37] A section of the Penal Law which created a presumption of fact against a defendant charged with the crime of obtaining property by means of a false statement of ability to pay was likewise sustained.[38]

The methods of dealing with convicted persons and others whom society feels must be institutionalized have brought before the courts a number of cases. The laws permitting the commitment of an insane person without notice, where it was felt that such information might produce undue excitement, were upheld[39] as was that part of the Code of Criminal Procedure, requiring a defendant acquitted on a plea of insanity to be committed to a state lunatic asylum without notice and hearing, if his discharge were deemed dangerous to the public peace and safety.[40]

[37] People v. Qualey 210 N. Y. 202 Section 221 b of Code of Criminal Procedure L. 1912, Ch. 290; People v. Vitusky 155 A. D. 139 1st Dept. Subd. 3 Section 8 Code of Civil Procedure.

[38] People ex rel. Woronoff v. Mallon (1918) 222 N. Y. 456 Section 442 Penal Law. The United States Supreme Court upheld the conviction of defendants who had been found guilty of conniving to withdraw a person from an insane asylum, who had been committed by a court order, under Sections 580 and 583, making criminal an agreement to commit an act for the perversion of justice or the due administration of the laws. Drew v. Thaw (1914) 235 U. S. 432.

[39] People ex rel. Andrews v. Zacker (1908) 126 A. D. 744 1st Dept. Section 62 of the Insanity Law amended by L. 1903, Ch. 146; Brayman v. Grant (1909) 130 A. D. 272 3rd Dept. In Chaloner v. Sherman (1917) 242 U. S. 455 the United States Supreme Court held that the omission of the New York statute concerning proceedings *de lunatico inquirendo* (Sections 2320 et seq. Code Civil Procedure) to provide expressly that notice of and opportunity to be heard at the inquisition should be afforded the alleged incompetent, was not in violation of the due process clause, as under decisions of the Court of Appeals such notice and opportunity were afforded by implication.

[40] People ex rel. Peabody v. Chanler (1909) 133 A. D. 159 2nd Dept. Section 454 Code of Criminal Procedure.

CIVIL LIBERTIES 71

The introduction of the indeterminate sentence was tested in the courts on three occasions. On the first, the law making it compulsory for certain offenses previously committed was approved, and not held in conflict with the clauses forbidding ex post facto punishments.[41] Another statute, authorizing this kind of sentence to Elmira Reformatory for such an offense as grand larceny in the second degree, was held not to encroach upon the judicial functions, nor to contravene Article 4, Section 5 of the State Constitution, vesting the pardoning power in the Governor, for, by the express terms of the statute, this power was reserved to the executive.[42] The third case resulted in the upholding of a law of 1915 providing such sentences for certain offenses in first class cities, and for the appointment of a parole commission, made applicable to crimes committed after the act was passed, but before the appointment of the commission.[43] The change of the sentence for robbery from a definite period of fifteen years to an indeterminate span, with a minimum of ten years and a maximum of fifteen, which unfavorably affected a convict's chances for parole, was nevertheless sustained, the court declaring that the right to parole was an act of grace and favor, and any subsequent legislation therefrom relating to its exercise afforded no basis for relief on the ground that it was ex post facto.[44]

The famous Baumes Law, decreeing increased punishment for one convicted of a felony who had been previously convicted, with life imprisonment made mandatory after the fourth

[41] People ex rel. Ammon v. Johnson (1906) 114 A. D. 876 2nd Dept. Ch. 425, L. 1901.

[42] People v. Madden (1907) 120 A. D. 338 1st Dept. Section 9, Ch. 711, L. 1887 (Section 24 Ch. 378 L. 1900, Section 700 Penal Code.)

[43] People ex rel. Cerzosie v. The Warden (1918) 224 N. Y. 307 L. 1915, Ch. 579. This law as amended by Ch. 287, L. 1916 providing for increased indeterminate sentences for offenses such as assault and disorderly conduct was approved in People ex rel. Berger v. The Warden (1917) 176 A. D. 602 1st Dept. and People ex rel. Liebowitz v. The Warden (1919) 186 A. D. 730.

[44] People ex rel. Kleinger v. Wilson (1938) 254 A. D. 406 3rd Dept. Correction Laws Section 230, Subd. 4-a, as added by L. 1933, Ch. 510.

such conviction, was challenged unsuccessfully in People v. Gowasky (1927).[45] Another law giving the Commissioner of Corrections the power to transfer a prisoner from a reformatory to a state prison was ruled not to be an unconstitutional delegation of judicial powers to an administrative official nor ex post facto as applied to the criminal.[46] An attempt of the legislature to place conditions on the commutation of sentences, by putting the persons affected under the jurisdiction of the parole board, was held to limit the constitutional authority of the Governor under Article 4, Section 3 in People ex rel. Ross v. Wilson (1937).[47]

A case occurring in the Magistrate's Court of New York City resulted in the decision that a law prohibiting the admittance to bail of any person charged with felony, until his fingerprints should have been taken to ascertain whether he had previously been convicted, was in violation of Article 1, Section 5, quoted above, as well as the due process clause.[48]

The whole question of the right to vote and the ballot was responsible for more laws being declared unconstitutional than either of the two categories just considered. Viewing the process of voting from registration to the time when the elector casts his vote, the cases may be further subdivided. An act of 1908 which required the electors in cities of one million or more to sign a public copy of the register when they could write, and to truthfully answer questions propounded to them when they could not, was held not to contravene Article 2,

[45] 244 N. Y. 451 Sections 1941, 1942, 1943, as amended by Ch. 457, L. 1926. Section 1941 of the Penal Law, when applied so as to cause a person who had been convicted of a previous offense for which he had been pardoned by the President to receive a longer sentence than for a first offense, was upheld by the United States Supreme Court in Corlesi v. New York (1914) 233 U. S. 51.

[46] People ex rel. Carnerale v. Brophy (1938) 277 N. Y. 667 Section 293 of Correction Law Ch. 455, L. 1931 (Cons. Laws, Ch. 43).

[47] 250 A. D. 143 3rd Dept. Section 218 Ch. 902, L. 1935.

[48] People v. Heron (1926) 127 Misc. 141 Ch. 14, L. 1926 enacting Section 552-a Code of Criminal Procedure.

Sections 1 and 4 or Article 3, Section 18.[49] The law of 1923 which abolished the former literacy test by the election board and substituted proofs by a certificate issued under the rules of the State Board of Regents was challenged to no avail on the grounds of violating both Article 2, Section 1 and Article 2, Section 6, which provided for bi-partisan election boards for the duty of registering voters and counting votes.[50] The Court of Appeals invalidated a law of 1911 which required voters outside of places with a population of five thousand or more, whose names did not appear on the poll book of the last general election, to register in person,[51] and one of 1913 requiring the affidavits of a voter and of two electors as the condition of registration, without a personal appearance at the first meeting of the registry board, in districts outside of places with a population of five thousand or over.[52] That part of the Election Law which excluded common law evidence of the right to vote including the testimony of the prospective elector's wife was also declared unconstitutional in 1906.[53]

[49] Matter of Ahern (1909) 195 N. Y. 493 L. 1908, Ch. 521. Article 2, Section 1 provided that every male citizen who satisfied the age, citizenship and residence requirements should be entitled to vote at elections while Article 2, Section 4 provided that laws should be made for ascertaining the citizens who should be entitled to the right of suffrage and for the registration of voters. Article 3, Section 18 prohibited the passage of a private or local bill concerned with the opening and conducting of elections or designating places of voting.

[50] People ex rel. Chadbourne v. Voorhis (1923) 236 N. Y. 437 Election Laws Section 166 amended L. 1923, Ch. 809.

[51] Matter of Fraser v. Brown (1911) 203 N. Y. 136 Section 6, Ch. 649, L. 1911.

[52] Matter of Ruppert v. Rees (1914) 212 N. Y. 514 Section 159 of Election Law as amended by Ch. 820 of L. 1913. The relevant portion of Article 2, Section 4 read "but voters not residing in such cities or villages [having 5,000 inhabitants or more] shall not be required to apply in person for registration at the first meeting of the officers having charge of the registry of voters."

[53] Matter of Morgan (1906) 114 A. D. 45 1st Dept. Section 31 Election Law amendment by L. 1905, Ch. 675. The remainder of the law providing that the affidavit of the Superintendent of Elections (based on inquiry of claimed residence) should be presumptive evidence against the elector was upheld.

74 JUDICIAL REVIEW OF LEGISLATION IN N. Y.

Disputes over nominating petitions resulted in the upsetting of several laws. One forbade a party committee to nominate a candidate of another party for the same office.[54] A second required independent nominations for the assembly to be signed by five hundred voters qualified as prescribed by statute.[55] The courts did uphold a law permitting an independent certificate of nomination to be made up of several sheets, and providing that no separate sheet should be received if five per cent of the names were fraudulent or forged. There was no compulsion for the nominators to sign separate sheets because they might all sign single sheets or each sign a sheet by himself.[56] Sanctioned also were statutes requiring fifteen hundred signatures to a petition for an independent nomination of a Supreme Court justice;[57] requiring five percent of the votes cast for governor at the last gubernatorial election in a Municipal Court district in Brooklyn for making an independent nomination for Municipal Court justice;[58] and increasing the minimum number of signatures required on independent nominating petitions for candidates in certain political units, including assembly and aldermanic districts, from five to seven per cent of

[54] In Re Callahan (1910) 200 N. Y. 59 Section 136 Election Laws (Cons. Laws, Ch. 17). In 1931 a section of the Election Law permitting the Supreme Court or a justice of this court to cancel the names on an enrollment list of a political party of those who were out of sympathy with the principles of the party, or who had made materially false statements in their enrollment declarations, was upheld. Matter of Newkirk 144 Misc. 765 Section 332 Election Law.

[55] People ex rel. Hotchkiss v. Smith (1912) 206 N. Y. 231 L. 1911, Ch. 891 Section 62, at time of case Section 122. Another part of Section 122, requiring one hundred electors to join in making a certificate for the independent nomination of ward officers in a city, including aldermen, was held valid in Matter of Independent Certificate (Aldermen of Cohoes) (1912) 78 Misc. 87 Albany Special Term.

[56] Matter of Burke (1911) 203 N. Y. 293 (Cons. Laws, Ch. 17) as amended by L. 1911, Ch. 649.

[57] Matter of O'Brien (1912) 152 A. D. 356 3rd Dept. Ch. 891, L. 1911.

[58] Matter of Richards (1917) 221 N. Y. 684 Section 122 of Election Law.

CIVIL LIBERTIES 75

the total vote for governor cast at the last election in the unit.[59]

Five decisions related to the make-up of the ballot itself. A prohibition in the New York City Charter against an election for vacancy in the Municipal Court, unless the vacancy occurred three months before the general election, combined with requirements for an appointment by the mayor for the interim, which would, on this particular occasion, have been about two years and five months, and then for an election for the full term, which might occur in an even-numbered year, was ruled unconstitutional in 1911.[60] A law of this same year requiring the name of the nominee to be printed only once on the ballot was invalidated in the case of Hopper v. Britt (1911).[61] The next year in a case with the same name, the section of the Election Law forbidding the name of a candidate to appear more than once on the ballot as a candidate for the same public office, or for the same party position, was also nullified by the court.[62] Another amendment to the Election Laws, passed twenty years later, which stipulated that the name of a person, nominated for an office by an independent body, should appear only once, in the column containing the names of the cadidates for other offices nominated by such party, unless the independent body should have nominated candidates for more than fifty per cent of the offices to be filled,[63] was held to dis-

[59] Matter of Howe v. Cohen (1935) 268 N. Y. 706 Subd. 4 Section 137 Election Law (Cons. Laws, Ch. 17) as amended by Section 8 of Ch. 955, L. 1935.

[60] Markland v. Scully 203 N. Y. 158 Ch. 603, Section 3, L. 1907 amended Section 1357 New York City Charter.

[61] 203 N. Y. 144 Section 12 Ch. 649, L. 1911.

[62] Matter of Hopper v. Britt (1912) Ch. 891, L. 1911, Section 58.

[63] Crane v. Voorhis (1931) 257 N. Y. 298 Section 249 Election Law (Cons. Laws, Ch. 17) amended L. 1931, Ch. 270. Section 249 Election Law as reenacted by L. 1922, Ch. 588 requiring that the names of candidates, nominated by a political party, and also by an independent body, should appear on the voting machine only in the party rows, was held unconstitutional in Matter of Gilfillan v. Commissioners of Elections (1924) 124 Misc. 628 Supreme Court Erie County. Affirmed in (1925) 212 A. D. 855,

criminate against the independent voters in violation of Article 1, Section 1. Under this law, the name of the candidate would have appeared in the party row with the emblem of the independent body nominating him alongside on the same row. It was not considered unconstitutional though to cause the names of the candidates for City Court in New York City to be grouped together with instructions to vote for only five.[64] In 1933 the Supreme Court held that a section of the Election Law should be liberally construed to permit the placing of the names, the emblems and the designating letters on ballots in order of sequence, both as regards independent political bodies as well as regular parties.[65]

The use of the voting machine was challenged but upheld by the courts.[66] Later it was decided that the machines did not have to contain the names of the candidates for presidential electors if their names were available in such manner as would permit a voter to write in the names of other candidates.[67]

Two other cases having a bearing on the subject matter of this chapter were Fawcett v. Andrews (1922) and Akely v. Kinnicutt (1924). In the first of these a law was held valid limiting the use of any family name or names in a business,

---

4th Dept. Affirmed again in (1925) 240 N. Y. 579. In Matter of Callahan (1929) 252 N. Y. 14 this law was held constitutional, except where its application would be unfair to and prejudicial to a particular class of voters. A memorandum decision of the Court of Appeals in Lynn v. Nichols (1930) 254 N. Y. 630 followed the Gilfillan case.

64 Matter of Walsh v. Boyle (1917) 179 A. D. 582 1st Dept. Ch. 537, L. 1916. The court held that the legislature had the power to fix the form of the ballot.

65 Matter of LaGuardia v. Cohen 149 Misc. 110 Section 249 Election Law. Supreme Court New York County. In addition, it was held that if the column of closed fists pointing to each separate row on the ballot with the name of the party placed on the fist were optional, it must nevertheless be used without discrimination.

66 Matter of Gerling v. Nichols (1924) 123 Misc. 811 Sections 243, 251, 256, 260 Election Law. Supreme Court Monroe Special Term.

67 Matter of Thomas v. Cohen (1933) 146 Misc. 836 Sections 290 et seq. Election Law. Supreme Court Kings County.

unless the name were the real name of the person conducting the business, or the business were being conducted by a successor in interest to the person using that name.[68] In the second a section of the Civil Practice Act was sustained, permitting persons to join in one action as plaintiffs, where a common question of law or fact would arise if separate actions were brought.[69]

Forty-nine of the sixty-six acts examined in this chapter were held constitutional, and seventeen, unconstitutional. The courts showed greatest watchfulness in protecting the rights of independent and minor party candidates to a place on the ballot. In the main, the judges did not disagree with the legislators as to the validity of laws affecting freedom of speech, press and religion. This was notably so in the unsettled period following World War 1, when the legislature enacted laws which, as administered, restricted organizations such as the Socialists on the one hand, and the Ku Klux Klan on the other. In so far as the legislature succumbed to hysteria, as critics assert, the courts did little to restrain its actions. To the extent that the legislature was exercising its powers legitimately, the courts assented, but this would have been the result without judicial review.

[68] 203 A. D. 591 1st Dept. Amendment of Section 440 Penal Law by Ch. 446, L. 1915.

[69] 238 N. Y. 471 Section 209 Civil Practice Act. It was held not violative of Article 1, Section 2.

CHAPTER IV
COMMERCE, PRIVILEGES AND CONTRACTS

CONSIDERED in the order of the situations in which the critics of judicial review concede its justifiability, a circumstance in which a state law conflicts with a clause or clauses of the Federal Constitution would take precedence over invalidation on grounds of violation of the State Constitution. The reasoning behind this viewpoint is similar to that which supports the Supreme Court's power over state statutes. If it is necessary, as Justice Holmes and others have declared, that the act of a subordinate legislature be reviewed by the Supreme Court under the Federal Constitution, in order to maintain uniformity and preserve the whole against the encroachments of one of its parts, logically it is felt that the subordinate judiciary ought to place the Constitution and laws of the Federal government paramount to the acts of the subordinate state legislatures. Indeed, they are bound by the Federal Constitution to do so.[1]

Difficulties, however, begin when the Supreme Court and the state courts disagree over the interpretation of the same clause in the Constitution. Since the " due process " clause appears in both the United States and New York Constitutions and has been under examination in such a great number of cases, discussion of this and closely allied subjects has been reserved for a later chapter. In the present one, four other important clauses of the Federal Constitution have been selected for consideration: the commerce clause, the privileges and immunities clauses, and the clause prohibiting the impairment of the obligation of contracts.

[1] Article 6 provided that " This Constitution, and the laws of the United States which shall be made in pursuance thereof; and all treaties made, or which shall be made, under the authority of the United States, shall be the supreme law of the land; and the judges in every state shall be bound thereby, anything in the Constitution or laws of any state to the contrary notwithstanding."

A. The Commerce Clause

Article 1, Section 8, Subdivision 3 provides that "the Congress shall have power to regulate commerce with foreign nations, and among the several states, and with the Indian tribes." In 1824, in the great case of Gibbons v. Ogden, involving a series of New York statutes, the Supreme Court had held that state laws affecting commerce, which were in conflict with congressional regulations, were unconstitutional.[2] In later cases, notably Cooley v. The Board of Wardens (1852), it had decided that a state might, on occasion, legislate concerning matters pertaining to interstate commerce upon which Congress had passed no law.[3] These decisions have had as their consequence two lines of decisions, one upholding and the other striking down the enactments of state legislatures. This has had its repercussions in the decisions of the state courts, though the latter have at times interpreted state laws challenged under the commerce clause more leniently or more strictly than the Federal courts.

In the following cases, which exclude all those relating to taxation, it may be seen that the commerce clause was not too high a barrier for most state legislation to hurdle, as far as the state courts were concerned. In only three instances did the courts find it necessary to hold statutes invalid. The substance of the decision in People v. Hudson River Connecting Railway (1920) was that a defendant, authorized by Congress in 1914 to build a bridge across the Hudson, could not be deprived of his franchise by a state law of 1917 seeking to repeal an earlier grant of permission by the state in 1913.[4] In Brood en Beschnit Fabrick v. Aluminum Company of America (1931), a section of the General Corporation Law, authorizing an action against one foreign corporation by another, was declared unconstitutional when construed to subject an inter-

[2] 9 Wheaton 1.
[3] 12 Howard 299.
[4] 228 N. Y. 203 Ch. 713, L. 1917.

state carrier to the necessity of defending suits, other than tort actions, in the courts of this state.[5] In Miele v. Chicago, Milwaukee, St. Paul and Pacific Rd. Co. (1934) another section of the General Corporation Law, permitting an action against a foreign corporation by a resident or by a domestic corporation, was considered null to the extent that it authorized a suit by a resident assignee of a cause of action accruing to a non-resident interstate carrier for damage to merchandise, since requiring the defendant to make a defense in New York would constitute an undue burden.[6]

The subject matter of the statutes which satisfied the courts as to their constitutionality included the following: providing compensation for the erection of telephone poles to individuals on the Tonawanda Reservation, as well as to the Council of the Seneca nation;[7] regulating the taking of deposits by certain persons, firms and corporations for transmission to foreign countries, by requiring the former to post a bond;[8] compelling foreign corporations (excepting moneyed and railroad ones) with an office for the transaction of business in the state to keep a stock book containing the names of stockholders, and imposing a penalty for a refusal to allow inspection;[9] requiring a company to erect roadways for pedes-

[5] 231 A D. 693 1st Dept. Subd. 4 Section 225 General Corporation Law.

[6] 151 Misc. 137 City Court of New York, New York County Section 224 General Corporation Law. However, the extension of the general jurisdiction of the courts of this state under Section 224 to transitory actions against a foreign corporation, where the subject of the action was a tort committed outside of the state, and the plaintiffs were residents of the state at the time the action was commenced, was held valid in Rojzenblitt v. Polish Trans-Atlantic Shipping Co. (1936) 162 Misc. 251 City Court of New York, New York County.

[7] Jemison v. The Bell Telephone Company of Buffalo (1906) 186 N. Y. 493, L. 1902, Ch. 296 amending Indian Law L. 1892, Ch. 679 adding Section 89.

[8] Musco v. United Security Company (1909) 186 N. Y. 459 Ch. 185, L. 1907.

[9] Hovey v. The DeLong Hook and Eye Company (1911) 147 A.D. 881 1st Dept. L. 1909, Ch. 61. Section 33 of Stock Corporation Law.

COMMERCE, PRIVILEGES AND CONTRACTS 81

trians and vehicles on a bridge across the Niagara River;[10] creating the Port Authority by interstate compact between New York and New Jersey, in order to remove artificial barriers to delay in the shipment of goods existing at the port of New York, and to confer special benefits upon the people of the two states and the country as well;[11] allowing an action against a foreign corporation to be maintained where it is doing business within the state;[12] serving process on non-resident defendants, including one engaged in interstate commerce at the time of a collision;[13] and ordering that the coal or coke, brought into the state by trucks, be weighed and accompanied by a certificate of origin.[14]

Four decisions were handed down affecting labor. The law directing railroad corporations to pay their employees semi-monthly in cash was upheld in New York Central and Hudson River Railroad Company v. Williams (1910).[15] The Court of Appeals also sustained the limiting of the hours of railroad employees in charge of block signal towers to an eight hour

[10] People v. International Bridge Company (1918) 223 N. Y. 137 Ch. 666, L. 1915.

[11] City of New York v. Willcox (1921) 115 Misc. 351 Supreme Court New York County L. 1921, Ch. 154. The sovereignty of the states was not relinquished or the equal protection clause violated, in the opinion of the court.

[12] Murnan v. Wabash Railway Company (1927) 220 A. D. 218 2nd Dept. Subd. 4 Section 47 General Corporation Law (as added by L. 1920, Ch. 916). Later it was decided that an interstate carrier doing business within New York might be sued by a foreign corporation or its assignee for failure to deliver in New York a shipment from another state. Jacobson v. Baltimore and Ohio Railroad Company (1936) 161 Misc. 268 City Court of New York Special Term New York County.

[13] Sweet v. Miller (1933) 147 Misc. 806 Supreme Court Erie County Section 52 Vehicle and Traffic Law.

[14] Rueffer v. Department of Agriculture and Markets (1938) 279 N. Y. 16 Article 16-a of Agriculture and Markets Law. (Cons. Laws, Ch. 69).

[15] 199 N. Y. 108 Sections 10 and 11 of the Labor Law. (Cons. Laws, Ch. 511.) This was affirmed by the United States Supreme Court in Erie Railroad Co. v. Williams (1914) 233 U. S. 685.

day. A federal act of March 4, 1907, to go into effect a year later, had set a nine hour day but no trespass was found by the judges on congressional powers. The United States Supreme Court, however, held the law unconstitutional.[16] Acting under Congressional authorization, the legislature passed a law giving the State Industrial Commission jurisdiction over cases involving workmen's compensation where the injury had been received in maritime employment. The Court of Appeals upheld this act, but the United States Supreme Court decided that Congress could not give away such jurisdiction.[17] Truck and bus drivers were required by a law passed in 1937 to take eight hours of rest after having been on duty continuously for ten hours, or at separate intervals, for ten hours in the aggregate or less in any fourteen consecutive hours, even though part of the time may have been outside of New York State. This was upheld in a lower court.[18]

Of the fifteen statutes considered, the state courts held twelve constitutional and three unconstitutional. Neither these three nor the two declared unconstitutional by the United States Supreme Court appear to manifest a spirit of revolt against Federal authority, or a desire to aggrandize the state at the expense of the Federal government. They seem rather to show the difficulty of determining the line of demarcation indicated by the words of the Federal Constitution. Men of equal honesty and integrity, whether legislators or judges, whether Federal or state officials, may differ on the interpretation of these words, without the conclusion being drawn that malignant

[16] People v. Erie Railroad Co. (1910) 198 N. Y. 369. Section 7-a of Labor Law (then Cons. Laws, Ch. 31, Section 8). Held unconstitutional in Erie Railroad Co. v. New York (1914) 233 U. S. 671.

[17] Matter of Stewart v. Knickerbocker Ice Co. (1919) 226 N. Y. 302. (Cons. Laws, Ch. 67.) Held unconstitutional in Knickerbocker Ice Co. v. Stewart (1920) 253 U. S. 149 United States Supreme Court. The Congressional Act had been passed in 1917.

[18] People v. Yarbrough (1938) 168 Misc. 769 City Magistrate's Court of New York, Borough of Manhattan, 1st District. Section 167 Labor Law, as amended by Ch 534, L. 1937.

forces are the motivating springs of action behind one or the other of the disagreeing factions.

B. The Privileges and Immunities Clauses

Article 4, Section 2 of the United States Constitution contains the provision that " The citizens of each state shall be entitled to all privileges and immunities of citizens in the several states," and Section 1 of the Fourteenth Amendment includes the prohibition that " No state shall make or enforce any law which shall abridge the privileges or immunities of citizens of the United States." Disregarding those cases concerned with taxation, it may be stated that these clauses failed to provide substantial grounds for the invalidation of legislation. In only one case, and that decided in a lower court, was an act declared unconstitutional for the principal reason of having violated these clauses. That portion of the act referred to above in the Musco case, regulating the transmission of deposits to foreign countries, which exempted transatlantic steamship companies and other persons and corporations from posting a bond was so held in 1908.[19]

Seven acts, each of which was declared valid by the courts, included the following provisions which had led to querying as to their consistency with the Constitution: 1. a section of the Stock Corporation Law subjecting a domestic corporation to a $100 payment and to liability for damages to stockholders for refusal to exhibit its stock book, while another section of the law subjected foreign corporations to a $50 payment alone;[20] 2. a section of the Forest, Fish and Game Law of 1902 prohibiting the sale of English pheasants, killed in another state, in New York City. This was held essential in order to accomplish the purposes of the act and prevent eva-

[19] Patti v. The United Surety Co. 61 Misc. 445 City Court of New York Special Term. It was held to violate the equal protection clause of the Fourteenth Amendment.

[20] Pelletreau v. Green Consolidated Gold Mining Co. (1906) 49 Misc. 233 L. 1890, Ch. 5(d) as amended L. 1897, Ch. 384 Supreme Court Appellate Term.

sion;[21] 3. a section of the Code of Criminal Procedure empowering a judge to issue a subpoena compelling a person within this state to appear in another state, as a witness in a felony action. The witness was to be given notice and opportunity to be heard, ample mileage and witness fees, and immunity from service of process. The basis of sustenance was the comity existing between the two neighboring states;[22] 4. a section of the Code of Civil Procedure stating when non-residents might sue foreign corporations in the courts of this state;[23] 5. a subdivision of the same code providing for service upon all foreign corporations, whether or not doing business within the state;[24] 6. the same subdivision as providing for the service of process upon an officer of a foreign corporation;[25] 7. and yet another section of this code barring the prosecution of an action, where the statute of limitations had

[21] People v. Waldorf-Astoria Hotel Co. (1907) 118 A. D. 723 1st Dept. Section 141 Forest, Fish and Game Law Ch. 194, L. 1902. The provisions of the Forest, Fish and Game Law, prohibiting the possession of game coming from without the state in the closed season, were held not violative of the due process clause, and a valid exercise of the police power in People ex rel. Hill v. Hesterberg (1906) 184 N. Y. 126 by the Court of Appeals. (L. 1900, Ch. 20, as amended by L. 1902, Ch. 194; L. 1902, Ch. 317 amended L. 1904, Ch. 588). This decision was affirmed by the United States Supreme Court in New York ex rel. Silz v. Hesterberg (1908) 211 U. S. 31.

[22] Commonwealth of Massachusetts v. Klaus (1911) 145 A. D. 798 1st Dept. Section 6182 Code of Criminal Procedure. L. 1902, Ch. 94.

[23] Johnson v. Victoria Chief Copper Mining and Smelting Co. (1912) 150 A. D. 653 1st Dept. Section 1780 Code of Civil Procedure. This section made actions of nonresidents against foreign corporations doing business in the state subject to dismissal at the discretion of the court. This was upheld by the United States Supreme Court as not violating the privileges clause in Douglas v. New York, New Haven and Hartford Railroad Co. (1929) 279 U. S. 577.

[24] Grant v. Cananea Consolidated Copper Co. (1907) 189 N. Y. 241; Pomeroy v. Hocking Valley Railway Co. (1917) 220 N. Y. 645. Subd. 1 Section 432 Code of Civil Procedure.

[25] Dollar Co. v. Canadian Car and Foundry Co. (1917) Section 432 Code of Civil Procedure Subd. 1,220 N. Y. 270.

run against it in the state where the cause of the action had originated.[26]

In the one case of the eight treated in which an act was held unconstitutional, there was an apparently rational basis for the discrimination which led to the ruling of invalidity. There is little evidence to warrant a charge that the legislature attempted to destroy the privileges and immunities of the citizens of the United States.

C. The Clause Prohibiting the Impairment of the Obligation of Contracts

" No state shall . . . pass any . . . law impairing the obligation of contracts " says Article 1, Section 10 of the United States Constitution. This simple statement has been one of the major clauses requiring interpretation by the courts in the past century and a half. An enormous amount of thought has gone into the explanation of what constitutes a contract, and what the precise meaning of impairment may be. Again two lines of decisions may be discerned, one upholding state laws affecting prior contracts as merely being concerned with the remedy, and not with the contract itself, while the other series has resulted in the annulment of state laws for violating this provision. At the same time, the courts have laid down the principle that contracts entered into after the passage of a law are done so with the recognition of the law being understood on the part of the contracting parties. At this point a digression becomes necessary upon certain principles which antedate 1906, but need to be considered for a fuller appreciation of the contracts clause.

For many years conservative jurists have sought some formula for the protection of vested rights within the words of the Constitution. The practice of declaring laws, which seemed to destroy rights of property considered sacrosanct, invalid on the ground of contravening natural law, without a basis in the

[26] Klotz v. Angle (1917) 220 N. Y. 347 Section 390a Code of Civil Procedure.

Constitution itself, had gradually been discarded with the upsurge of the Jacksonian revolution, and though appearing sporadically in decisions since, has not been of marked importance. The idea that constitutional conventions, springing from the people themselves, could do anything in a sovereign capacity had forced the judges to seek support for their notions of what was just in the phrases of the documents emerging from those assemblies. The first clause seized upon for a large scale use as a judicial weapon was the contract clause in the Federal Constitution. The first state law ever nullified by the United States Supreme Court was held to conflict with this clause.[27] In New York, the first law " construed " so as to save its constitutionality had been a case involving vested rights, but use had not been made of the contracts clause.[28] Further developments, notably Marshall's interpretation of the word " contract " to include charters from the state in the Dartmouth College case (1819), had led to a situation in which that clause took on great significance.[29] The opinion of the Supreme Court under Taney in the Charles River Bridge case, that such grants by the state should be construed strictly, had modified the importance of the clause to a degree, but was by no means a complete reversal.[30] The effect of these decisions led the states to include reservation clauses in the acts of incorporation passed in the early decades of the nineteenth century. New York adopted such a clause in 1827.[31] Later New York, as well as several other states, included such a reservation in its constitution. Article 8, Section 1 of the Constitution of 1846 provided that "All general laws and special acts passed pursuant to this section [on incorporation] may be

[27] Fletcher v. Peck (1810) 6 Cranch 87.
[28] Gardner v. Newburgh (1816) 2 Johnson Chancery 162.
[29] Dartmouth College v. Woodward (1819) 4 Wheat. 518.
[30] Charles River Bridge v. Warren Bridge (1837) 11 Pet. 420.
[31] Benjamin F. Wright, *The Contract Clause of the Constitution* (Cambridge, 1938), p. 59.

altered from time to time, or repealed."[32] This development did not produce any precipitate decline in cases arising under the clause. When it was realized, however, the protection of various rights, considered important by the judges, as well as important interests outside the courts, demanded a more adequate legal device, the search continued. The result was the change in meaning of the due process clause as construed by the courts, discussed later.[33]

Although over forty cases in this category were decided in the courts in these years, only six acts were held invalid. A statute of 1845 which repealed the ferry clauses of the ancient charters of New York City in so far as the power to establish ferries to Long Island had been unexecuted, and those sections of the Banking Law which authorized a person who claimed to be the owner of a certificate of deposit alleged to have been lost or destroyed to maintain a proceeding to enforce payment thereof, were both upheld in the same year.[34] In the latter case it was held that since the legislature could not cancel the rights of the bona fide holder of the certificate, and since therefore the liability was imposed upon the maker of the certificate of deposit of paying the amount of the certificate a second time to a holder in good faith who might produce it, the maker's freedom of contract was thus impaired. In Saratoga State Waters Corporation v. Pratt (1920), a law of 1917 that attempted to confirm the acts of the defendants in preventing the plaintiff from entering rights granted by an agree-

[32] New York State Constitutional Convention Committee, Vol. I, *New York State Constitution Annotated* (New York, 1938) Part 2, p. 67; Wright, *op. cit.*, pp. 84-85.

[33] E. S. Corwin, "The Establishment of Judicial Review," *op. cit.*, See Foreword note 2, *supra*. "The Doctrine of Due Process of Law Before the Civil War." *Harvard Law Review*, 24: 366-385, 460-479 (March and April, 1911).

[34] Matter of Wheeler (1909) 62 Misc. 37 Supreme Court Kings Special Term Ch. 352, L. 1845; Matter of Ellard (1909) 62 Misc. 374 Supreme Court New York Special Term. Sections 227 to 238 Banking Law, L. 1899, Ch. 451, as amended by L. 1901, Chapters 171, 503.

ment between the commissioners of the state reservation at Saratoga Springs and itself, under the authority of an earlier law, was declared invalid.[35] The Russian revolution made its effects felt in New York, when a life insurance company refused to pay on a policy contracted with a Russian citizen before November 7, 1917. The justification was a law of 1926 providing for a stay of action on such contracts, as the United States government had not recognized the government of Russia which had existed since that date. The Court of Appeals considered the statute a violation of the contracts clause.[36] An amendment to the Statute of Frauds, making a "contract to bequeath property" void unless in writing, was judged unconstitutional as applied to a prior agreement. This was viewed as an unreasonable alteration of the law of evidence, resulting in the destruction or serious impairment of the remedy upon a contract.[37] In 1935 the Appellate Division with brief comment ruled that Section 1077-h of the Civil Practice Act, in so far as it purported to authorize the vacatur of a judgment of foreclosure and sale theretofore entered, was not within the legislative power, which could not be used to destroy rights vesting as a consequence of the entry of the judgment.[38]

[35] 227 N. Y. 429, Ch. 204, L. 1917. Earlier authority granted by Ch. 569, L. 1909 as amended by Ch. 394, L. 1911.

[36] Sliosberg v. New York Life Insurance Co. (1927) 244 N. Y. 482. Section 169a of Civil Practice Act added by Ch. 232, L. 1926 providing for a stay of action upon contracts for insurance made prior to Nov. 7, 1917 payable in Russian rubles or to be performed within the territory of the former Russian Empire.

[37] Ralph v. Cronk (1934) 150 Misc. 69. Amendment of 1933 to Section 31 Personal Property Law L. 1933, Ch. 616 amending Statute of Frauds (Personal Property Law Section 31; Subds. 1, 7). As applied prospectively the law was held constitutional in Doyle v. Gleason (1934) 152 Misc. 641 Supreme Court Cayuga Co. where it was remarked that whether Subd. 7 were construed only as a rule of evidence or as a rule of substantive law, if construed to bar the performance of a valid contract made previous to its enactment, it would violate the contract clause.

[38] Raphael v. Goldman Furniture Co. (1935) 246 A. D. 548 2nd Dept.

COMMERCE, PRIVILEGES AND CONTRACTS 89

In chronological order of the decisions, the acts deemed satisfactory as far as the constitutional requirements were concerned were as follows: an act of 1896, declaring incest a crime, construed not to be retroactive;[39] the permission granted to a municipality in 1905 to require a street railway to change its tracks, when necessary for street improvements;[40] an amendment to the Code of Civil Procedure allowing an execution against wages on a judgment obtained before its passage;[41] a prohibition in 1896 against the farming out of prison labor as applied to a contract for such labor, which included a provision for rescission in case of legislation;[42] the requirement in 1885 that the plan of a company to build independent lines for the conduction of electricity be approved by the commissioners of electrical subways, despite an earlier permission granted by a board of appeals in 1883;[43] a prohibition against a foreign stock corporation maintaining an action upon any contract made by it in New York State, unless it had procured a certificate authorizing it to do business before

[39] Weisberg v. Weisberg (1906) 112 A. D. 231 1st Dept. L. 1893, Ch. 601 L. 1896, Ch. 272 Section 2. Section 302 of Penal Code.

[40] People ex rel. City of Geneva v. Geneva, Waterloo, Seneca Falls and Cayuga Lake Traction Co. (1908) 112 A. D. 581. L. 1897 amended by L. 1905, Ch. 462. Any contract rights acquired by such railway company under a municipal franchise were held subject to the police power of the municipality and the obligations of such a contract were not impaired within the meaning of the Constitution by requiring the company to alter its tracks as in this case.

[41] Myers v. Moran (1906) 113 A. D. 427 2nd Dept. amendment to Section 1391 Code of Civil Procedure. A statute exempting property from execution was not viewed as a contract between the state and the judgment debtor and might be changed by subsequent legislation. The general rule against retroactive construction did not control a statute affecting a remedy or a rule of procedure affecting a right.

[42] Mills Co. v. State of New York (1906) 110 A. D. 843 3rd Dept. L. 1896, Ch. 429. Article 3, Section 29 of the Constitution had gone into effect prohibiting such labor as well and this too was not seen as conflicting with the Federal Constitution.

[43] People ex rel. New York Electric Lines Co. v. Ellison (1906) 115 A. D. 254 1st Dept. Ch. 499, L. 1885.

making the contract, which was not held applicable to a contract made before the law was passed;[44] the provision limiting the amount of compensation to be paid by life insurance companies for new business, not construed as retroactive;[45] the requirement that a company authorized to maintain hydrants for distributing water in Jamaica secure a permit from the borough president of Queens Borough before the pavement or surface of the street should be disturbed;[46] the enfranchisement of the policy holders of a life insurance company, the power to do which had been reserved in its charter of 1853;[47] the requirement that the surety of an administrator be cited on a voluntary accounting of an estate, as applied to a surety whose bond had been executed before the amendment;[48] the provision that the Public Service Commission might change a railroad rate found excessive " notwithstanding that a higher rate, fare or charge has been heretofore authorized by statute ";[49] the law making rebates unlawful, which was not held to affect certain accrued rights under a contract;[50] the limitation of fares on certain electrical railways, which had previously been six cents, to five cents;[51] the interpretation of

[44] McNamara v. Keene (1906) 49 Misc. 452 Supreme Court Appellate Term L. 1901, Ch. 538 amendment to Section 15 Stock Corporations Law.

[45] Boswell v. Security Mutual Life Insurance Co. (1908) 193 N. Y. 465 Section 97 Insurance Law. L. 1906, Ch. 326.

[46] Jamaica Water Supply Co. v. City of New York (1908) 57 Misc. 475 Supreme Court Queens Special Term. L. 1901, Ch. 466, Section 391.

[47] Lord v. Equitable Life Assurance Co. of United States (1909) 194 N. Y. 212 L. 1906, Ch. 326 Section 13.

[48] Cookman v. Stoddard (1909) 132 A. D. 480 4th Dept. Section 2728 Code of Civil Procedure. Ch. 686, L. 1893 amended by L. 1894, Ch. 421 and L. 1895, Ch. 426. There was held to be no impairment of the obligation of contracts expressed in the bond as the amendment affected the procedure only.

[49] People ex rel. Delaware and Hudson Co. v. The Public Service Commission (1910) 140 A. D. 839 3rd Dept. Section 49 Public Service Commission Law (Cons. Laws, Ch. 48); L. 1910, Ch. 480.

[50] Baird v. Erie Railroad Co. (1911) 148 A. D. 452 4th Dept. Public Service Commission Law, L. 1907, Ch. 429.

[51] People ex rel. Cohoes Railway Co. v. The Public Service Commission (1911) 143 A. D. 769 3rd Dept. Ch. 358, L. 1905.

COMMERCE, PRIVILEGES AND CONTRACTS 91

the act incorporating New Rochelle as having repealed previous laws entitling a land owner to damages resulting from a change of a street grade;[52] the requirement that the court annul alimony on the remarriage of the wife, not to be applied retroactively;[53] the authorization of an execution against the income from trust funds, not held applicable retroactively;[54] the construction that a fraternal beneficiary order could not deprive a member, upon reaching a stated age, of certain payments on a policy after receiving two annual payments on his certificate;[55] the interpretation of the law permitting the issuing of an execution against the income of a trust fund created by a will, probated before the enactment of the statute;[56] the proviso that a contract for the conditional sale of goods and chattels to be attached to a building should be void, as against a subsequent bona fide purchaser of the premises, unless the contract had been filed and indexed before the date of delivery;[57] the authorization given to a court in matrimonial actions to modify a decree respecting the education and main-

[52] Matter of Lawton v. City of New Rochelle (1908) 123 A. D. 832 2nd Dept. Ch. 128, L. 1899 dissolving the Village of New Rochelle, repealing L. 1883, Ch. 113 and L. 1884, Ch. 281. The change of the street grade had taken place in 1904.

[53] Krauss v. Krauss No. 1 (1908) 127 A.D. 740 1st Dept. Amendment to Section 1771 Code of Civil Procedure by Ch. 339, L. 1904.

[54] Demuth v. Kemp (1909) 130 A. D. 546 1st Dept. Section 1391 Code of Civil Procedure as amended by Ch. 461, L. 1903.

[55] People ex rel. Mount v. Chapter General of America, Knights of St. John of Malta (1909) 132 A. D. 410 2nd Dept. Order incorporated under L. 1881, Ch. 256.

[56] Brearley School Limited v. Ward (1911) 201 N. Y. 358 Section 1391 Code of Civil Procedure as amended by Chapter 148, L. 1908; followed in Smith v. Endicott Johnson Corporation (1921) 199 A. D. 198 3rd Dept. wherein a garnishee execution remedial process had been issued by a court against an employer without notice to the judgment debtor.

[57] Central Union Gas Co. v. Browning (1911) 146 A. D. 783 1st Dept. Section 112 of Lien Law reenacted Section 62 Personal Property Law (Cons. Laws, Ch. 41; L. 1909, Ch. 45).

tenance of the children of a marriage;[58] the law governing the commissions of trustees, where the instrument of trust provided no specific compensation, not held applicable to a prior contract as to compensation made by the parties themselves;[59] the requirement that persons selling transportation tickets to or from foreign countries, who in conjunction with their business received money to transmit to such countries, furnish a bond as a condition for the faithful transmission of the money, with a later amendment compelling a bond also where money, was received on deposit;[60] the law permitting the cancellation and retirement of the bonds given by private bankers to do the business of receiving deposits for safe-keeping;[61] a law transferring powers from certain commissioners in Monroe County to collectors appointed by the county judge, the intent of which was construed by the court as not doing away with the commissioner's power and duty to reassess and raise by tax sufficient moneys to pay bonds originally issued to pay for a sewer and remaining unpaid;[62] the law fixing the price of the gas furnished to the City of New York as a consumer, not held as dissolving the city's obligations under prior contracts;[63] the permission given the Superintendent of Banks, by an amendment to the Banking Law, to enforce the individual liability of shareholders, and rendering it unnecessary

[58] White v. White (1912) 154 A. D. 250 2nd Dept. Section 1771 Code of Civil Procedure Ch. 297, L. 1908.

[59] The Miami Valley Gas and Fuel Co. v. Mills (1913) 157 A. D. 542 1st Dept. amendment to Section 3320 Code of Civil Procedure L. 1904, Ch. 755; reenacted L. 1909, Ch. 65.

[60] Goldberg v. People's Security Co. (1914) 162 A. D. 385 1st Dept. Ch. 479, L. 1908 amending Ch. 185, L. 1907; also upheld in Russo v. Illinois Surety Co. (1910) 141 A. D. 690 2nd Dept.

[61] Greenspan v. Olivier (1914) 164 A. D. 535 3rd Dept. Ch. 369, L. 1914 repealing Ch. 348, L. 1910.

[62] People ex rel. Equitable Life Assurance Society v. Pierce (1918) 104 Misc. 343 Supreme Court Monroe Equity Term.

[63] Kings County Lighting Co. v. The City of New York (1916) 176 A. D. 175 2nd Dept. Ch. 736, L. 1905.

COMMERCE, PRIVILEGES AND CONTRACTS 93

first to recover a judgment where the Superintendent was involved, as applied to a contract contained in a special act between the state and a trust company and its shareholders reserving the right to amend to the state;[64] the Arbitration Law as applied to pre-existing contracts, but not to pending actions;[65] a provision for adding any power or purpose to the charter of a corporation, which addition, at the time of the alteration, might apply to corporations engaged in a business of the same general character;[66] the statute prohibiting holders of bank stock from entering into voting trust agreements;[67] a provision that the trustees of a hospital were to be elected by the remaining members of the board, thus disfranchising the members of a charitable corporation;[68] the law providing for interest on awards and in contract cases, as applied to all

[64] Skinner v. Schwab (1919) 188 A. D. 457 1st Dept. Ch. 143, L. 1908 amending Section 18 of the former Banking Law.

[65] Matter of Berkowitz v. Arbid and Houlberg Inc. (1921) 230 N. Y. 261 L. 1920, Ch. 275. Nor did it violate Article 1, Section 2 requiring trial by jury, nor Article 6, Section 1 dealing with the courts. The application of this law to maritime contracts, to require the compulsory specific performance of arbitration agreements, was upheld in Red Cross Line v. Atlantic Fruit Co. (1924) 264 U. S. 109.

[66] Hollender v. Rochester Food Products Corporation (1924) 124 Misc. 130 Supreme Court Monroe County. Section 18 Stock Corporation Law of 1909, at the time of case Section 5, L. 1923. In 1927 the United States Supreme Court upheld a section of the Personal Property Law providing that whenever articles, sold on condition that the title should remain in the vendor until payment of the price, were retaken by the vendor, they should be retained for thirty days during which the vendee might comply with the contract and recover the property, and that after the expiration of that period, if the contract were not complied with, the vendor might cause the articles to be sold at public auction, and that unless sold within thirty days after expiration, the vendee might receive the amount paid on the articles under the contract. Stewart and Co. v. Rivara 274 U. S. 64 Section 65 Personal Property Law.

[67] Matter of Morse (1928) 247 N. Y. 290 Ch. 120, L. 1925. Although retroactive, this was considered within the reserve power of the legislature and no property interest was held involved.

[68] Matter of Mt. Sinai Hospital (1928) 250 N. Y. 103 Ch. 17, L. 1925. This too was passed under the reserve power of the legislature.

actions brought after the act went into effect, irrespective of when the cause of action arose;[69] the section of the Civil Practice Act authorizing the set-off of the market value of the real property in an action to recover the indebtedness secured by a mortgage, the section to apply for a limited period during a declared emergency;[70] a section of the Insurance Law providing that the beneficiary of a life insurance policy, other than the insured or his executors, was entitled to the proceeds as against the creditors of the insured;[71] a subdivision of the Decedent Estate Law authorizing the election by a testator's surviving spouse to take a share of the estate, as in intestacy, as applied to a surviving husband who had executed a separation agreement with his wife before the act took effect;[72] an amendment to the Decedent Estate Law precluding the introduction of evidence, other than a demonstration of the existence of a written ante-nuptial agreement, to prove that there had been a promise to leave money in consideration of marriage, if not applied to the case at bar;[73] an article of the Insurance Law, pursuant to which a liquidation order had been entered in respect to insurance companies, construed as not automatically causing the liability of sureties on a bond,

[69] Preston Co. v. Funkhouser (1933) 261 N. Y. 140 Section 480 of Civil Practice Act as amended by Ch. 623, L. 1927. The court's opinion was that a new and more adequate remedy was afforded. Affirmed in Funkhouser v. Preston Co. (1933) 290 U. S. 163 by United States Supreme Court.

[70] Klinke v. Samuels (1934) 264 N. Y. 144 Section 1083-b of Civil Practice Act. Chapters 793 and 794, L. 1933. This section as well as Section 1083-a was upheld also in Honeyman v. Hanan (1937) 275 N. Y. 382. This latter case was affirmed by the United States Supreme Court in (1937) 302 U. S. 375.

[71] Addiss v. Selig (1934) 264 N. Y. 274 Section 55-a of Insurance Law. (Cons. Laws, Ch. 28).

[72] Matter of Sacks (1935) 155 Misc. 233 Surrogate's Court Kings County. Affirmed in 246 A. D. 546 (1935) 2nd Dept. Subd. 9, Section 18, Decedent Estate Law.

[73] Matter of Goldberg (1935) 157 Misc.. 49 Surrogate's Court Kings County Ch. 459, L. 1932 amendment to Section 35 Decedent Estate Law.

covering a temporary administrator of an estate, to cease;[74] the law abolishing the cause of action for breach of promise of marriage;[75] a section of the Civil Practice Act giving the court authority to order installment payments by a judgment debtor, applying to judgments in existence prior to the date the act became effective;[76] a section of the Decedent Estate Law pursuant to which an executor and trustee was permitted to enforce the immediate reimbursement by insurance companies of amounts representing estate taxes paid out of the true estate assets, in the proportion that the insurance funds included in the tax estate bore to the whole tax estate, irrespective of whether under the terms of the policies the proceeds thereof were payable in bulk on the death of the decedent, or by annuity or installment payments, and notwithstanding the general assets of the companies were the sole source out of which the contracts would be performed;[77] an expressly retroactive provision that an attorney or any one of his employees were not to be disqualified from becoming a witness in any proceeding concerning the validity or construction of a will;[78] a

[74] Matter of Erlanger (1934) 153 Misc. 573 Surrogate's Court New York County. Article XI Insurance Law, Ch. 191, L. 1932.

[75] Fearon v. Treanor (1936) 272 N. Y. 268 Article 2-A of Civil Practice Act. L. 1935, Ch. 263. This was also held constitutional as applying to actions for alienation of affections in Hanfgarn v. Mark 274 N. Y. 22 after having been previously declared unconstitutional under the same title. 248 A. D. 325 2nd Dept. (1936) affirmed without opinion in 272 N. Y. 671.

[76] Compton and Co. v. Williams (1936) 248 A. D. 545 4th Dept. Section 793 Civil Practice Act added by Ch. 630, L. 1935. The legislature, the Appellate Division held, had the power to alter, modify or change the remedies given for a party to enforce an obligation, and unless it was apparent from the language of the statute that the law-making body intended otherwise, a change in procedure would be held to apply to pending actions or proceedings.

[77] Matter of Scott (1936) 158 Misc. 401 Section 124 Decedent Estate Law. It was remarked that the essential attributes of the sovereign power were deemed written into every contract.

[78] Matter of Casper (1936) 161 Misc. 199 Surrogate's Court Westchester County. Section 354 Civil Practice Act, as amended by Ch. 493, L. 1936. This was regarded as a rule of evidence, not taking away or impairing rights vested under any prior law.

section of the Insurance Law directing that an insurance company should not hand over liability insurance to a judgment creditor, as applied to policies written before its enactment;[79] the Mortgage Commission Act allowing the commission to borrow a stated sum of money on the security of property foreclosed to pay taxes and to rehabilitate the property;[80] the extension in 1936 of the emergency mortgage moratorium to July 1, 1937,[81] and in 1937 to July 1, 1938;[82] the limitation of the right of a plaintiff in action to foreclose a mortgage on real property to enter a deficiency judgment;[83] and an amendment to the Stock Corporation Law authorizing a gas and electric corporation to merge any other gas and electric corporation of which it owned at least ninety-five per cent of the stock, and also empowering a gas and electric corporation owning ninety-five per cent of the stock of any district steam corporation to merge such corporation where previously the ownership of all stock was required.[84]

[79] Associated Indemnity Corporation v Chais (1936) 161 Misc. 763 Supreme Court Appellate Term 1st Dept. The view of the judges was that this did not violate any constitutional right of the judgment creditor, although its claim arose in 1932 and the policy of insurance involved predated the enactment of the statute.

[80] Mortgage Commn. v. Daly (1937) 165 Misc. 666 Supreme Court Special Term Queens County following Wolff v. Mortgage Commission (1936) 270 N. Y. 428; Matter of Mortgage Commission (1175 Evergreen Avenue) (1936) 270 N. Y. 436, affirmed 299 U. S. 521 (1936); Moore v. Barker (1936) 270 N. Y. 648. L. 1935, Ch. 19.

[81] Kane v. Bowers, Brennan and Ricoro Estates Inc. (1938) 276 N. Y. 665, Sections 1083-a and 1083-b of Civil Practice Act. Ch. 87, L. 1936 as applied to a final judgment made before passage.

[82] McGuire and Co. v. Lent and Lent (1936) 277 N. Y. 694, Ch. 820, L. 1937. The mortgage moratorium had originally been established by Ch. 793, L. 1933 adding Sections 1077-a to 1077-s to the Civil Practice Act.

[83] Honeyman v. Clark (1938) 278 N. Y. 467 Section 1083-a Civil Practice Act.

[84] Alpren v. Consolidated Edison Co. of New York Inc. (1938) 168 Misc. 381 Supreme Court Special Term New York County. Ch. 778, L. 1936 and Ch. 815, L. 1937 amending Stock Corporation Law Section 85, Subd. 1.

COMMERCE, PRIVILEGES AND CONTRACTS

An enumeration shows forty-six acts held constitutional and six held unconstitutional. At least nine of the acts were construed as not having a retroactive application, but no evidence was apparent that the legislature would have been in disagreement with the interpretations of the courts in these cases. The most important legislation during this period, including the acts passed after the depression of 1929 restricting the rights of mortgagees to recover their property, was sustained. The distance between the acts held unconstitutional and those held constitutional was more of a line than a gulf. The former acts were not such clear-cut cases of violation that a rational argument for sustaining them based on the police power, the right to change the remedy or some other line derived from the Constitution could not be constructed. This is not to ignore the possible or actual injustice of the acts, but to say that, if the courts had been willing, it would not have been too difficult to reconcile these six with the Constitution.

CHAPTER V
JUST COMPENSATION

THE last clause of Article 1, Section 6 of the 1894 Constitution stated: " Nor shall private property be taken for public use without just compensation." [1]

Article 1, Section 7 read:

> When private property shall be taken for any public use, the compensation to be made therefor, when such compensation is not made by the state, shall be ascertained by a jury, or by not less than three commissioners appointed by a court of record, as shall be prescribed by law. Private roads may be opened in the manner to be prescribed by law; but in every case the necessity of the road and the amount of all damage to be sustained by the opening thereof shall be first determined by a jury of freeholders, and such amount, together with the expenses of the proceeding, shall be paid by the person to be benefited. General laws may be passed permitting the owners or occupants of agricultural lands to construct and maintain for the drainage thereof, necessary drains, ditches and dikes upon the lands of others, under proper restrictions and with just compensation but no special laws shall be enacted for such purposes.[2]

In 1913 the text was amended by adding after the words *ascertained by a jury*:

> or by the Supreme Court with or without a jury but not with a referee

and the following paragraph:

> The legislature may authorize cities to take more land and property than is needed for actual construction in the laying out, widening, extending or relocating parks, public places, highways or streets; provided, however, that the additional land and property so authorized to be taken shall be no more

[1] New York State Constitution Annotated, *op. cit.*, Part 2, p. 105.
[2] *Ibid.*

than sufficient to form suitable building sites abutting on such park, public place, highway or street. After so much of the land and property has been appropriated for such park, public place, highway or street as is needed therefor, the remainder may be sold or leased.[3]

In 1919 the following words were added after the word *benefited* in the first paragraph: " The use of property for the drainage of swamp or agricultural lands is declared to be a public use and " followed by the insertion after the words *owners or occupants of* " swamp or." Finally after the word *restrictions* the words " on-making " were substituted and after *just compensation* there was added " and such compensation, together with the cost of such drainage may be assessed, wholly or partly, against any property benefited thereby; "[4] Briefly this declared the use of property for drainage a public use and allowed compensation to be assessed against the property benefited.

In 1927 the words " and counties " was inserted after the word *cities* in the second paragraph.[5] In short this extended the power of condemnation previously allowed to cities, to counties.

In 1933 there was added after the word *referee*:

> or in proceedings affecting property located within the City of New York and to be acquired by the City of New York, by a term of said court to consist of one or more justices thereof without a jury, .[6]

A long history of interpretation is connected with this clause starting from such cases as Gardner v. Newburgh, to which reference has already been made,[7] and People v. Platt

---

[3] Amendments Proposed, *op. cit.*, pp. 31-32.

[4] *Ibid.*, p. 35.

[5] *Ibid.*, p. 36.

[6] *Ibid.*, p. 38.

[7] See Chapter IV note 28 supra.

(1819),[8] the latter being the first case in which a state statute was definitely held unconstitutional by a New York court. Although there was still discussion of the meaning of the words as applied to concrete cases, the significance of this section as an obstacle to legislation had become secondary by 1906 as compared with other parts of the Constitution. The conservatism of spirit embodied in this clause, as well as the contracts clause, was preserved, however, in decisions based on the due process and other clauses. In those cases which have been chosen for discussion here, the majority resulted in the upholding of the constitutionality of the challenged laws.

Six cases have been found in which the court decided that an act or part of an act was in conflict with this provision. In three of these the question at issue involved the nature of just compensation. In 1902 the legislature had directed the state engineer to locate a disputed boundary line and appropriated forty thousand dollars for the purposes of the act. In 1903 the taking of land was authorized after trespass. Neither of these laws, the Court of Appeals held, could authorize the use of eminent domain without compensation nor afford protection to wrongdoers as against the owner.[9] A section of the New York City Charter which authorized the setting off of benefits against an award for land to be taken for waterfront improvements was held unconstitutional especially where the city acquired the fee and was under no obligation to continue the public use.[10] Those sections of a law of 1924 requiring a commission to acquire real estate for park purposes "from moneys or property on hand or appropriated for its use" did not satisfy the Court of Appeals as to their validity.[11]

[8] People v. Platt (1819) 17 Johnson 195.

[9] Litchfield v. Bond (1906) 186 N. Y. 66. L. 1902, Ch. 473.

[10] Matter of City of New York (North River Waterfront) (1907) 190 N.Y. 350. Section 822 of City Charter, L. 1901, Ch. 466.

[11] Pauchogue Land Corporation v. Long Island Park Commission (1926) 243 N.Y. 15. Sections 16-19 of Ch. 112, L. 1924 and Section 59 of Conservation Law, limited by Section 8 of Act of 1924 which included the above requirement.

The thorny problem of exactly what constituted a public use, which historically came to the fore in Taylor v. Porter (1843), one of the celebrated precursors of the substantive interpretation of the due process clause,[12] led the court in two cases to disapprove acts of the legislature. One was a law of 1907, repealed in 1913, granting a company the control over the navigation of the St. Lawrence River for the purpose of operating dams, canals, reservoirs etc., near Long Sault Island or for the development of electrical power.[13] The other allowed the removal of timber from land which had been conveyed to the state in a compromise of an action between the state and the company involved.[14] This law was also challenged as conflicting with Article 7, Section 7 which read at that time as follows:

> The lands of the state, now owned or hereafter acquired, constituting the forest preserve as now fixed by law, shall be forever kept as wild forest land. They shall not be leased, sold or exchanged, or be taken by any corporation, public or private, nor shall the timber thereon be sold, removed or destroyed.[15]

The procedure, established by an act of 1907, for the acquirement of land by Rochester outside of its limits was not considered impartial by the Court of Appeals. It was required that one of the three commissioners be a resident freeholder of the City of Rochester, and the right of appeal from the decision of the common council of that city in the event that the council disapproved of the commissioners' report was withheld from the landowners.[16]

[12] Corwin, "The Doctrine of Due Process of Law before the Civil War," *op. cit.*, passim. See Chapter IV, note 33 supra.

[13] Matter of Long Sault Development Company (1914) 212 N.Y. 1. Ch. 355, L. 1907 repealed by Ch. 452, L. 1913.

[14] People v. Santa Clara Lumber Company (1914) 213 N.Y. 61. Section 20, Ch. 220, L. 1897 as amended by Ch. 135, L. 1898.

[15] New York State Constitution Annotated, *op. cit.*, Part 2, p. 141.

[16] City of Rochester v. Holder (1918) 224 N.Y. 386. L. 1907, Ch. 438 of Charter).

In a seventh case, an amendment to the Barge Canal Act by which private bridges and their franchises were made subject to condemnation for the Barge Canal was held to be in direct conflict with Article 7, Section 4 requiring a vote by the people on debts contracted by the state with certain exceptions.[17]

Grouping the acts held constitutional according to whether the point at issue was a matter of just compensation, of public use or of procedure, the largest number are found under the first heading. These included the following: a law of 1890 allowing the immediate possession of condemned land to be ordered, if the public interests would be prejudiced by delay, and if the sum stated in the answer (by the owner) as the value of the property were deposited;[18] an authorization to a municipality to close streets without compensating owners of land when total access to their property was not cut off;[19] the

[17] Halfmoon Bridge Company v. The Canal Board (1915) 91 Misc. 600 Supreme Court Saratoga Trial Term. L. 1913, Ch. 801 amending The Barge Canal Act (L. 1903, Ch. 147).

[18] Matter of Niagara, Lockport and Ontario Power Company (1906) 111 A. D. 686 4th Dept. Section 3380 Code of Civil Procedure incorporated by Ch. 95, L. 1890.

[19] Reis v. City of New York (1906) 113 A.D. 464 2nd Dept. Section 442 Greater New York Charter.

A law empowering New York City to acquire lands for its new water supply under an act authorizing it to acquire property in the watershed previously granted to a water company, which had made no further use of the grant beyond filing a map, was upheld by the United States Supreme Court in Ramapo Water Co. v. City of New York (1915) 236 U. S. 579. Ch. 724, L. 1905. The court remarked that the company had no right to exclude the rest of the world from whatever watershed it chose. However, in 1926 the United States Supreme Court decided that grants by New York City, of land under navigable waters, to private persons, made on valuable consideration and for the public purpose of harbor development might be regained by the state and city only through condemnation proceedings. Hence Chapter 574, L. 1871 amending Section 99 of an act of 1870, establishing a bulkhead line and forbidding solid filling of the land beyond that line, did not meet the requirements of the Constitution. Appleby v. City of New York, 271, U. S. 364; Appleby v. Delaney, 271 U. S. 403.

statutes requiring a change in the viaduct structure in Park Avenue, into which just compensation had been read by a previous decision of the United States Supreme Court;[20] the establishment of a commission for the regulation of the flow of watercourses, the powers of which were later transferred to the State Water Supply Commission, with power to condemn lands in accordance with the condemnation law;[21] the act giving authority to the Board of Creeks and Park Commissioner of Ithaca to control the flow of water in creeks under which act the banks of a creek had been raised, closing certain overflows for flood-water channels, and casting water upon the plaintiff's premises in time of flood, compensation having been granted by the court's construction;[22] a section of the Code of Civil Procedure providing for the immediate possession by the condemnor prior to compensation for the lands taken;[23] the removal in 1897 of restrictions established in 1868

[20] Foster v. New York Central and Hudson River Railroad Company (1907) 118 A. D. 143 1st Dept. Ch. 102, L. 1872, Ch. 339, L. 1892, Ch. 548, L. 1894, Ch. 613, L. 1898; following Muhlker v. Harlem Railroad Company (1905) 197 U. S. 544. The acquisition by the city of the spur of the elevated railroad running from 42nd Street and Park Avenue to 42nd Street and Third Avenue under a law, one provision of which stated that the court was to "ascertain and estimate the compensation which ought justly to be made by the City of New York to the respective owners of the real property to be acquired," was upheld in Roberts v. New York City (1935) 295 U. S. 264 by the United States Supreme Court, which considered such a system of condemnation at least fair upon its face. Section 1001 New York City Charter, L. 1915, Ch. 606.

[21] State Water Supply Commission v. Curtis (1908) 192 N. Y. 139 Ch. 734, L. 1904. It was held that compensation was made before the possession of the land and that notice was provided.
A somewhat similar law, giving commissioners of the Palisades Interstate Park the power to acquire lands by entry and appropriation, was upheld by the United States Supreme Court in White v. Sparkill Realty Co. (1930) 280 U. S. 500. Sections 59 and 761 Conservation Law, L. 1928, Ch. 242.

[22] Brown v. City of Ithaca (1911) 148 A. D. 477 3rd Dept. Ch. 345, L. 1906.

[23] Long Island Railroad Company v. Jones (1912) 151 A. D. 407 2nd Dept. Section 3380 Code of Civil Procedure. The constitutional provision, it was held, did not require compensation to precede possession, although title did not pass until the compensation was actually received.

against the erection of certain buildings, such as slaughterhouses and others considered dangerous, noxious or offensive, in a locality in Brooklyn;[24] and a section of the Conservation Law giving the owner of the major part of the head and volume of the usable flow of a stream rights withheld from the owner of a minor part.[25]

Five acts classed under the heading of public use were: a law authorizing water to be taken from the Niagara River, held not to violate Article 1, Section 9 of the 1846 Constitution which declared that:

> The assent of two-thirds of the members elected to each branch of the legislature shall be requisite to every bill appropriating the public moneys or property for local or private purposes;[26]

parts of an act, which lacked the two-thirds vote required by Article 1, Section 9 just quoted, granting a construction company rights to land under water;[27] the appropriation of land by the Forest Preserve Board giving a claimant the right to take and remove certain spruce timber upon the conditions stated;[28] the establishing of a public park and memorial for

[24] Hall v. House of St. Giles the Cripple (1915) 91 Misc. 122 Supreme Court Kings Special Term, L. 1897, Ch. 702, Section 4. Justice Kelby stated in his opinion that "the legislature cannot permanently incumber, for private esthetic benefit, its trusteeship over public property."

[25] People ex rel. Horton v. Prendergast (1928) 248 N. Y. 215. Section 624, Subd. 3, Conservation Law, also challenged for violating the clause in the Fourteenth Amendment guaranteeing equal protection of the laws.

[26] Niagara County Irrigation and Water Supply Company v. College Heights Land Company (1906) 111 A. D. 770 4th Dept. Ch. 259, L. 1891, Sections 4 and 6. (the charter of the first named company). The state, it was decided, holds the bed not as proprietor but as sovereign in trust.

[27] First Construction Company of Brooklyn v. New York (1917) 221 N. Y. 295. L. 1884, Ch. 494.

[28] Taggart's Paper Company v. State of New York (1919) 187 A. D. 843 3rd Dept. Ch. 130, L. 1908. The court ruled that costs might properly be denied.

JUST COMPENSATION

Theodore Roosevelt, the land acquired for which being considered taken for a public purpose;[29] and an article of the State Housing Law granting a municipal housing authority the power of eminent domain to carry out slum clearing and reconstruction projects.[30]

Considerations of proper procedure in this type of case were involved in the suits in which the following three acts were sustained: the amendment to the New York City Charter giving discretionary powers to the Commissioner of Docks, with the approval of the Sinking Fund Commissioners, to acquire by purchase or condemnation land within certain boundaries;[31] the sections of the New York City Charter under which the owner of land was liable to assessment for prospective injury to buildings not taken for a street improvement, the lands ceded for the improvement not being liable to this assessment;[32] and the section of the same charter making confirmation by the Board of Assessors of an award to a property owner, in proceedings involving a change of street grade, final and conclusive upon all parties and persons with respect to the amount of damages sustained.[33]

---

[29] Roosevelt Memorial Association of Oyster Bay v. Jones (1926) 244 N. Y. 538. Ch. 429, L. 1919.

[30] Matter of New York City Housing Authority v. Muller (1936) 270 N. Y. 333. Article 5 State Housing Law Ch. 823, L. 1926; amended L. 1934, Ch. 4. Also challenged under the due process clause.

[31] Matter of City of New York (Brooklyn Ferry) (1910) 140 A. D. 238 2nd Dept. Section 824a New York Charter as amended by L. 1907, Ch. 450 and by Ch. 331, L. 1909. The land was not taken perforce by the act.

[32] Matter of City of New York (Tibbett Avenue) (1914) 162 A. D. 398 1st Dept. Sections 979, 980 Greater New York Charter. (Street improvement undertaken under L. 1897, Ch. 378).

[33] McEwan v. The City of New York (1934) 242 A. D. 559 1st Dept. Section 950 of the Greater New York Charter, also challenged under the due process clause. A similar law was upheld by the United States Supreme Court in Crane v. Hablo (1922) 259 U. S. 142. It stated that the confirmation of an award in this type of proceeding by the Board of Revision of Assessments should be final and conclusive, except for lack of jurisdiction, fraud, or wilful misconduct. L. 1918, Ch. 619.

The courts, in fifteen of the twenty-two cases included in this chapter, held that the legislature had not violated any constitutional provision. In the seven others, the decisions were based upon clauses of the Constitution which were subject to diverse interpretations. As there has been no universal agreement about the meaning of "just compensation," of "public use," or of similar expressions, the acts held unconstitutional in these seven do not prove that the legislature ever attempted to seize private property in deliberate violation of the Constitution.

CHAPTER VI
TITLES

Article 3, Section 16 of the State Constitution read as follows:

> No private or local bill, which may be passed by the Legislature, shall embrace more than one subject, and that shall be expressed in the title.

Article 3, Section 17 declared that:

> No act shall be passed which shall provide that any existing law, or any part thereof, shall be made or deemed a part of said act, or which shall enact that any existing law, or part thereof, shall be applicable, except by inserting it in such act.

These two provisions, the first placed in the Constitution of 1846 and the second added in 1874, were designed to prevent the passing of legislation desired by special interests without adequate consideration. In the latter part of the nineteenth century many acts were found in conflict with these sections, particularly the former.[1] However, in the years under consideration, less than ten instances have been found where this was the primary ground for an act being held invalid.

Provisions of the charter of Yonkers, requiring the filing of notices of mechanics' liens in that city in the office of the city clerk, were not mentioned in the title, reading " An act to revise the charter of the City of Yonkers " and hence were held invalid.[2] " An act to amend the municipal court act of the City of New York with reference to rules of court and appeals " attempted to repeal Section 3 of the Municipal Court Act of

---

[1] This statement is based on unpublished research of my own but may be substantiated by Lincoln, *op. cit.*, Vol. 4, pp. 377 to 410 containing an annotation of Article 3, Section 16, and pp. 410 to 415 annotating Article 3, Section 17 to 1905.

[2] Tommasi v. Archibald (1906) 114 A. D. 838 2nd Dept. L. 1895, Ch. 635, Section 3, Title 12.

the City of New York which provided for the removal of cases to the City Court. It was held invalid in the same year as the preceding act.[3] Section 5 of a law of 1893 entitled "An act to incorporate the Economic Power and Construction Company" authorized the company to exercise the right of eminent domain. Section 6 authorized it to lease or sell its property or franchise. In 1909 this was held to be a private act and these grants not expressed in the title.[4] The title of a law passed in 1872 was "An act supplemental to an act entitled ' An act for the appointment of commissioners to lay out a plan for roads and streets in the towns of Kings County, passed May 7, 1869 '." It authorized and empowered the town survey commissioners of Kings County to designate, on the maps to be filed by them, the bulkhead and pierhead lines which were to form the termination of the streets and avenues laid out by them, along the waterfront of the district under their jurisdiction on Gravesend and Jamaica Bays. The act to which it was supplementary mentioned what the court considered only one subject and the act itself was viewed as a local one, thus making the act of 1872 unconstitutional. Even conceding that but one subject was embraced within the statute, it was held not to be expressed within the title.[5] An act of 1884, confirming previous grants of a franchise to land, on the condition of filling in the land and erecting docks, contained a grant of land in fee which had not been filled in. This purpose was not expressed in the title.[6] "An act" of 1900 "to legalize the erection and maintenance of the dam heretofore erected by the

[3] Bonagur v. Orlandi, Supreme Court Appellate Term, 1st Dept. Ch. 598, L. 1904. (1906) 51 Misc. 582.

[4] Economic Power and Construction Company v. Buffalo 195 N. Y. 286. L. 1893, Ch. 459.

[5] People v. Ireland Realty Company (1916) 96 Misc. 18 Supreme Court Kings Special Term. L. 1872, Ch. 331, supplementary to Ch. 670, L. 1869.

[6] First Construction Company of Brooklyn v. State of New York (1917) 221 N. Y. 295 L. 1884, Ch. 494. The rest of this act was held constitutional and has been dealt with above. See note 27, Chapter V supra.

Hudson River Water-Power and Paper Company, now known and designated as the Duncan Company, across the Hudson River at Mechanicville, Saratoga County " embraced an authorization to the company to forever maintain the dam, and to flood back up the river so far as it owned the adjacent upland, or had rights of fluvage thereon, for the purpose of maintaining the pond formed thereby, and also a grant to the predecessor of any interest of the state in the land under the waters of the river covered by the dam, the building and work of the predecessor connected therewith. Not only was this in violation of Article 3, Section 16, but it was void because it attempted to alienate the sovereign right of the state.[7] An act of 1919 authorizing the trustees of Wilson to borrow money for discharging certain debts, when construed to deal with claims lacking legal obligation, was held not to express the subject.[8] In so far as a statute of 1911 purported to make the loss sustained by a delay on a contract the legal obligation of a village, where the title did not indicate the inclusion of a distinct cause of action for the work covered by the contract, it was unconstitutional, but a cause of action for work covered by the contract was well pleaded where reasonable conpensation for additional work, labor and services was mentioned in the title.[9] In 1929 the Court of Appeals held that the insertion of Section 14b, allowing any person who had served on a city police force for twenty years, and as police commissioner or a deputy police commissioner for three years, and who was then serving in the latter capacity, to be retired and granted a pension equal to one-half the salary of police commissioner or deputy police commissioner upon the payment of a proportionate amount of his salary, from the date of his appointment as commissioner to the date of his retirement, in an amendment of 1924 to a law of

[7] West Virginia Pulp and Paper Company of Delaware v. Peck (1918) 104 Misc. 172 Supreme Court Saratoga Special Term. Ch. 683, L. 1900.

[8] Matter of Dean (1920) 230 N. Y. 1, L. 1919, Ch. 399. Certificates of indebtedness had been issued for invalid assessments.

[9] Gaynor v. Village of Port Chester (1921) 231 N. Y. 451, Ch. 513, L. 1911.

1909, bearing the title "An act in relation to cities, constituting Chapter 21 of the Consolidated Laws," also contravened this section.[10]

Two acts were in conflict with Article 3, Section 17. The first of these involved an attempt by the legislature to make the codes established by the Federal government under the National Industrial Recovery Act applicable to intra-state industry. The act provided that those codes, filed with the Secretary of State of New York and which had been approved by the President under the act, should be the standard of fair competition for intra-state transactions in trade and industry. This was held to violate both Article 3, Section 17 and Article 3, Section 1, which states that "The legislative power of this State shall be vested in the Senate and Assembly."[11] The Court of Appeals also prevented an attempt by the legislature to make the provisions of law which required the issuance of permanent teaching certificates to those who had served a probationary period in schools in a city of 400,000 or more applicable to those teachers who were employed by the New York City Board of Higher Education.[12]

The following acts were challenged under Article 3, Section 16 but were sustained: "An act to authorize the City of Elmira to issue its bonds for the construction of a bridge or the reconstructing and repairing of an existing bridge across the Chemung River in the City of Elmira," the title expressing enough of the general purpose of the act;[13] "An act to ratify a certain

[10] Schieffelin v. Warren (1929) 250 N. Y. 396, Ch. 509, L. 1924 amending Ch. 26, L. 1909.

[11] Darweger v. Staats (1935) 267 N. Y. 290, Ch. 781, L. 1933.

[12] Matter of Becker v. Eisner (1938) 277 N. Y. 143, Section 1143 of the Education Law as amended by Ch. 873, L. 1935.

[13] City of Elmira v. Seymour (1906) 111 A. D. 199 3rd Dept. Ch. 476, L. 1905. In order to be constitutional, the court stated, it was not necessary that the title of a bill should be the best that could be selected, nor was it necessary to set forth in the title the various details of the object or purpose to be accomplished by the bill; it was sufficient if the title properly expressed the general purpose of the bill so as to apprise the public of the interests affected thereby.

contract entered into by and between the city of Buffalo, and the Buffalo Railway Company, the Crosstown Street Railway Company of Buffalo and the West Side Street Railway Co. and to carry the same into full force and effect" held explicit;[14] an act of 1900 ratifying and confirming a revised constitution adopted in 1895 by the Seneca Nation of Indians, which included a provision dealing with the Surrogates' courts;[15] an act of 1855 ratifying and confirming an agreement whereby a railroad was given forever the exclusive right to use and occupy a strip thirty feet in width in the center of Atlantic Avenue, and providing for the carrying out of the proposed agreement, held to deal with but one subject, the title merely being very specific;[16] "An act to provide for the expense of widening Livingston Street in the Borough of Brooklyn, City of New York," which placed the total expense of the improvement on New York City;[17] "An act to establish the public service commissions and prescribing their powers and duties, and to provide for the regulation and control of certain public service corporations and making an appropriation therefor," which was held to be a general act;[18] the insertion in the Insurance Law of a section limiting the amount of new business which a domestic insurance corporation might do yearly;[19] "An act to amend Chapter 423 of Laws of 1903

[14] Smith v. City of Buffalo (1906) 51 Misc. 244. Supreme Court Erie Special Term. Ch. 151, L. 1892.

[15] Jimeson v. Lehley (1906) 51 Misc. 352. Supreme Court Erie Special Term. Ch. 252, L. 1900.

[16] Leffman v. Long Island Railroad Company (1907) 120 A.D. 528, 2nd Dept. Ch. 475, L. 1855.

[17] Matter of Lockitt (1908) 58 Misc. 5. Supreme Court Kings Special Term. L. 1907, Ch. 91. No objection was found on the grounds of the just compensation or public use clauses.

[18] Gubner v. McClellan (1909) 130 A.D. 716 1st Dept. Ch. 429, L. 1907.

[19] Bush v. New York Life Insurance Company (1909) 135 A. D. 447 1st Dept. Section 96 Insurance Law. Ch. 326, L. 1906 reenacted in Cons. Laws, Ch. 28; L. 1909, Ch. 33. The legislature had the reserve right under Article 6, Section 1, of amending or annulling corporation charters. The law was also questioned unsuccessfully because companies doing half their business in industrial insurance were excepted.

entitled 'An act to provide for the abolition, discontinuance and avoidance of certain grade crossings in the City of New York'" of 1905, which included provisions for acquiring property rights and making compensation;[20] "An act to provide for the election and to prescribe the terms and compensation of the town trustees in the town of Southampton," etc. which reduced the number of trustees in the town from twelve to five;[21] the act creating the Long Sault Development Company and empowering it to build a dam in the St. Lawrence River which included provisions dealing with tolls;[22] "An act to incorporate the Electric Water Power Company of Oneonta, Otsego County," which included the provision that "Such corporation may acquire lands by condemnation in the manner provided by the Condemnation Law of the State for any of the purposes herein specified;[23] an act for the control of the waters of the Allegany River and Olean Creek by acquiring lands for that purpose which included the way and the manner in which the subject was to be handled;[24] "An act to amend the Education Law, in relation to the assessment and collection of school taxes in the County of Suffolk," held to embrace but one subject,

[20] People ex rel. Olin v. Hennessy (1912) 206 N. Y. 33. Ch. 634, L. 1905.

[21] People ex rel. Squires v. Hand (1913) 158 A. D. 510 2nd Dept. Ch. 133, L. 1902. Nor did it violate the contract clause.

[22] Matter of Long Sault Development Company v. Kennedy (1913) 158 A. D. 398 3rd Dept. Ch. 355, L. 1907. This was held to be the same subject as that of the bridge although, the court noted, that if the provision were unconstitutional the rest would still be valid and not violative of Article 7, Section 7 or of Article 3, Section 18.

[23] Oneonta Light and Power Company v. Schwarzenbach (1914) 164 A. D. 548 3rd Dept. Ch. 234, L. 1898. This act was also considered in harmony with Article 3, Section 18 forbidding the legislature to pass a private or local bill granting any private corporation "any exclusive privilege, immunity or franchise whatever" and Article 8, Section 1 providing that corporations should not be created by special act.

[24] Flood Abatement Commission v. Merritt (1916) 94 Misc. 388, Supreme Court Cattaraugus Special Term. Ch. 717, L. 1915. Nor did this law violate Article 3, Section 18 or Article 8, Section 10 discussed supra.

and that expressed in the title;[25] a section of the Town Law, authorizing a town to acquire lands by condemnation for park purposes, and providing for the appointment of appraisers, which was held to be a general law;[26] " An act to amend the Conservation Law, in relation to the powers of the Water Power and Control Commission as to the water supply of the City of Rochester " which included a requirement that the city pay indirect damages for the additional water supply gained by the taking of Honeoya Lake and a tract of land adjacent;[27] " An act to amend the Public Service Commission Law, in relation to the powers and duties of the Board of Transportation " held to be a general act amending a general law, and " An act to amend Chapter three hundred and seventy-nine of the Laws of nineteen hundred and twenty-nine entitled ' An act to authorize the Land Board to release and surrender to the City of New York a part of the premises, with structures thereon, demised by the lease of Ward's Island made by the City of New York to the State of New York ', in relation to the type of bridge to be constructed " over the rivers, between Manhattan, The Bronx and Queens;[28] an act, in relation to sewage disposal in Nassau County, under which a judge was to authorize the site chosen by sewage commissioners of the

[25] Ruland v. Tuthill (1919) 187 A. D. 20 2nd Dept. Ch. 518, L. 1918. The law was enacted for the purpose of readjusting the burden of taxation among school districts as it would have been if the unit system, which had been repealed after being in operation for about nine months, had never been created. The legislature had the power to readjust and correct inequalities by a retroactive law.

[26] Matter of Town of Tonawanda (1926) 127 Misc. 852 Supreme Court Erie County Section 512-a Town Law added by L. 1923, Ch. 795. On another issue raised, the court stated that compensation had to be given.

[27] Matter of Supervisors of Ontario County v. Water Power and Control Commission (1929) 227 A. D. 345 3rd Dept. Ch. 862, L. 1928. The act did not infringe on Home Rule or violate due process of law.

[28] Robia Holding Corporation v. Walker (1930) 230 A. D. 666 1st Dept. Ch. 373, L. 1930 and Ch. 437, L. 1930.

sewage district for the erection of a sewage disposal plant;[29] the addition of Section 23 to the Transportation Corporation Law under which the franchises of omnibus routes had been issued by the Board of Railroad Commissioners and its successor the Public Service Commission;[30] and "An act * * * in relation to a free public library in the City of Buffalo" which contained a provision for authorizing a contract between the city and the library, for the support of the latter, and in which city there were two, not one, free libraries.[31]

An amendment to the Farms and Markets Law providing penalties of $25 to $100 for the first violation, and of $200 for the second violation of the law providing a twelve month limit for keeping food products in cold storage, discussed in Chapter X, was challenged as a violation of Article 3, Section 17, but was sustained.[32]

In summary, eighteen acts were challenged under Article 3, Section 16, and sustained, while eight failed to meet the test. Under Article 3, Section 17, two were found unconstitutional, and one, constitutional. The most important casualty was the act making the code under the N.I.R.A. applicable within the state, and in that case the question of delegation of legislative power weighed more heavily than the phraseology of the title. The courts have appreciated, in general, the difficulties a too literal interpretation of these clauses would place on the legislature.

[29] Matter of Jordan v. Smith (1930) 137 Misc. 341, affirmed 254 N. Y. 585 (1930). Section 249-a Town Law (as added by L. 1929, Ch. 693). Other objections to the law which were not convincing to the court were that the power conferred was not judicial, and that the act violated the due process and just compensation clauses.

[30] City of New York v. Fifth Avenue Coach Company (1933) 262 N. Y. 481, Ch. 657, L. 1900. [General Laws Chapter 40.]

[31] Matter of Buffalo Library v. Wanamaker (1937) 162 Misc. 26 Supreme Court Erie County, Ch. 16, L. 1897.

[32] People v. Buffalo Cold Storage Co. (1920) 113 Misc. 479 Supreme Court Erie Special Term. Section 58, Ch. 69 Cons. Laws—Farms and Markets Law, added to Cons. Laws by Ch. 802, L. 1917. See People v. Finkelstein Chapter X, note 17 infra.

CHAPTER VII
HOME RULE

IN the first half of the nineteenth century, the local offices of municipalities and of counties, previously appointive, were made elective.[1] This lone restriction on the powers of the legislature did not prevent interference in the affairs of the cities as they grew in size and wealth, thus becoming tempting targets for rapacious and patronage-hungry legislators.[2] Most of these legislative acts were upheld by the courts, one of the most notable of which was the act of 1857 creating the Metropolitan Police District. This act transferred the control of the police functions of New York City to a commission which supervised a district comprising that city, but also including four neighboring counties. In this way the constitutional restrictions were successfully circumvented.[3] Similar types of legislation followed. The reaction to this found its voice in debates in the Convention of 1867 and in the reports of various investigating bodies.[4] In 1874 the legislature was forbidden by constitutional amendment to pass private or local bills on a number of topics.[5] These restrictions will be dealt with in the next chapter, but here it may be noted that among them were prohibitions against the incorporation of villages, the location or change of county seats and provision for the election of members of boards of supervisors.

The flood of special legislation continued, nevertheless, and in 1894 the Constitutional Convention adopted a requirement

[1] Article 4, Section 10, New York Constitution of 1821 as amended in 1833 and 1839. New York State Constitution Annotated, *op. cit.*, Pt. II, pp. 42-43.

[2] Howard L. McBain, *The Law and the Practice of Municipal Home Rule*, (New York, 1916), pp. 5-10.

[3] People ex rel. Wood v. Draper (1857) 15 N. Y. 532.

[4] McBain, *op. cit.*, pp. 8-10.

[5] Article 3, Section 18 Constitution of 1846 as amended in 1874.

designed to correct the situation. The cities of the state were divided into three classes based on population. In the first class were cities with a population of 250,000 and over, changed in 1907 to those over 175,000. At that time only New York, Buffalo and Rochester had attained that figure. In the second class were cities whose population ranged from 50,000 to 175,000, and the remaining cities formed the third class. The convention declared that laws " relating to the property, affairs, or government of cities and the several departments thereof . . . which relate to a single city, or to less than all the cities of a class, shall be deemed special laws." The legislature was forbidden to pass such laws without submitting them to the local authorities of the cities concerned for their consideration. In the first class cities a bill of this type was submitted to the mayor, and in the other cities to the mayor and council. These authorities were required, after public notice and a public hearing, to accept or reject the bill. If, however, the bill was returned without having been accepted or within fifteen days was not returned, it might again be passed by the legislature, subject in the same manner as other bills to the governor's action. If such a bill applied to more than one city, it had to be submitted for acceptance to the mayors of each city to which it related.[6] In 1921 a decision of the Court of Appeals held that the fact that the legislature had repassed an act before the fifteen days allowed the mayor of New York City to consider and return it, when the mayor had sent the bill back before the fifteen days had gone by, did not make the act unconstitutional. The bill had been returned to the governor instead of the legislature, but this was unimportant. It was also held that the time of transmission was determined not by the date of receipt, but by the date of dispatch.[7]

The restrictions so imposed did not prevent the legislature from passing general laws relating to the property, affairs and government of cities. Despite this, and the fact that the legis-

[6] Article 12, Section 2 Constitution of 1894, McBain, *op. cit.*, pp. 101-105.
[7] People ex rel. Boyle v. Cruise 231 N. Y. 639. Ch. 670, L. 1921.

lature might by a simple majority repass special acts following a suspensory veto by a city or cities, the situation from the standpoint of those advocating home rule for cities showed great improvement after 1894 as contrasted with that of the years before.[8] However, the demands for the conferring of positive powers on the cities themselves continued, as well as the desire to make the negative restrictions on the legislature stronger. Since Article 3, Section 1 stating that " The legislative power of this state shall be vested in the senate and assembly " had been interpreted as barring the delegation of legislative power, the statutes passed before the Home Rule Amendment of 1923 did not satisfy the proponents of this reform.

Among these statutes were the General Municipal Law of 1892 into which a number of previous enactments had been incorporated relating to " counties, towns, cities, and villages, defining and declaring their rights, privileges, limitations, and liabilities as municipal corporations; "[9] the General City Law of 1900 containing the so-called Home Rule Act granting every city " power to regulate, manage, and control its property and local affairs," and " all the rights, privileges, and jurisdiction necessary and proper for carrying such power into execution; "[10] the Second Class Cities Law of 1909 outlining general charter provisions for that class of cities;[11] and the Optional City

[8] McBain, *op. cit.*, pp. 103-105. From 1902 to 1914 the legislature allowed 524 vetoes by the cities of the state to stand effective.

[9] L. 1892, Ch. 685, consolidated with later acts relating to municipal corporations by L. 1909, Ch. 29. New York State Constitutional Convention Committee, Vol. II, *Problems Relating to Home Rule and Local Government*, (Albany, 1938) p. 19. Hereinafter cited as Home Rule Problems.

[10] *Ibid.*, The General City Law was originally Ch. 22 of General Laws, L. 1900, Ch. 327, later, L. 1909, Ch. 26.

The Home Rule Act was Article 2-A of the General City Law added by L. 1913, Ch. 247.

[11] *Ibid.*, L. 1909, Ch. 55; derived from the Second Class Cities Law, L. 1906, Ch. 473; provisions of this law relating to the repair and construction of tenement houses and other buildings were held to be concerned with the public health and safety and not to violate Article 12, Section 2, which was passed after the law, in House v. Bodour (1938) 168 Misc. 766. Municipal Court, City of Syracuse.

Government Law of 1914, under which cities were given the option of adopting one of a number of simplified forms of government.[12]

The Home Rule Law of 1913 was sustained in the same year by the Supreme Court, despite the contention that " Though in form a general law it was a mere device or subterfuge to circumvent the operation of Section 2 of Article XII of the Constitution." [13] The Optional City Government Law was likewise upheld as not violating Article 3, Section 1 or Article 12, Sections 1 and 2.[14]

In 1923 the Home Rule Amendment was adopted. Because of the importance of this landmark as a basis for judicial decisions, it is here given in full, the date on the left representing the date of adoption of the particular section to which it applies:

Article 12

1894 Sec. 1. It shall be the duty of the legislature to provide the organization of cities and incorporated villages, to restrict their power of taxation, assessment, borrowing money, contracting debts, and loaning their credit, so as to prevent abuses in assessments and in contracting debt by such municipal corporations;

1905 and the legislature may regulate and fix the wages or salaries, the hours of work or labor, and make provision for the protection welfare and safety of persons employed by the state or by any county, city, town, village or other civil division of the state, or by any contractor or sub-contractor performing work, labor or services for the state, or for any county, city, town, village or other civil division thereof.

---

12 *Ibid.,* L. 1914, Ch. 444 applying to second and third class cities; extended to all cities by amendment, L. 1935, Ch. 407.

13 Hammitt v. Gaynor (1913) 82 Misc. 196 New York Special Term; affirmed without opinion 185 A. D. 909. See note 10 supra.

14 Cleveland v. City of Watertown (1917) 222 N. Y. 159. See note 12 supra.

1923   Sec. 2. The legislature shall not pass any law relating to the property, affairs or government of cities, which shall be special or local either in its terms or in its effect, but shall act in relation to the property, affairs or government of any city only by general laws which shall in terms and in effect apply alike to all cities except on message from the Governor declaring that an emergency exists and the concurrent action of two-thirds of the members of each house of the legislature.

1923   Sec. 3. Every city shall have power to adopt and amend local laws not inconsistent with the constitution and laws of the state, relating to the powers, duties, qualifications, number, mode of selection and removal, terms of office and compensation of all officers and employees of the city, the transaction of its business, the incurring of its obligations, the presentation, ascertainment and discharge of claims against it, the acquisition, care, management and use of its streets and property, the wages or salaries, the hours of work or labor, and the protection, welfare and safety of persons employed by any contractor or sub-contractor for performing work, labor or services for it, and government and regulation of the conduct of its inhabitants and the protection of their property, safety and health. The legislature shall, at its next session after this section shall become part of the constitution, provide by general law for carrying into effect the provisions of this section.

1923   Sec. 4. The provisions of this article shall not be deemed to restrict the power of the legislature to enact laws relating to matters other than the property, affairs or government of cities.

1923   Sec. 5. The legislature may by general laws confer on cities such further powers of local legislation and administration as it may from time to time, deem expedient.

1923   Sec. 6. All elections of city officers, including supervisors and judicial officers of inferior local courts, elected in any city or part of a city, and of county officers elected in the counties of New York and Kings, and in all counties whose boundaries are the same as those of a city, except to fill vacancies, shall be held on the Tuesday succeeding the first

Monday in November in an odd numbered year, and the term of every such officer shall expire at the end of an odd numbered year. The terms of office of all such officers elected before the first day of January, one thousand eight hundred ninety five, whose successors have not then been elected which under existing laws would expire with an even numbered year, or in an odd numbered year and before the end thereof, are extended to and including the last day of December next following the time when such terms would otherwise expire; the terms of office of all such officers which under existing laws would expire in an even-numbered year and before the end thereof, are abridged so as to expire at the end of the preceding year. This section shall not apply [to any city of third class or] 1923 to elections of any judicial officer, except judges and justices of inferior local courts.

1923   Sec. 7. The provisions of this article shall not affect any existing provision of law; but all existing charters and other laws shall continue in force until repealed, amended, modified or superseded in accordance with the provisions of this article. Nothing in this article contained shall apply to or affect the maintenance, support, or administration of the public school systems in the several cities of the state, as required or provided by Article 9 of the Constitution.[15]

It will be seen that the grant of power to the cities under Section 3 did not cover the area forbidden to the state by Section 2. However, Section 5 could enable the gap to be filled. Since the amendment was not self-executing, the legislature passed an enabling act in 1924.[16] This law gave the city legislative bodies the power to pass local laws " in relation to the property, affairs or government of the city relating to . . ." a list of items which was reproduced from Article 12, Sec-

[15] Joseph D. McGoldrick, *Law and Practice of Municipal Home Rule, 1916-1930*, (New York, 1933) pp. 385-387. This text may also be found in Home Rule Problems, *op. cit.*, pp. 255-257.

[16] L. 1924, Ch. 363. McGoldrick, *op. cit.*, p. 272; Home Rule Problems, *op. cit.*, p. 19.

tion 3.[17] Both the Home Rule Amendment and the Home Rule Law were challenged on the ground that the former had been improperly passed. The basis of this contention was that Article 12, upon which the amendment was to operate, was not the same in both years that the amendment was acted upon by the legislature. A minor amendment had been adopted in 1922, between the first passage of the amendment in the same year and its repassage in 1923. Another objection to the amendment was that it had not been entered upon the journals of the Senate and Assembly properly, only the title having been entered. Although these contentions were accepted by the Appellate Division, the Court of Appeals held them to be of no avail against the law, considering the first objection about the change in amendment immaterial.[18]

In 1927 Section 8 was added to Article 12, reading as follows:

> No territory shall be annexed to any city until the people of the territory proposed to be annexed shall have consented to such annexation by a majority vote on a referendum called for that purpose.[19]

Meanwhile, a movement for county home rule had gotten under way. Enthusiasm for this type of reform was not so great because the county had generally been regarded as an administrative division of the state, while cities were more likely to be natural economic and social units. In 1921 an amendment was adopted which allowed the legislature to provide forms of government for either Westchester or Nassau Counties, or both, subject to adoption by the county electors, at a

17 McGoldrick, *op. cit.*, p. 272; Home Rule Problems, *op. cit.*, p. 25.

18 Browne v. City of New York (1925) 213 A. D. 206 1st Dept.; 241 N. Y. 96 (1925) Court of Appeals. The resuit of the case in both courts was the same, as far as the validity of four local laws of New York City, attempting to establish a municipal bus system, were concerned. They were held beyond the power of the city to enact.

19 Home Rule Problems, *op. cit.*, p. 257.

general election, in an odd-numbered year. The form of government might transfer functions exercised by the towns or town officers to the county or to county officers. However, the legislature might amend or modify the plan.[20] In 1929 the power of the legislature was further restricted by requiring that laws dealing with the abolition or creation of an elective office, changing the voting or veto power, the method of removal, the term of office or reducing the salary of an elective officer during his term of office, diminishing the powers of such an officer, changing a legislative body or providing a new charter were to require approval by the county electorate. In addition, special or local laws affecting Westchester or Nassau Counties had to be referred after passage by both branches of the legislature to the board of supervisors or other governing elective body of the county for a public hearing. If the board accepted the bill, it was to go to the governor, not to take effect until sixty days after his approval or after final adoption by the legislature in the event of his disapproval. If within the sixty days, a petition should be filed by a number of electors equal to five per cent of the gubernatorial vote in the county at the last election, the proposed law had to be approved by the electors of the county. If the board did not accept the bill it might be repassed by the legislature, but was not to take effect until approved by the county electors.[21]

In 1935 county home rule was extended, first by law, and then in greater measure by amendment, to all the counties of the state. The law was held constitutional the next year. As legislation to implement this amendment was not passed until 1937, it added little to the number of cases occurring in the period under study. For the sake of completeness and because of its potentialities as a restriction on the powers of the legislature, it is given below. The following is the text of Article 3, Section 26 as it read in 1938:

20 Article 3, Section 26, as amended in 1921. Amendments proposed, *op. cit.*, pp. 239-40.

21 *Ibid.*, pp. 244-46.

HOME RULE

Subdivision 1. There shall be in each county, except in a county wholly included in a city, a board of supervisors, or other elective body, to be composed of such members and elected in such manner for such period as is or may be provided by law.

2. The legislature shall provide by law for the organization and government of counties and shall provide by law alternative forms of government for counties except counties wholly included in a city and for the submission of one or more such forms of government to the electors residing in such counties. No such form of government shall become operative in any such county unless and until adopted at a general election held in such county by receiving a majority of the total votes cast thereon in (1) the county, (2) every city containing more than twenty-five per centum of the population of the county according to the last preceding federal census, and (3) that part of the county, if any, outside of such cities. Any such form of government shall set forth the structure of the county government and the manner in which it is to function. Any such form of government may provide for the appointment of any county officers or their selection by any method of nomination and election, or the abolition of their offices, and may also provide for the exercise by the board of supervisors or other elective body of powers of local legislation and administration and the transfer of any or all of the functions and duties of the county and the cities, towns, villages, districts and other units of government contained in such county to each other or to the state, and for the abolition of offices, departments, agencies or units of government when all of their functions are so transferred without regard to the provisions of Article 10 or any other provisions of this constitution inconsistent herewith. The boards of supervisors or other elective bodies of any two or more such counties may by agreement provide for the discharge within the territorial limits of such counties or parts thereof of one or more governmental functions.

3. Nothing herein contained shall be deemed to impair or restrict the existing power of the legislature to enact laws

relating to the government of a county or the cities, towns, villages, districts or other units of government therein contained until the adoption of a form of government by such county pursuant to subdivision 2 of this section.

4. After the adoption of a form of government by a county pursuant to subdivision 2 of this section, the legislature shall not pass any law relating to the property, affairs or government of such county which shall be special or local either in its terms or in its effects, but shall set in relation to the property, affairs or government of any such county only by general laws which shall in terms and in effect apply alike to all such counties except on message from the governor declaring that an emergency exists and the concurrent action of two-thirds of the members of each house of the legislature and no law, special or local in its terms or in its effect, which abolishes or creates an elective office or changes the voting or veto power of or the method of removing an elective officer, changes the term of office or reduces the salary of an elective officer during his term of office, abolishes, transfers or curtails any power of an elective officer, changes the form or composition of the elective body of any such county, or provides a new form of government for such county, shall become effective without adoption by the electors of such county in the manner prescribed in subdivision 2 of this section for the adoption of a form of government for such county pursuant thereto. Nothing herein contained shall impair or restrict the power of the legislature to enact laws relating to matter other than the property, affairs or government of such county.

5. If under a form of government, adopted by a county pursuant to subdivision 2 of this section, the board of supervisors be abolished, the powers and duties of the board of supervisors, as prescribed by the constitution, or by statute if not provided for by such form of government, shall devolve upon the elective body in such county.

6. In a city which includes an entire county, or two or more entire counties, the powers and duties of a board of supervisors may be devolved upon the municipal assembly, common council, board of aldermen or other legislative body of the city.

7. Existing laws applicable to the government of counties

and the cities, towns, villages, districts and other units of government therein contained shall continue in force until repealed, amended, modified or superseded by law or by a form of government and nothing contained in this section shall be construed to impair the provisions of Article 12 of this constitution.[22]

In 1911 the Court of Appeals declared that the attempt of the legislature to create an area known as Sylvan Beach was not warranted by the Constitution which only authorized the creation of counties, cities, towns and villages as civil divisions for political purposes.[23] This did not prevent the legislature from establishing the Buffalo Sewer Authority in 1935 and providing for its powers and duties.[24] By 1938 twenty-two authorities had been created for various purposes. Although not possessing the power to levy taxes or make assessments, they do have the power of eminent domain and are allowed to charge for their services. In addition, their obligations are tax-free.[25] Another objection to the Buffalo Sewer Authority was that its nature was local rather than general, but the court held that the sewage situation in Buffalo was a menace to the people of the state, thus providing the basis for sustaining the law.[26]

The court upheld the authorization of a county or other district to purchase and operate a light or power plant. The

[22] Article 3, Section 26. Home Rule Problems, *op. cit.*, pp. 257-259; Amendments Proposed, *op. cit.*, pp. 261-65. In Matter of Burke v. Krug (1936) 272 N. Y. 575, Ch. 879, L. 1936, providing alternative forms of county government for certain counties and for submisssion of the same was held not to violate Article 12 or Article 3, Sections 16 and 20 of the State Constitution.

[23] People ex rel. Hon Yost v. Becker 203 N. Y. 201. Ch. 812, L. 1896 and Ch. 361, L. 1901.

[24] Robertson v. Zimmerman 268 N. Y. 352. Ch. 349, L. 1935; Smith v. Zimmerman 268 N. Y. 491. Ch. 342, L. 1935.

[25] New York State Constitutional Convention Committee, Vol. IV, *State and Local Government in New York*, (Abany, 1938) pp. 189-193. Hereinafter referred to as State and Local Government.

[26] Judges Lehman and O'Brien concurred on the basis of the decision in Adler v. Deegan discussed in note 54 infra.

provision, in Article VIII, Section 10, barring local units of government from lending money or credit in aid of any individual, association or corporation or becoming indebted except for county, city, town or village purposes, was held inapplicable to assessments for benefits. However, the part of the act under which taxation to pay the bonds issued for the light and power plant would fall upon parts of the county outside of the district to be benefited was held unconstitutional.[27]

Besides authorities, there have also been created in New York school districts under the Education Law, and since 1880 a number of special improvement districts, such as fire, lighting, highway, park and water districts. These latter were created in most cases upon petition to the town or county boards, as the case may be. There is no record of any challenge in the courts to the creation of this type of local division.[28]

Under Article 3, Section 18, given in full in the next chapter, the legislature is prohibited from passing a private or local bill incorporating a village. This was held to forbid the amendment by the legislature of the charter of the Village of Cornwall, in order to ratify proceedings taken by that village for the annexation of territory. The court asserted that " If the day after a village is incorporated the legislature may under the guise of an amendment alter its charter by a special act [the] purpose [of the constitutional provision] is frustrated." [29] Similarly an act relating to Williamsville, a village incorporated under the General Village Law, which, according to the court, had become its charter, was held unconstitutional.[30]

[27] Gaynor v. Marohn (1935) 268 N. Y. 417, Ch. 842, L. 1935; Section 14 held unconstitutional.

[28] A description of these districts as they existed to 1938 is included in State and Local Government, *op. cit.*, pp. 164-186.

[29] Abell v. Clarkson (1923) 237 N. Y. 85. Ch. 20, L. 1923.

[30] Magrum v. Village of Williamsville (1934) 241 A. D. 55 4th Dept. Ch. 601, L. 1933. The act also was held to violate Article 3, Section 16 because the title gave no intimation of the creation of an obligation on the village's part to pay back money which had been collected for taxes levied and assessed under the General Village Law.

In two cases the question was raised as to whether the legislature had improperly delegated the legislative power vested in it. A county board of supervisors was permitted to submit the question of the establishment of county hospitals to the voters by an act of 1914, without violating the Constitution in the judgment of the Appellate Division.[31] Later the Village of Peekskill was validly delegated power, by a law of 1917, to permit the erection and maintenance of gasoline pumps in the public streets.[32]

The most frequent type of decision dealt with local offices. In 1906 the laws establishing the Metropolitan Elections District and creating the office of State Superintendent of Elections, to be filled by appointment by the governor, were upheld, since the office was considered new in name and essentially new in functions.[33] The sections of the New York City Charter providing for the removal of county officers and of the mayor by the governor after a hearing were sustained, that referring to the county officers in 1909, and the other in 1932.[34] So too were the following: a section of the Village Law providing that in case of a tie vote, the Board of Trustees should select a village officer by lot;[35] a section of the Revised Charter of Ithaca abolishing the office of justice of the peace in that city;[36] laws which fixed the terms of the Bronx County Sheriff, District Attorney, County Clerk and Register of Deeds at four, in-

---

[31] Smith v. Smith (1916) 174 A. D. 473, 2nd Dept. Ch. 323, L. 1914.

[32] Matter of McCoy (1925) 241 N. Y. 71. L. 1917, Ch. 198, Section 3, Subd. 7. The alleged objection was that public property was being used for private gain.

[33] Matter of Morgan 186 N. Y. 202. L. 1898, Ch. 676; L. 1905, Ch. 689.

[34] People v. Ahearn 196 N. Y. 221. Section 382 New York Charter, Ch. 466, L. 1901; Matter of Donnelly v. Roosevelt (In Re Walker) (1932) 144 Misc. 525. Supreme Court Albany County. Section 122 Greater New York Charter, Ch. 466, L. 1901.

[35] Matter of Frame (1910) 69 Misc. 568. Supreme Court Onondaga Special Term for Motions. Section 53, Village Law.

[36] Reid v. Stevens (1910) 70 Misc. 177. County Court Tompkins County. Ch. 503, L. 1908; Section 233 Revised Charter of Ithaca.

stead of three, years;[37] the statute abolishing the office of coroner and establishing that of chief medical examiner;[38] the law validating the action of the voters of the town of Brookhaven rescinding a prior resolution making the office of superintendent of highways appointive, and again making it an elective office;[39] the act abolishing the offices of the former trustees of the town of Huntington and transferring their duties to the town officials;[40] the section of the New York City Charter entitling the Commissioners of Public Works of Manhattan and Bronx Boroughs to vote in the absence of the Borough President at sessions of the Board of Estimate and Apportionment;[41] that section of the Education Law under which a District Superintendent of schools was elected by school directors elected by the people of Huntington;[42] and a section of the Utica City Court Act providing that in case of a vacancy in that court, the office

[37] Matter of O'Brien v. Boyle (1916) 219 N. Y. 195. L. 1912, Ch. 548, Section 3. Bronx County had been formed from New York County and Article 12, Section 3 of the 1894 Constitution required that elections of county officers in New York and Kings Counties should be held in an odd-numbered year.

[38] Matter of Senior v. Boyle (1917) 221 N. Y. 414. Ch. 284, L. 1915. The coroner was not an officer mentioned in the 1894 Constitution.

[39] People ex rel. Dare v. Howell (1916) 174 A. D. 118 2nd Dept. affirmed (1917) 220 N. Y. 593. Ch. 48, L. 1916. This was not viewed as an attempt to substitute an election by the legislature for one by the qualified town electors.

[40] Sammis v. Huntington (1919) 186 A. D. 463 2nd Dept. Ch. 492, L. 1872.

[41] Matter of Richmond Railways Inc. v. Gilchrist (1929) 225 A. D. 371. 1st Dept. Sections 74, 226 Greater New York Charter; L. 1901, Ch. 466 as added to by L. 1914, Ch. 467. The Board of Estimate was the upper branch of the legislative body of New York City, the Board of Aldermen being the lower. The former consisted of the three city-wide elected officers—the Mayor, the Comptroller, the President of the Board of Aldermen—each with three votes and the five borough presidents elected by their respective boroughs, those of Manhattan and Brooklyn having two votes and the others, one.

[42] Gwynne v. Board of Education of Union Free School District No. 3 (1931) 234 A. D. 629 2nd Dept. Section 129 Education Law.

should be filled for a full term at the next annual election, when construed to mean that the election could take place in the year the vacancy occurred, although it was even-numbered.[43]

The court held unconstitutional a section of the Public Health Law requiring the State Commissioner of Health to appoint the village health officer on the nomination of the local Board of Health, because the office had not been provided for by the State Constitution, and therefore the officer had to be elected by the village electors or appointed by the village authorities.[44] A section of the Election Law, under which the nomination to the office of Commissioner of Elections was restricted to those whose names were submitted by political parties, was held to destroy the power of selection of the Mayor and contravene Article X, Section 2.[45] An act of 1914 establishing a receiver of taxes, elected or appointed in each town to collect all the taxes within the town, was viewed as depriving the incorporated villages of their rights to assess and collect taxes for village purposes by the Court of Appeals.[46] The laws providing for the appointment of the Commissioner of Jurors of Albany County by the resident Supreme Court justices were considered in violation of Article X, Section 2, since the position was a county office existing prior to January 1, 1895 and the appointment could not be made by state officers.[47] So much of the section of the New York City Charter as provided that a vacancy in the borough presidency should be filled for the un-

[43] Matter of Brown v. Sisti (1936) 160 Misc. 332. Supreme Court Oneida County, Section 20 Utica City Court Act; Ch. 586, L. 1925 amending Ch. 103, L. 1882.

[44] Matter of Towne v. Porter (1908) 128 A. D. 717 3rd Dept. Section 20 Public Health Law.

[45] Matter of Kane (1911) 71 Misc. 163. Supreme Court Kings Special Term. Section 194 Election Law.

[46] People ex rel. Pelham v. Village of Pelham (1915) 215 N. Y. 374. Westchester County Tax Act; L. 1914, Ch. 510.

[47] Wendell v. Lavin (1927) 246 N. Y. 115. Ch. 441, L. 1899 and Ch. 320, L. 1900.

expired term by appointment was adjudged in conflict with Article X, Section 5, stating that:

> in case of elective officers, no person appointed to fill a vacancy shall hold his office by virtue of such appointment longer than the commencement of the political year next succeeding the first annual election after the happening of the vacancy.[48]

A provision of the Town Law that a person appointed to fill a vacancy in a town elective office was to hold until commencement of the calendar year after the first biennial town election was also held to violate this last section.[49]

In 1907 legislation had been enacted authorizing a contract between New York City and Mount Kisco, a village in Westchester County, for sewage disposal, empowering that city to make connection between the village and the city's sewage system at the expense of the villagers, if the latter failed to make the connection themselves. The persons acting for New York City in this matter were held by the Appellate Division not to be village officers unknown at the time the Constitution was put into effect. Hence, they were not required to be elected by the villagers.[50] A section of the Greater New York Charter providing for the assessment and taxation of lands outside of New York City, in Yonkers, taken in connection with the water supply of New York City by its officers, did not relate to the property, affairs or government of Yonkers, in the view of the Appellate Division, because the city officers were considered agents of the state.[51]

The New York legislature, in common with those of other states, had recourse to the device of classification in order to

[48] Needleman v. Voorhis (1930) 254 N. Y. 339. Section 382 New York City Charter; Ch. 466, L. 1901.

[49] Mott v. Krug (1938) 278 N. Y. 457. Subd. 5, Section 64 Town Law (Cons. Laws, Ch. 62).

[50] Mead v. Turner (1909) 134 A. D. 691 2nd Dept. Ch. 428, L. 1907.

[51] People ex rel. City of New York v. Neville (1918) 183 A. D. 799 2nd Dept. Section 480 Greater New York Charter, L. 1901, Ch. 466. The law had not been transmitted for the acceptance of the mayor.

overcome the limitations on its power to pass special legislation. Among the laws sustained which had been passed in accordance with this method were the laws of 1905 transferring certain cities then in the third class to the second class, without submission to those cities for approval,[52] and of 1914 authorizing a city of the second or third class to adopt a simplified form of government.[53] More significance has been attached to those laws affecting New York City, which since its consolidation in 1898 has had over half the state's population. Several laws which by their terms could only have been applicable to that city at the time of passage have been upheld. The most outstanding was the Multiple Dwelling Law of 1929, upheld in the same year in Adler v. Deegan.[54] The act referred to applied only to cities of 800,000 or over. It established standards of construction for such dwellings, including height and size of lot. There were three majority opinions, and two dissenting. Two of the majority opinions were written by Judges Pound and Crane, both of whom were Republicans, Judge Crane coming from Brooklyn. The third, however, was written by Chief Judge Cardozo, who was a Democrat from New York City. The basis of this opinion lay in the fact that, although the law dealt with matters of local concern, the questions of health involved made them a matter of state concern. The classification adopted by the legislature was therefore considered reasonable. Discussing the standard for determining the line of demarcation between the two spheres of action, Cardozo declared " that if the subject be in a substantial degree a matter of state concern, the Legislature may act, though intermingled with it are concerns of the locality." The city, however, in his opinion, was free to act until the state had intervened.[55] The dissenting opinions, written by Judges Leh-

[52] Koster v. Coyne (1906) 110 A. D. 742 2nd Dept. Ch. 501, L. 1905.

[53] Ch. 444, L. 1914. Cleveland v. City of Watertown, cited in note 14 supra.

[54] 251 N. Y. 467. Ch. 713, L. 1929.

[55] *Ibid.,* at p. 491.

man and O'Brien, both Democrats, held that the law did affect the " property, affairs or government " of New York City in violation of the Home Rule Amendment. Judge Lehman's test was " Whether the subject matter of the law relates to the government of the city or to its affairs or property." [56] This was almost the direct opposite of Cardozo's criterion.

The other cases on the subject seemed to follow the same general pattern of confirming the powers of the state legislature, and construing strictly the restrictions embodied in Article 12. The laws passed during the depression authorizing cities with a population of one million or more to impose taxes on public utilities for the relief of the unemployed were upheld.[57] These decisions had as precedents cases which occurred before the passage of the Home Rule Amendment involving the interpretation of what were general and what were local laws. As some of these cases were concerned with Article 3, Section 18, they will be dealt with later.

These decisions do not mean that the legislature was given a completely clean slate by the courts. A law was passed in 1925 providing that claims for indemnification against New York City barred by the Statute of Limitations might again be presented or prosecuted. The provisions were so hedged about that the claims of only one company would have been subject to the act. The Court of Appeals considered the act a violation of Article 12, Section 2 because the prescribed conditions were so narrow that the act was not general.[58] It also disapproved a law passed in 1936, directing the submission of the question of the three platoon system for members of the fire department to the voters of the city with a population of one million or over.[59]

56 *Ibid.*, at p. 496.

57 New York Steam Corporation v. City of New York (1935) 268 N. Y. 137. Ch. 815, L. 1933;
Garfield v. New York Telephone Co. (1935) 268 N. Y. 549. Ch. 873, L. 1934. Taxes were allowed upon receipts from telephone service.

58 Matter of City of New York (1927) 246 N. Y. 72. Ch. 602, L. 1925.

59 Osborn v. Cohen (1936) 272 N. Y. 55. Ch. 886, L. 1936.

Another case which has assumed prominence in discussions of home rule is City of New York v. Village of Lawrence (1929). Here a law defining the boundary line between the City of New York and the town of Hempstead, in adjoining Nassau County, was held constitutional, although the topic certainly pertained to the property, affairs and/or government of New York City. The question of the boundary lines between two subdivisions of the state was thought of such importance to the state that it was not felt that such a matter could be left to the local units of government.[60] Fourteen years earlier the Appellate Division had upheld an act, providing for the taking into the City of Schenectady of portions of towns containing a school district, which exempted the city from liability upon the bonds issued subsequent to January 1, 1915 for the construction of a school house in the portion of the school district not included by the act in the City of Schenectady.[61]

The legislature was allowed to pass special laws, upon an emergency message from the governor, by a two-thirds vote. This did not prove the barrier that it might appear at first glance. From 1924, when the amendment became effective, through 1937, 1,067 such laws were passed.[62] In 1934 the legislature had authorized the mayor of New York City to appoint a charter revision commission by this means. This was questioned because Article 12, Section 3 granted the city the power to adopt and amend local laws, not inconsistent with the Constitution and laws of the state, relating to a number of subjects which have already been given above.[63] The law was upheld by the Court of Appeals.[64] The New York

---

[60] 250 N. Y. 429. Ch. 802, L. 1928.

[61] People ex rel. Welch v. Dunn (1915) 168 A. D. 678 3rd Dept. Ch. 58, L. 1914.

[62] Home Rule Problems, *op. cit.*, p. 264. See discussion on pp. 68-70 and tables on pp. 264-269.

[63] See p. 119 of this chapter, supra.

[64] Matter of Mooney v. Cohen (1936) 272 N. Y. 33. Ch. 867, L. 1934, as amended by Chapter 293, L. 1935.

City Economy Act, which conferred powers on that city's Board of Estimate and Apportionment to abolish certain positions, although the budget for the current fiscal year had been adopted as provided in the charter, was another instance of emergency legislation upheld by the courts.[65] In 1936 another emergency law was held valid which took a portion of the town of Wawayanda and made it part of the City of Middletown, subject to the consent of the residents.[66]

Three years earlier, Article 12, Section 3 had been construed as allowing laws to be enacted permitting a city to assume liability for injury to an innocent bystander from the act of a policeman in making an arrest.[67] Other state laws allowing cities to assume various powers have already been discussed.[68] Further mention will be made in the next chapter of decisions under other sections of the Constitution.[69] The assumptions of powers by the cities themselves, without the sanction of statutes under Article 12, Section 3, will not be dealt with as has been explained in the Foreword. It is appropriate to note, nevertheless, that from 1924 through 1936, 1,844 local laws were passed by the cities.[70] A number of these local laws have been declared unconstitutional, thus making the benefits to the cities under the Home Rule Amendment appear smaller than had been hoped by advocates of the reform.[71]

65 Matter of Levinson v. Rice (1934) 152 Misc. 813. Ch. 178, L. 1934.

66 People ex rel. City of Middletown v. McBride (1936) 272 N. Y. 563. Ch. 574, L. 1931.

67 Matter of Evans v. Berry (1933) 262 N. Y. 61. Sections 11 and 31 of City Home Rule Law (Cons. Laws, Ch. 76, amended L. 1928, Ch. 670; L. 1929, Ch. 646) and Section 20 of General City Law (Cons. Laws, Ch. 21).

68 See Gaynor v. Marohn, note 27 supra, and Robertson v. Zimmerman, note 24 supra.

69 See cases in Chapter VIII infra.

70 Home Rule Problems, *op. cit.*, p. 71.

71 *Ibid.*, pp. 64-72.

A doctrinaire democrat might find some justification for limiting the powers of the New York legislature in the matter of control over the affairs of the large cities of the state, especially New York City. That city, containing more than one-half the population of the state, is underrepresented in the legislature. In actual practice, the legislature has given heed to many of the requests of the cities. It is, furthermore, difficult to draw the line between matter of general and of local concern. That the courts recognized these conditions is shown by the fact that they upheld thirty-one of the forty-three laws challenged. The question, though, cannot help come to mind, whether in the event that the legislature were apportioned on the basis of population alone, complaints about legislative inroads on the affairs of the cities would not lessen, and the calls for judicial review subside.

CHAPTER VIII
LOCAL AND SPECIAL ACTS

IN 1874 there was added to the Constitution, after a lengthy series of legislative abuses, a section restricting the type of legislation which might be passed.[1] The text of this section as incorporated in the Constitution of 1894 read as follows:

ARTICLE III

Section 18. The legislature shall not pass a private or local bill in any of the following cases:

Changing the names of persons.

Laying out, opening, altering, working or discontinuing roads, highways or alleys, or for draining swamps or other low lands.

Locating or changing county seats.

Providing for changes of venue in civil or criminal cases.

Incorporating villages.

Providing for election of members of boards of supervisors.

Selecting, drawing, summoning or impaneling grand or petit jurors.

Regulating the rate of interest on money.

The opening and conducting of elections or designating places of voting.

Creating, increasing or decreasing fees, percentage or allowances of public officers, during the terms for which said officers are elected or appointed.

Granting to any corporation, association or individual the right to lay down railroad tracks.

Granting to any private corporation, association or individual any exclusive privilege, immunity or franchise whatever.

Providing for building bridges, and chartering companies for such purposes, except on the Hudson River below Waterford, and on the East River, or over the waters forming a part of the boundaries of the State.

---

[1] New York State Constitution Annotated, *op. cit.*, pp. 52-53.

The Legislature shall pass general laws providing for the cases enumerated in this section, and for all other cases which in its judgment may be provided for by general laws. But no law shall authorize the construction or operation of a street railroad except upon the condition that the consent of the owners of one-half in value of the property bounded on, and the consent also of the local authorities having the control of, that portion of a street or highway upon which it is proposed to construct or operate such railroad be first obtained, or in case the consent of such property owners cannot be obtained, the Appellate Division of the Supreme Court, in the department in which it is proposed to be constructed, may, upon application, appoint three commissioners who shall determine, after a hearing of all parties interested whether such railroad ought to be constructed or operated, and their determination, confirmed by the court, may be taken in lieu of the consent of the property owners.[2]

In 1901 this section was amended to include a prohibition against " Granting to any person, association, firm or corporation, an exemption from taxation on real or personal property." [3]

Other restrictions on the legislature have been and will be mentioned. Another significant one in connection with local and special bills is contained in Article 8, Section 10. The most important sentence in this long amendment, for the present purposes, states:

No county, city, town or village shall hereafter give any money or property, or loan its money or credit to or in aid of any individual, association or corporation, or become directly or indirectly the owner of stock in, or bonds of, any association or corporation; nor shall any such county, city, town, or village be allowed to incur any indebtedness except for county, city, town or village purposes.[4]

[2] Amendments Proposed, *op. cit.*, pp. 216-17.

[3] *Ibid.*, p. 218.

[4] *Ibid.*, p. 653 as in 1894. The word "or" was inserted before the last mention of "town" in 1905, *ibid.*, p. 656 and eliminated in 1908, *ibid.*, p. 666.

The most important acts declared unconstitutional because of conflict with Article 3, Section 18 were passed in 1897 and 1899. In the former year the Atlantic Avenue Improvement Act required that steam railroad tracks, formerly maintained and operated over a strip of that avenue, should be removed from the surface of the street and put below or above. In 1899 a statute provided that whenever the tracks of any steam railroad should have been placed below or above street level by legal requirement, the right of the railroad company to maintain and operate a surface passenger railway within the limits of the right of way so depressed or elevated, with all tracks necessary to secure the continuous operation of the surface railroad, should not be curtailed. The Court of Appeals ruled that a street surface railroad could not be operated on the surface of the strip from which the steam railroad had been removed, without the consents required in Article 3, Section 18.[5]

The other acts which came before the courts passed the test of constitutionality successfully. In chronological order these were: an act of 1899 authorizing the board of supervisors of Essex County to change the location of the county buildings from Elizabethtown to Westport;[6] an act of 1892 ratifying the so-called " Milburn agreement " under which the extension of street railways in Buffalo was allowed with the consent of the local authorities;[7] a law of 1902 providing for the appointment of a commissioner of jurors for Kings County and a law of 1901, amended in 1904, applicable to counties of one million or more permitting a court " by reason of the importance or intricacy of a case " to order the trial to be had by a special jury;[8] a law of 1895 authorizing the city of Rochester

[5] Matter of Long Island Railroad Company (1907) 189 N. Y. 428. L. 1897, Ch. 499 and L. 1899, Ch. 497.

[6] Stanton v. The Board of Supervisors of the County of Essex (1906) 112 A. D. 877 3rd Dept. L. 1899, Ch. 133.

[7] Kuhn v. Knight (1906) 115 A. D. 837 4th Dept. Ch. 151, L. 1892.

[8] Coler v. Brooklyn Daily Eagle (1909) 133 A. D. 300 2nd Dept. Ch. 564, L. 1902; Ch. 602, L. 1901, amended by Ch. 458, L. 1904.

to take the shores of Hemlock Lake, land belonging to the state, in order to prevent the pollution of the city water supply, an action which had as its result the incidental change of highways;[9] a subdivision of the Town Law under which the supervisor of Rye was entitled to commissions for paying out money for park purposes, these functions being held separate from the duties of a park commissioner, thus avoiding the restriction against increasing the fees of public officers during their terms;[10] the laws of 1909 and 1912 authorizing contracts between New York City and the Interborough Rapid Transit Company and the Brooklyn Union Elevated Railroad Company for the construction and operation of subways;[11] the section of the charter of Rochester empowering the common council to discontinue streets and providing for the allowance of damages;[12] the "act to amend the election law in relation to the commissioner of elections in Niagara County" requiring the county judge and county clerk to appoint the commissioner of elections, which in effect removed the then existing board;[13] the law providing that after April 3, 1917 biennial town meetings in towns in Nassau County were to occur on the first Tuesday after the first Monday in odd-numbered years;[14] the law of 1921 by which the Transit Commission

[9] City of Rochester v. Gray (1909) 133 A. D. 852, Ch. 1018, L. 1895.

[10] People ex rel. Studwell v. Archer (1910) 142 A. D. 71 2nd Dept. Subd. 3, Section 85 of Town Law (Cons. Laws, Ch. 62 [L. 1909, Ch. 63], as amended by L. 1909, Ch. 491).

[11] Admiral Realty Company v. The City of New York (1912) 206 N. Y. 110, L. 1909, Ch. 498 and L. 1912, Ch. 226. Nor did these laws violate Article 8, Section 10; Ch. 226, L. 1912 also upheld in Hopper v. Willcox (1913) 155 A. D. 213 1st Dept.

[12] Matter of Joiner Street (City of Rochester) (1917) 177 A. D. 361 4th Dept. Section 121 of Rochester Charter (L. 1907, Ch. 755.)

[13] Vroman v. Fish (1919) 224 N. Y. 540, Ch. 202, L. 1917. This act did not violate Article 3, Section 16 relating to titles discussed above in Chapter V or Article 12, Section 2 referred to in Chapter VI.

[14] People ex rel. Cotte v. Gilbert (1919) 226 N. Y. 103, Ch. 126, L. 1917, later Section 588 of Town Law.

was delegated the power to demand and receive appropriations from the New York City Board of Estimate and Apportionment, to properly perform its duties;[15] the provisions of the Long Beach Charter making the term of supervisor four years, instead of two, as in the General City Law;[16] the act of 1927 authorizing the Commissioners of the Sinking Fund of New York City to sell land acquired for park purposes in Brooklyn to the Polytechnic Institute of Brooklyn;[17] the law of 1935 providing time to make application for the remission of the forfeiture of bail, where the principal had later appeared, and the charges had been dismissed, and to vacate the judgment should be extended one year, despite the expiration described in Section 598 of the Code of Criminal Procedure;[18] the 1931 enactment specifying the fees to which the county treasurer of Monroe County was entitled on tax sales, when applied to the incumbent at the time the statute became effective;[19] the section of the Mortgage Commission Act exempting the State Mortgage Commission from paying a fee, specified in the Civil Practice Act, for placing a cause concerning a plan of read-

[15] Matter of McAneny v. Board of Estimate (1922) 232 N. Y. 377, Ch. 134, L. 1921 as amended by Ch. 335, L. 1921. It was held that the Appellate Division had the discretion to decide whether the appropriations demanded were necessary and that the Home Rule provisions were not violated as the offices of the Transit Commissioners were new.

[16] Matter of Knob v. Cheshire (1927) 246 N. Y. 533, L. 1922, Ch. 625.

[17] Blank v. Walker (1930) 253 N. Y. 513, Act of March 16, 1927.

[18] Matter of Rosenthal (1935) 269 N. Y. 584, Ch. 16, L. 1935.

[19] Matter of Bareham v. The Board of Supervisors of the County of Monroe (1936) 247 A. D. 534 4th Dept. L. 1931, Ch. 171. The legislature was not barred from increasing the compensation of county officers during their term of office. Article 3, Section 23 provided that Article 3, Section 18 should not apply to any bill or the amendments to any bill reported to the legislature by commissioners appointed pursuant to law to revise the statutes. Article 3, Section 28 forbidding the legislature from granting extra compensation to any public officer or servant was not violated as the work was performed after the enactment of the statute. It consisted of the advertisement and sale of property for unpaid taxes.

LOCAL AND SPECIAL ACTS 141

justment of a mortgage on a special term calendar;[20] and the law of 1933 exempting the properties of the Buffalo and Fort Erie Public Bridge Authority from taxation.[21]

Article 8, Section 10 was responsible for the invalidation of five laws. These included a 1905 law authorizing the payment by New York City of damages to the purchaser of lands, the value of which had been lessened by a change of street grade;[22] a section of a 1907 act permitting the application of village funds for streets used by, but not owned by, the public;[23] a section of the Village Law requiring the amount of taxes unpaid by a village to be paid out of the moneys in the county treasury raised for contingent expenses;[24] a section of the Civil Service Law so far as it made a city pay an illegally ousted employee, who had been reinstated by order of the Supreme Court, the salary he would have earned between the date of his removal and the date of his restoration, less the amount he might have received from other employment;[25]

[20] Matter of Bond and Mortgage Guarantee Company (1936) 249 A. D. 25 2nd Dept. Section 27-a Mortgage Commission Act (added by L. 1936, Ch. 514). The fee had been specified in Subd. 2, Section 1551-a of the Civil Practice Act. The county clerk had no right to question the constitutionality of this legislation as he was merely relieved of collecting fees or subsidiary compensation.

[21] People ex rel. Buffalo and Fort Erie Public Bridge Authority v. Davis (1938) 277 N. Y. 292, Ch. 824, L. 1933. The act creating this authority was passed at an extraordinary session of the legislature but the court held that it did not violate Article 4, Section 4 stating that "At extraordinary sessions no subject shall be acted upon, except such as the governor may recommend for consideration."

[22] People ex rel. City of New York v. Stillings (1909) 134 A. D. 480 1st Dept. Ch. 747, L. 1905. This was regarded as a gift from the city funds.

[23] Smith v. Smythe (1910) 197 N. Y. 457, Section 170 added to General Village Law by Ch. 93, L. 1907.

[24] Kenmore v. Erie (1930) 252 N. Y. 437, Section 126D of Village Law (Cons. Laws Ch. 64; amended L. 1927, Ch. 650).

[25] Mullane v. McKenzie (1936) 269 N. Y. 369, Section 23 of Civil Service Law (Cons. Laws Ch. 7; amended L. 1935, Ch. 734). The court stated that this provision was in violation of Article 8, Section 10 or a grant of extra compensation in violation of Article 3, Section 28 referred to in note 19 supra.

142   JUDICIAL REVIEW OF LEGISLATION IN N. Y.

and a subdivision of the Education Law empowering the Board of Education of the city school district of Troy to issue bonds to pay a portion of the cost of a new high school, which would increase the indebtedness of the city beyond the limit set by the article.[26]

In thirteen cases the challenged acts were upheld. In this group were: a law of 1906 exempting veteran firemen's associations from the payment of water rates;[27] a provision in the charter of Tonawanda that the Board of Public Works might sell to a corporation or individual outside of the city the right to make connection with the mains for the purpose of drawing water therefrom, and fix the prices and conditions therefor, if the supply for the city should not in consequence be insufficient;[28] a statute authorizing the construction of a sewer in the Bronx River Valley in order to drain a large and thickly populated part of Westchester County, and providing for the issuance of bonds by the county for its construction;[29] sections of the Railroad Law authorizing the Public Service Commission to eliminate dangerous grade crossings and impose a proportion of the cost upon the state and the village where the

[26] McCabe v. Gross (1937) 274 N. Y. 39, Subd. 6 of Section 879 of the Education Law (Cons. Laws Ch. 16, amended L. 1937, Ch. 20). The provision was that no "city shall be allowed to become indebted for any purpose or in any manner to an amount which, including existing indebtedness, shall exceed ten per centum of the assessed valuation." The court held that nothing in Article 9, Section 1 requiring the legislature to provide for the maintenance of a system of free common schools authorized disregard of this restriction. The school district referred to was wholly within the limits of the city.

[27] People ex rel. Veteran Volunteer Firemen v. Metz (1907) 128 A. D. 565 2nd Dept. Ch. 440, L. 1906. Charitable organizations had been previously exempted by Ch. 696, L. 1887. A municipality, it was ruled, might fulfill honorable obligations founded upon public service.

[28] Simson v. Parker (1907) 190 N. Y. 19. The authority granted, in the court's opinion, was to sell merely the surplus water, property for which the city had no use.

[29] Horton v. Andras (1908) 191 N. Y. 231, L. 1905, Ch. 646.

crossing was;[30] a section of the Highway Law providing for the payment of interest by any county, city, town or village on awards for damages sustained by reason of the change of grade of a street or highway;[31] the charter of the newly incorporated city of White Plains challenged on the alleged grounds that it permitted excessive indebtedness;[32] a law ratifying the employment by the authorities of the village of Port Chester of a certified public accountant to make audit of receipts of taxes;[33] sections of the New York City Charter and of the General City Law, interpreted as conferring upon the city the power to expend its funds upon a public celebration;[34] the statute authorizing the development and use by the city of Oswego of the waters of the Oswego River at Barge Canal dam No. 6 in that city, and erecting the Water Service Commission of that city;[35] enactments empowering cities to es-

[30] Matter of New York City and Hudson River Railroad Company (Village of Ossining) (1910) 136 A. D. 760 2nd Dept. Sections 62-66 of the Railroad Law, L. 1897, Ch. 754, amended by L. 1899, Ch. 359. There was no conflict with Article 8, Section 9 stating that neither the credit nor the money of the state shall be given or loaned to or in aid of any association, corporation, or private undertaking. The law was considered an exercise of the police power.

[31] People ex rel. Central Trust Company v. Prendergast (1911) 202 N. Y. 188, Ch. 701, L. 1910 adding Section 59a to the Highway Law (Cons. Laws Ch. 25). This was viewed as a general and not a local or city law. Furthermore, it was considered to be supported by a moral obligation.

[32] People ex rel. Haight v. Brown (1915) 216 N. Y. 674, L. 1915, Ch. 351. The objections based on the fact that the limit on a city's debt would be exceeded were declared to be prematurely raised.

[33] Gaynor v. Village of Port Chester (1920) 230 N. Y. 210, L. 1911, Ch. 513. Article 3, Section 20 requiring the assent of two-thirds of the members elected to each branch of the legislature for every bill appropriating public moneys or property for local or private purposes was not violated by this law.

[34] Schieffelin v. Hylan (1923) 236 N. Y. 254, Section 39 of New York City Charter (L. 1901, Ch. 466) and Sections 19, 20 (Subds. 13, 16) and 21 of the General City Law (Cons. Laws Ch. 21).

[35] People's Gas and Electric Company v. The City of Oswego (1924) 238 N. Y. 606, Ch. 349, L. 1915.

tablish and maintain airports;[36] a subdivision of the Buffalo Charter granting pensions to members of the police department holding ranks superior to that of captain, who had served ten years on the force, and one year in a position superior to captain;[37] a section of the Lockport Charter prescribing that the Board of Supervisors of Niagara County should collect the amount estimated by the city as necessary for the support of the poor, and settle with the treasurer of Lockport as to the sums to be retained by the latter officer;[38] and the statute permitting counties, with the consent of the Water Power and Control Commission, to create county water authorities.[39]

These restrictions accounted for but six decisions invalidating legislation, while in twenty-nine, the laws were upheld. The judges appear to have been reluctant to apply a strict interpretation of these limitations, which might have prevented the legislature from acting in a number of local matters requiring its attention.

36 Hesse v. Rath (1928) 249 N. Y. 436, L. 1928, Ch. 647.

37 Matter of Carr. v. Roesch (1930) Subd 3, Section 464 Buffalo Charter, 231 A. D. 19 affirmed 255 N. Y. 44. Article 3, Section 28 referred to in note 19 supra was not violated.

38 County of Niagara v. City of Lockport (1934) 264 N. Y. 423, Section 304 of Lockport Charter (L. 1911, Ch. 870).

39 Matter of County of Suffolk v. Water Power and Control Commission (1935) 269 N. Y. 158, Ch. 847, L. 1934. This was not an unlawful delegation of legislative power or a violation of the debt limit for counties set in the article under consideration.

CHAPTER IX

DUE PROCESS, EQUAL PROTECTION AND FREEDOM OF CONTRACT

THE importance of the concepts of due process of law, of equal protection of the laws and of freedom of contract is familiar to all students of constitutional history. The interpretation and development of these concepts by the courts have been treated in numerous books and articles.[1] Because of the interrelation of the three it seems suitable to group them for discussion.

The phrase " due process of law " appears in the Fifth and Fourteenth Amendments of the United States Constitution and in Article 1, Section 6 of the New York State Constitution. In the last two instances it is applicable to New York State. The relevant clause in the Fourteenth Amendment declares " Nor shall any State deprive any person of life, liberty or property, without due process of law; ".[2] In the state constitution it appears " No person shall be. . . nor be deprived of life, liberty, or property without due process of law; ".[3] The identity of these phrases makes it difficult in the absence of a judicial discussion to tell whether a law is being disposed of under the Federal or State provisions separately. In most instances it has not appeared necessary to the court to so differentiate and hence the cases are treated under the one topic. However, the state courts have the right to interpret their own constitution differently than the Federal courts, even though the words are the same, and have on occasion done so.[4] Since appeals may be

[1] On due process the standard treatise for the history up to its date of publication is Rodney L. Mott, *Due Process of Law*, (Indianapolis, 1926). An article dealing with significant phases, including some of the early cases in New York, is that by Edward S. Corwin, " Due Process of Law before the Civil War " *Harvard Law Review* 24:366,460. (1911).

[2] Article 14, Section 1.

[3] Article 1, Section 6 Constitution of 1894.

[4] See Ives v. South Buffalo Railway Company (1911) 201 N. Y. 271 discussed *infra*.

taken to the United States Supreme Court from the highest state court, whether the state law has been affirmed under the United States Constitution, or following an act of 1914, has been declared unconstitutional, it is possible for a law to be held in conflict with due process by the state courts and not by the Federal, and vice versa.[5]

One of the major themes in constitutional history has been the conflict between due process of law and the police power. The restrictions implied in the clause which originally had been given a procedural meaning by the courts, applying only to the judicial and administrative procedures whereby laws were carried out, were expanded in the latter half of the nineteenth century, when the judges gradually adopted a substantive interpretation of the clause. This meant in practice that the substance of the laws themselves was to be examined to see if conflict could be found with those beliefs held by the judges as to what constituted a reasonable law.[6] As some of the enactments conflicted with the beliefs of the judges adhering to the philosophy of laissez faire, as exemplified and incorporated in the works of such legal commentators as Thomas M. Cooley, they were held invalid under the due process clause.[7] For the

[5] Section 25 of the Judiciary Act of 1789 allowed appeals from state court decisions holding acts valid under the United States Constitution to be taken to the United States Supreme Court. The essence of this has been preserved in United States Code, Tit. 28, Section 344(a). In 1914 the law was changed following agitation springing from the fact that some state courts were holding laws invalid under the United States Constitution, when similar acts affirmed in other states were held valid by the United States Supreme Court. The Supreme Court may now bring a case in which a law has been declared unconstitutional by the state court because of violation of the United States Constitution before it by writ of certiorari. United States Code Tit. 28, Section 344(b). A demand for this change had been incorporated in the Progressive Party platform for 1912. Walter W. Spooner and Ray B. Smith, *Political and Governmental History of the State of New York* (Syracuse, 1922), Volume VI, National Political Parties with their Platforms, p. 415.

[6] See Mott, *op. cit.*, passim. How a number of noted lawyers contributed to this development is described in Benjamin R. Twiss, *Lawyers and the Constitution, How Laissez Faire Came to the Supreme Court* (Princeton, 1942).

DUE PROCESS, EQUAL PROTECTION   147

purposes of treatment here the cases in which enactments passed to safeguard the health, safety, morals or general welfare of the people under the police power were under attack have been separated arbitrarily from the others arising under the due process clause, and are dealt with in the following chapter. A full appreciation of the meaning of the clause as interpreted by the New York courts requires a consideration of both sets of cases.

Five cases occurred in which statutes were held not to fulfill the procedural requirements of the clause.[8] The first was a law of 1902 providing, among other things, that if a warehouseman should make known to the claimant of a chattel the name and address of the depositor, he should not be made defendant in an action for conversion or replevin unless he had some other claim on the chattel than for charges growing out of its care and custody.[9] The other acts were: a provision of the Corrupt Practices Act requiring a person or committee to file a statement of campaign expenditures with a Supreme Court justice after an application had been made to that court, and a judgment issued requiring such filing, or else be adjudged guilty of a contempt of court;[10] an amendment to the Decedent Estate Law permitting the revival of suits against a foreign representative, whether executor or administrator of a deceased person's estate, for a judgment *in personam,* drawing no distinction between a case where assets existed and where they did not;[11] two parts of the Surrogate's Court Act requiring no

[7] A leading example in New York was In Re Jacobs (1881) 98 N. Y. 98 in which a law prohibiting the manufacture of cigars in tenement houses was declared unconstitutional by the New York Court of Appeals. This roused the ire of Theodore Roosevelt.

[8] Exclusive of those dealt with in the chapter on Civil Liberties.

[9] Lissner v. Cohen (1906) 49 Misc. 272 Supreme Court Appellate Term, L. 1902, Ch. 608.

[10] Matter of Lance (1907) 55 Misc. 13 Supreme Court Clinton Special Term, L. 1906, Ch. 502.

[11] McMaster v. Gould (1925) 240 N. Y. 379, Ch. 253, L. 1925 amending Section 160 of the Decedent Estate Law.

distribution of the assets of an estate, without the reservation of sufficient money to pay a contingent or unliquidated claim, filed in an affidavit as provided in the act, and requiring that if such a claim had not become fixed and liquidated, a sum sufficient to satisfy it should be retained in the hands of the accounting party, as directed in the decree on a final accounting, for such period as the court might deem proper for the purpose of being applied to the payment of such claim when fixed and liquidated;[12] and an amendment to the Surrogate's Court Act providing that if the name or whereabouts of a person interested in an estate up to the extent of $500 could not be ascertained, the service of citation on him might be dispensed with by the Surrogate, in which case, however, the decree settling the account was not to be conclusive against that person unless, before its entry he should appear, waive or be duly served.[13]

The twelve cases in which the courts affirmed the validity of the legislation presented for their consideration involved the following: the removal of the liability of a city for injuries from snow and ice on a sidewalk, unless written notice were given to the common council, and there had been failure to have the snow or ice removed and the place made fairly safe within a reasonable time after receipt of such notice;[14] the section of the Code of Civil Procedure authorizing the apprehension of a person who had refused to obey a subpoena of the State Superintendent of Banks without notice;[15] sections of the Code of Criminal Procedure not providing notice to a pledgee holding stolen property of a hearing and determina-

[12] Matter of Littleton (1927) 129 Misc. 845 Surrogate's Court Westchester County. First and last parts of last paragraph of Section 207 Surrogate's Court Act added in L. 1921, Ch. 629.

[13] In Re Calvin's Estate (1934) 153 Misc. 11 Surrogate's Court Monroe County, L. 1932, Ch. 420 amending Surrogate's Court Act.

[14] MacMullen v. Middletown (1907) 187 N. Y. 37, Section 30 Charter of Middletown, L. 1902, Ch. 572.

[15] Matter of Union Bank No. 2 (1911) 147 A. D. 593 2nd Dept. Section 855 Code of Civil Procedure.

tion to be made by the Magistrate's Court as to its disposition:[16] the practice adopted for proceedings before the State Workmen's Compensation Commission, and the provision that a claim was to be presumed to come within the provisions of the act, in the absence of substantial evidence to the contrary;[17] a section of the Code of Civil Procedure allowing executors or administrators appointed in any other state, territory or district of the United States, or in any foreign country, to sue or be sued in any court in the state in the capacity of such representatives;[18] the section of the Civil Practice Act allowing the sequestration of a defendant's property in an action for divorce or separation where the defendant could not be personally served and there was property within the state;[19] the article of the Real Property Law, the so-called Torrens Law, permitting service of notice of registration of land by publication and registered mail;[20] the sections of the Code of Criminal Procedure providing for the seizure of property of an absconding parent or spouse, leaving children or mate destitute, without notice being given;[21] a section of the Buffalo Charter allowing service for the foreclosure of a tax certificate to be made by mailing a copy of the summons and complaint,

[16] People ex rel. Simpson Company v. Kempner (1913) 154 A. D. 674 2nd Dept. Sections 687, 806-809 Code of Criminal Procedure.

[17] Matter of McQueeney v. Sutphen and Myer (1915) 167 A. D. 528 3rd Dept. Section 2 Group 20 Workmen's Compensation Law authorized by Article 1, Section 19 of the Constitution. The portions objected to provided that there should be an award on mere proof of injury in a list of occupations including the manufacture of glass products, porcelain and pottery.

[18] Helme v. Buckalew (1920) 191 A. D. 59 1st Dept. Section 1836-a Code of Civil Procedure, L. 1911, Ch. 631.

[19] Matthews v. Matthews (1925) 240 N. Y. 28, Ch. 51, L. 1923 amending Article 70 of Civil Practice Act by inserting Section 1171-a; Geary v. Geary (1936) 272 N. Y. 390 where it was ruled that the seizure must precede an adjudication as to an alimony award.

[20] City of New York v. Wright (1926) 243 N. Y. 80 (Cons. Laws Ch. 50).

[21] Coler v. The Corn Exchange Bank (1928) 250 N. Y. 136, Sections 921-925 Code of Criminal Procedure.

and by publishing in a newspaper and in an official publication;[22] the requirement in the Charter of Rochester that a claim must be presented within thirty days where a nuisance was continuing;[23] the section of the Arbitration Law providing that an award in an arbitration proceeding was to be enforceable without a previous application to the Supreme Court or to a judge thereof, but that before final judgment in proceedings to carry the award into effect, the party not participating might apply for a determination, whether the contract was made or the submission entered into, and whether the arbitrators were appointed or acted pursuant to contract;[24] and the portion of the Civil Practice Act letting the issue of making a contract to arbitrate be tried before a court or a jury, the court holding that this issue could be asserted and determined in opposition to an application to confirm an award, adequate remedy thereby being provided.[25]

The spectacular significance of this clause lies, as has been indicated, in its substantive interpretation and not in the procedural matters just treated. Here the New York courts had early taken leadership. In 1856 a prohibition statute, passed the year before, was held to violate due process of law because the rights of owners in liquor, existing at the time the act was passed, were thereby destroyed.[26] Again in the 1880's, in three celebrated cases, the Court of Appeals had held invalid laws

[22] City of Buffalo v. Hawks (1929) 226 A. D. 480 4th Dept. Section 643-a Buffalo Charter (as added by Ch. 532, L. 1929).

[23] Thomann v. City of Rochester (1930) 230 A. D. 612 4th Dept. L. 1907, Ch. 755, Second 632.

[24] Matter of Finsilver, Still and Morse Inc. v. Goldberg, Maas and Company Inc. (1930) 253 N. Y. 382, Section 4a of Arbitration Law (Cons. Laws Ch. 72 amended L. 1927, Ch. 352).

[25] Schafran and Finkel Inc. v. Lowenstein and Sons Inc. (1938) 254 A. D. 218 1st Dept. Section 1458 Civil Practice Act, Ch. 341, L. 1937.

[26] Wynehamer v. People (1856) 13 N. Y. 378. Commentary on this may be found in the two articles by Corwin referred to in Foreword note 5 and note 1 of this chapter supra.

forbidding the manufacture of tobacco in tenement houses,[27] prohibiting the manufacture and sale of oleomargarine,[28] and banning the offer of gifts or prizes as an inducement to the purchase of food.[29] Other decisions less famous were also handed down. This led to a reputation of conservatism on the part of the New York courts.[30] The basis of these last-mentioned decisions was that the constitutional right of liberty included the freedom to pursue an occupation and make contracts which were not harmful to public policy, as well as freedom from bodily restraint.

In the early years of the twentieth century, the New York courts upset laws attempting to regulate the wages and hours of labor for employees on public works.[31] In order to circumvent these decisions the constitution of New York was amended to provide:

> The legislature may regulate and fix the wages or salaries, the hours of work or labor, and make provision for the protection, welfare and safety of persons employed by the State or by any county, city, town, village or other civil division of the State, or by any contractor or sub-contractor performing work, labor or services for the State, or for any county, city, town, village or any other civil division thereof.[32]

[27] In Re Jacobs (1881) 98 N. Y. 98 referred to in note 7 supra.

[28] People v. Marx (1885) 99 N. Y. 377. A similar statute brought to the United States Supreme Court from another state was held constitutional in Power v. Pennsylvania 127 U. S. 678.

[29] People v. Gillson (1889) 109 N. Y. 389.

[30] See remarks of former Governor George H. Hoadly of Ohio, then a lawyer in New York, in "The Constitutional Guarantees of the Right of Property as Affected by Recent Decisions," a paper read before the American Social Science Association. (Saratoga Springs, 1889) p. 51.

[31] In People ex rel. Rodgers v. Coler (1901) 166 N. Y. 1 and People ex rel. Treat v. Coler (1901) 166 N. Y. 144 the statutes provided that contractors on public works should pay the prevailing local wage to laborers. In People v. Orange County Road Construction Company (1903) 175 N. Y. 84 and in People ex rel. Cossey v. Grout (1904) 179 N. Y. 417 the statutes prescribed an eight hour day for laborers on public works. Here again the United States Supreme Court upheld such a law in Atkin v. Kansas (1903) 191 U. S. 207.

[32] Article 12, Section 1, as amended in 1905.

Following this amendment, an act of 1906 which provided that a municipal contractor could not recover for his work where he had violated his contract by having his men labor more than eight hours a day was sustained.[33]

If the United States Supreme Court had been more inclined to uphold the constitutionality of state laws regulating industrial and labor conditions of the types considered than the courts of New York and of certain other states, the decision handed down in Lochner v. New York (1905) proved an exception to the rule. Here the New York Court of Appeals had sustained a law forbidding more than ten hours work for employees in bakeries.[34] The Supreme Court reversed the decision and held the law unconstitutional by a vote of five to four. This case occasioned a great number of comments and is included in many treatments on the subject of constitutional history.[35] The influence of this case was manifested in the New York courts in the decision of the Court of Appeals in People v. Williams (1907), where the provisions of the Labor Law prohibiting the employment of an adult female in a factory before six A. M. or after nine P. M. were invalidated as arbitrarily taking away the right of a woman to labor without reference to the number of hours worked or the healthfulness of the occupation.[36] Eight years later this ruling was specifically reversed in People v. Charles Schweinler Press (1915) where the law forbade women to work in factories before six in the morning or after ten in the evening.[37] In the same year

[33] People ex rel. Williams Engineering and Contracting Company v. Metz (1908) 193 N. Y. 148, L. 1906, Ch. 506 Section 3 amending Labor Law. This law did not conflict with the equal protection clause.

[34] People v. Lochner (1904) 177 N. Y. 145. This was a four to three decision upholding an Appellate Division ruling viewing the law as valid by a vote of three to two. 73 A. D. 120 (1902).

[35] Particular attention has been paid to Justice Holmes' remark in his dissenting opinion that the Fourteenth Amendment was not intended to read Herbert Spencer's Social Statics into the Constitution.

[36] 189 N. Y. 131, Section 77 of Labor Law.

[37] 214 N. Y. 395. Amendment to Labor Law, L. 1913, Ch. 83.

a ban on women working after ten or before seven in mercantile establishments was also held valid.[38] Changes both in personnel and in the evidence presented to the court, as well as developments in the political arena discussed below, contribute toward an explanation of this reversal of opinion.

A year before the Williams case a section of the Penal Code attempting in substance to outlaw the "yellow dog" contract was also held to be an unauthorized restraint upon the freedom to contract.[39] These decisions were followed by one of the most famous cases in the history of New York. In 1911 the Court of Appeals, by a unanimous vote, declared the Workmen's Compensation Act, passed the year before, unconstitutional in Ives v. South Buffalo Railway Company.[40] This law, based on the findings of the Wainwright Commission, enumerated a list of hazardous occupations in which compensation for injuries by employers was made compulsory. Such compensation was made elective in a number of other occupations. The decision in the case was written by Judge Werner, Chief Judge Cullen writing a concurring opinion. It was competent, according to the court, for the legislature to abolish the old defenses available to employers in suits against them by employees for damages, such as the fellow servant rule, under which the employer was not liable for injuries sustained because of the carelessness or negligence of a fellow servant, providing reasonable care had been exercised in the latter's selection; and the doctrine of contributory negligence, according to which a plaintiff for damages had to establish his own freedom from negligence. For the legislature, however, to impose a liability on the employer based solely upon the legisla-

[38] People ex rel. Krohn v. The Warden 215 N. Y. 201, Subd. 2, Section 161 Labor Law.

[39] People v. Marcus (1906) 185 N. Y. 257, Section 171a of Penal Code. In effect an enactment that a person should not make the employment of another person conditional upon the employee not joining or becoming a member of a labor organization.

[40] 201 N. Y. 271, Article 14-a of Labor Law, L. 1910, Ch. 674.

tive determination that his business was inherently dangerous was a deprivation of property without due process of law. To the contention that the United States Supreme Court had upheld statutes of a similar nature, the court indicated in response that it would not necessarily be bound by the decisions of that body as far as its own interpretations of the due process clause were concerned. Desirable and well intentioned as the legislation might be, the court ruled that it was bound by the Constitution, which prohibited that sort of enactment.

The opinion resulted in an outcry against both the specific decision and the general power of the courts as exercised in other cases, including those mentioned previously. A group of prominent lawyers, including Roscoe Pound and Ernst Freund, issued a protest, stating " that a compensation plan as moderate and carefully guarded as that embodied in the law of New York is entirely constitutional, and they regard it as their duty to inform the public that there is a professional opinion entitled to consideration which differs from that expressed by the Court of Appeals of New York, and which may and should be urged upon the courts of other jurisdictions." [41] Viewed against the background of the progressive movement then flourishing in the country, the case assumed perhaps even greater significance. Theodore Roosevelt, then back from Africa, proceeded to criticize the Ives and other decisions both in New York and elsewhere, and in February, 1912, speaking before the Ohio Constitutional Convention, made his proposal for the recall of judicial decisions, a proposal which, by alienating his more conservative followers, is considered to have been partly responsible for his defeat in the presidential race of that year.[42]

[41] Boudin, *op. cit.*, pp. 444-457. The statement is appended on pp. 455-457. It appeared originally in *The Outlook* 98: 710.

[42] Jackson H. Ralston, *Study and Report for American Federation of Labor upon Judicial Control over Legislatures as to Constitutional Questions* (Washington, 1919) pp. 53-54; a collection of the speeches made by Theodore Roosevelt in the campaign of 1912, a number of which express his opinions on the judiciary at this time, may be found in Theodore Roosevelt, *Progressive Principles* (New York, 1913).

DUE PROCESS, EQUAL PROTECTION 155

Meanwhile the Supreme Court had been handing down a number of liberal decisions. In 1908 after the presentation to the court of an impressive brief containing a mass of sociological data by Louis D. Brandeis, an Oregon law limiting the working hours for women to ten a day was upheld.[43] In the following years the court sustained similar types of laws in other states.[44] The influence of Muller v. Oregon was partly responsible for the reversal of the Williams case in People v. Charles Schweinler Press, mentioned above.[45] In addition liberalism was being shown in the courts on other issues. In 1911 Justice Holmes had declared that the police power was shaped " by the prevailing morality or the strong and preponderant opinion" as to what is "greatly and immediately necessary to the public welfare." [46]

It is not surprising then to find that after the Ives case, the New York Constitution was amended to read as follows:

> Nothing contained in this Constitution shall be construed to limit the power of the Legislature to enact laws for the protection of the lives, health or safety of employees; or for the payment, either by employers, or by employers and employees or otherwise, either directly or through a State or other system of insurance, or otherwise, of compensation for

---

[43] Muller v. Oregon 208 U. S. 412.

[44] Among the cases where acts were sustained were: Sturges and Burn Manufacturing Company v. Beauchamp (1913) 231 U. S. 320 upholding an Illinois Child Labor Law; Riley v. Massachusetts (1914) 232 U. S. 671—a fifty-six hours of labor per week statute for women; Hawley v. Walker (1914) 232 U. S. 718—a nine hour per day statute for women; Miller v. Wilson (1915) 236 U. S. 373 and Bosley v. McLaughlin (1915) 236 U. S. 385—a California statute providing for forty-eight hours of work per week for women. Evan Haynes, Chapter VII "Are Elected Judges with Short Terms More Liberal Than Appointed Judges with Secure Tenure?" *The Selection and Tenure of Judges* (The National Conference of Judicial Councils, 1944) p. 193..

[45] See note 37 supra.

[46] Noble State Bank v. Haskell 219 U. S. 104 quoted in John R. Commons and John B. Andrews, *Principles of Labor Legislation*, Fourth Revised Edition (New York, 1936), p. 528.

156 JUDICIAL REVIEW OF LEGISLATION IN N. Y.

injuries to employees or for death of employees resulting from such injuries without regard to fault as a cause thereof, except where the injury is occasioned by the willful intention of the injured employee to bring about the injury or death of himself or of another, or where the injury results solely from the intoxication of the injured employee while on duty; or for the adjustment determination and settlement, with or without trial by jury, of issues which may arise under such legislation; or to provide that the right of such compensation, and the remedy therefor shall be exclusive of all other rights and remedies for injuries to employees or for death resulting from such injuries; or to provide that the amount of such compensation for death shall not exceed a fixed or determinable sum; provided that all moneys paid by an employer to his employees or their legal representatives, by reason of the enactment of any of the laws herein authorized, shall be held to be a proper charge in the cost of operating the business of the employer.[47]

In 1914 the legislature again passed a Workmen's Compensation Law which was held constitutional the following year in Matter of Jensen v. Southern Pacific Company.[48] Of course, the amendment to the State Constitution could not have overcome any conflict with the Fourteenth Amendment, but in 1917 the United States Supreme Court upheld the laws of New York and Washington, thus removing doubt on that score.[49]

[47] New York State Constitutional Convention Committee, Vol. VI, *Problems Relating to Bill of Rights and General Welfare* (Albany, 1938), p. 288.

[48] 215 N. Y. 514 (1915) (Cons. Laws Ch. 67, L. 1914, Ch. 41). The court ruled that this law applied to accidental injuries in interstate work except where Congress had established a rule of liability or a method of compensation. This decision was reversed in Southern Pacific Co. v. Jensen (1917) 244 U. S. 205 in which the act was held unconstitutional as applied to a stevedore engaged in unloading an interstate ship at a wharf in navigable waters.

[49] New York Central Railroad Company v. White (1917) 243 U. S. 188.

The United States Supreme Court also upheld an amendment to the Workmen's Compensation Law providing that in case of an injury resulting in serious facial or head disfigurement, the Workmen's Compensation Com-

DUE PROCESS, EQUAL PROTECTION 157

Since then the laws passed relating to workmen's compensation have been generally sustained. Among them were: a section requiring an award of nine hundred dollars to the state treasurer in the absence of any beneficiary of a deceased employee;[50] another denying a husband the right to recover for the loss of his wife's services in the event of her being injured in the course of her employment, and becoming entitled to compensation;[51] another making a contractor, who had subcontracted any part of a contract involving a hazardous employment, liable for compensation to any employee injured in such employment, unless the subcontractor had secured compensation for the employee;[52] the requirement that, in proceedings to ascertain the award to be made for partial disability, the wage earning capacity of the injured employee was to be determined by his actual, and not potential, earnings;[53] and a provision that compensation should not be payable for partial disability due to silicosis or another dust disease.[54]

---

mission might, in its discretion, make such compensation as it might deem proper in view of the nature of the disfigurement, but not to exceed $3,500. A point to be noted is that this award was not based exclusively on loss of earning power. New York Central Railroad Company v. Bionc (1919) 250 U. S. 596, affirming 226 N. Y. 199. Ch. 222, L. 1916.

The extension of workmen's compensation to all employments in which four or more workmen were employed, excepting farm labor and domestic service, was likewise sustained by the same court in Ward and Gow v. Krinsky (1922) 259 U. S. 503, affirming 231 N. Y. 525, against contentions of violating both the due process and equal protection clauses. Ch. 634, L. 1918.

50 Matter of Claim of McNamara v. New York State Railways (1922) 233 N. Y. 681. Subd. 8, Section 15 Workmen's Compensation Law.

51 Swan v. Woolworth Co. (1927) 129 Misc. 500. Supreme Court Monroe County. Section 11 Workmen's Compensation Law, L. 1922, Ch. 615.

52 Matter of Claim of Anttonen v. Lakso Builders Inc. (1933) 261 N. Y. 545. Section 56 Workmen's Compensation Law (Cons. Laws, Ch. 67).

53 Matter of Claim of Dalberth v. Iuppa and Battle Company (1933) 262 N. Y. 537, 564; Matter of Claim of Boscarino v. Miller Cabinet Company (1933) 263 N. Y. 581, 608. Subd. 5-a of Section 15 Workmen's Compensation Law (Cons. Laws, Ch. 67) L. 1930, Ch. 316, Section 2.

54 Debusto v. Dupont Denemours and Co., Inc. (1938) 167 Misc. 920. Supreme Court Niagara County, Section 66, Article 4-A Workmen's Compensation Law (L. 1936, Ch. 887).

The Appellate Division held in 1919 that a section of the Workmen's Compensation Law might not be construed to permit the adoption of a resolution, arbitrarily, without notice and hearing, that every mutual association and every self-insurer should, on or before a certain date, pay into the aggregate trust fund of the State Insurance Fund the present value as of that date of the installments of compensation under every award against such carrier for death claims arising from accidents occurring between July 1 and December 31, 1917.[55] A special act for the relief of a claimant whose claim had been barred under the Workmen's Compensation Law was held to violate the equal protection clause.[56]

An issue closely related to that of maximum hours is minimum wages. The attitude of the United States Supreme Court again had an influence on the New York judges. In 1923 an act of Congress which authorized a commission to establish a "living" wage for female employees in the District of Columbia was held to violate the Fifth Amendment.[57] This aroused controversy in view of previous decisions indicating a liberal attitude to such regulations, which seemed to show that the Supreme Court recognized a connection between conditions of work and the use of the police power to protect the health of employees.[58] The Supreme Court continued to maintain the same view on minimum wage legislation throughout the 1920's, which was largely responsible for the fact that in 1936 the Court of Appeals, by a vote of four to three, held void the law of 1933 establishing minimum wage standards

[55] Sperduto v. New York City Interborough Railroad Company (1919) 186 A. D. 145 3rd Dept. Section 27 Workmen's Compensation Law as amended by Ch. 703, L. 1917.

[56] Decker v. Pouvailsmith Corporation (1929) 252 N. Y. 1. Ch. 702, L. 1927.

[57] Adkins v. Children's Hospital (1923) 261 U. S. 525.

[58] In 1917 a ten-hour law of Oregon applying generally had been upheld in Bunting v. Oregon 243 U. S. 426.

for women.[59] This decision was affirmed the same year by the United States Supreme Court,[60] but the latter reversed its stand when a Washington minimum wage law was passed upon the next year.[61] In 1927, however, the Court of Appeals had upheld a provision of the Labor Law for the payment of the prevailing rate of wages on public works, which phrase was held to be intelligible. Authority for this law had been incorporated in the Constitution by the amendment of 1905 quoted above.[62] Going beyond the scope of time covered in this chapter, the record shows that New York amended its minimum wage law in 1944 to include men as well as women and children.[63]

In 1915 the section of the Labor Law requiring that employees be given one day of rest in seven was challenged. This provision was found unobjectionable, but another law delegating the power of exemption to the Commissioner of Labor for those not working more than eight hours a day was considered an improper delegation of legislative power.[64]

It was not considered a violation of the clause securing equal protection of the laws to exempt labor unions [65] and farmers'

[59] People ex rel. Tipaldo v. Morehead (1936) 270 N. Y. 233. Ch. 584, L. 1933 (Cons. Laws, Ch. 31, Article 19).

[60] Morehead v. New York (1936) 298 U. S. 587.

[61] West Coast Hotel Company v. Parrish (1937) 300 U. S. 379. The statute was upheld on the basis of the police power because of the interrelation of wages and health, which was deemed paramount to the liberty of contract of the wage earner. Both cases were decided by a vote of five to four, Justice Roberts alone changing sides.

[62] Campbell v. City of New York 244 N. Y. 317. Section 220 Labor Law (Cons. Laws, Ch. 31). This law had been reenacted several times. L. 1906, Ch. 506; L. 1909, Ch. 212; L. 1913, Ch. 494; L. 1916, Ch. 152; L. 1921, Ch. 642. See note 32 supra for text of the amendment.

[63] MacDonald, *op. cit.*, p. 575.

[64] People v. Klinck Packing Company 214 N. Y. 121. Labor Law (L. 1913, Ch. 740) Section 8a held valid; L. 1914, Ch. 396 held void.

[65] Williams v. Quill (1938) 277 N. Y. 1. Subd. 2 Section 340 General Business Law (Cons. Laws, Ch. 20).

cooperatives [66] from the anti-trust laws of the state. In the case deciding the last point, Referee Merwin, upon whose report the decision was based, declared:

> The legislature, backed by public opinion, has determined that the State can afford to give special treatment to this class of producers. It is a question not of technical constitutional law, but of social policy.[67]

An effort to upset a section of the Inferior Criminal Courts Act of the City of New York, a provision of which stated that if the mother of a child born out of wedlock were married, both she and her husband might testify to non-access to each other for the purposes of proving paternity, because it applied only to the City of New York and not to the entire state, was thwarted in 1934.[68] It was held that the constitutional question had not been raised in the lower courts.

In 1936 a law of 1935, in so far as it made unlawful the sale of commodities including books bearing the trademark or name of the publisher at a price lower than that fixed in a contract between the publisher and another retailer, under a different section of the act making such contracts lawful, was ruled a violation of the due process clause.[69] The next year, however, following a decision of the United States Supreme Court holding such legislation constitutional,[70] the Court of

[66] Barnes v. Dairymen's League Cooperative Association, Inc., (1927) 220 A. D. 624 4th Dept. Section 340 of General Business Law as amended by. L. 1921, Ch. 712 and Penal Law Section 582 as amended by L. 1918, Ch. 491.

[67] *Ibid.*, at p. 638.

[68] Commissioner of Public Welfare v. Jackson 265 N. Y. 469. Provision in Section 67 of the Inferior Criminal Courts Act of the City of New York (As amended by L. 1930, Ch. 434 and L. 1933, Ch. 746).

[69] Doubleday Doran and Company v. Macy and Company 269 N. Y. 272. Section 2, Ch. 976, L. 1935; Seeck and Kade Inc. v. Tomshinsky (1935) 269 N. Y. 613.

[70] Old Dearborn Distributing Co. v. Seagram Distillers Corporation (1936) 299 U. S. 183.

Appeals held the same section of the law just mentioned valid out of respect to the national tribunal.[71]

In 1938 the lower courts upheld two acts in decisions from which there is no record of appeal. This is perhaps significant of the change in attitude toward governmental regulation of economic activities, because both were examples of that type of legislation. In the first, it was made unlawful to ask or receive any return or contribution from the wages of any workman engaged in the performance of personal services, at the prevailing rate of wages, upon the representation that failure to comply with the request would prevent the workman from obtaining or keeping employment.[72] In the second, the maximum fee an employment agency could charge for placement of a seamstress, among several other types of workers, was fixed at an amount not exceeding ten per cent of the first month's wages.[73]

Since the due process and equal protection clauses have been the staple arguments of attorneys combating many of the acts to which reference has been made in other chapters, conclusions about these clauses based on only the cases treated in this chapter are necessarily of limited value. Nevertheless, some of the most spectacular cases have been included in the preceeding pages. Furthermore, the impact on the judiciary of a strong and continuing demand for certain kinds of laws is well illustrated here by the change in attitude on acts regulating maximum hours, minimum wages and workmen's compensation. Throughout the period, in questions of both procedure and substance, the judges were in agreement with the legislature on constitutional principles in the majority of cases presented

[71] Bourjois Sales Corporation v. Dorfman (1937) 273 N. Y. 167. Section 2, Ch. 976, L. 1935.

[72] People v. Desowitz (Complaint of Rabinowitz) 166 Misc. 1. Section 962 Penal Law. City Magistrates' Court of New York Borough of Manhattan 7th District.

[73] Abbye Employment Agency, Inc. v. Robinson 166 Misc. 820. Supreme Court Appellate Term 1st District. Section 185 General Business Law.

for decision. They were inclined to accept the legislative standards of classification under the equal protection clause and the legislature's right to restrict the liberty of contract in the interest of the police power. This will be made more evident by a survey of the decisions in the following chapter. The combination of fear of encroaching paternalism and a respect felt toward some of the more conservative opinions of the United States Supreme Court on the part of the state judges prevented the two branches of government from arriving at complete harmony on interpretations of these ambiguous clauses. The legislation which provoked disagreement seems mild in retrospect, though undoubtedly taking on fearsome aspects in the prevailing climate of opinion. That the judges themselves, however, in most instances did not believe the legislature was seeking to tear up these constitutional restrictions, would seem to be plain from the tally showing twenty-eight acts sustained to thirteen held unconstitutional.

CHAPTER X
POLICE POWER

As the years of the twentieth century rolled on, further and further demands were made that the legislature exercise its recognized powers to protect the health, safety, morals and welfare of the people of the state. In order to consider the courts' reaction to the legislative acts passed in response to these demands, it has appeared best to divide the cases into two broad categories, those in which the legislature attempted to regulate particular industries which possessed an influence on the people's health and welfare; and those enactments establishing standards for the professions and occupations which directly or indirectly affected the people's interests.

The most important branch of agriculture in New York State has been the dairying industry. Many cases have been found dealing with this leading economic activity. We have already referred to the case of People v. Marx [1] in which the legislative attempt to prohibit the sale of oleomargarine was prevented by the Court of Appeals. Other laws regulating the sale of imitations of butter were later upheld, however.[2] The only noteworthy law concerned with dairying held invalid after 1905 was a section of the Agriculture Law permitting the Commissioner of Agriculture to revoke a license to purchase milk, where the licensee had given evidence of his inability to properly conduct his business, or of an intent to defraud customers, because notice of the time and place of hearing of the proceedings to revoke the license was not given the licensee.[3]

[1] People v. Marx 99 N. Y. 377.

[2] People v. Arensberg 105 N. Y. 123.

[3] People ex rel. Levy Dairy Co. v. Wilson (1917) 179 A. D. 416 3rd Dept. Section 57 Agriculture Law.
The United States Supreme Court held unconstitutional a prohibition against the sale of milk imported from another state, unless the price paid in that other state to the producer was up to the minimum prescribed by New York for purchase from local producers, in Baldwin v. Seelig (1935)

The other laws affecting the subject of dairying were held constitutional. In the order of their appearance before the courts, they were: a section of the Agricultural Law prohibiting the selling of milk deprived of its richness, but otherwise not unwholesome;[4] another section of the same law, the validity of which was saved by construing it as only prohibiting the sale of oleomargarine made by artificial means to resemble butter;[5] a law of 1911 providing that the consumer should rinse the

---

294 U. S. 511. Section 258 (m) (4), Article 21-a Agriculture and Markets Law, L. 1934, Ch. 126 formerly Section 312 (g), Article 25, L. 1933, Ch. 158. It was considered a burden on interstate commerce, whether applied to milk sold by the importer in the cans in which it was imported, or to milk sold by him in bottles into which it was put after importation.

However, a part of the Milk Control Law discriminating between dealers who had well advertised trade names and those who had not, by allowing the latter to sell bottled milk in New York City at a price one cent less per quart than the price prescribed for the former, was not found violative of the equal protection clause in Borden's Farm Product Company Inc. v. Ten Eyck (1936) 297 U. S. 251. Milk Control Law of April 10, 1933 (reenacted by L. 1934, Ch. 126). The court found that in practice no gain or loss occurred to the company as such had been the trade practice before the act.

On the same day, though, that section of the Milk Control Act discriminating between milk dealers without well advertised trade names who were in the business before April 10, 1933 and those in that class who entered it later, by granting the former this privilege of selling milk at a cent less than those with well advertised trade names, while denying this privilege to the later entrants, was held unconstitutional in Mayflower Farms v. Ten Eyck 297 U. S. 266. Milk Control Act as amended, effective April 1, 1934.

[4] People v. Koster (1907) 121 A. D. 852 1st Dept. Section 22 Agriculture Law (L. 1893, Ch. 388 as amended by Ch. 602, L. 1905).

In St. John v. New York (1906) this law, as it had been amended in 1898 to provide that producing vendors might show that the milk sold or offered for sale by them was in the same condition as when it left the herd, had been held valid by the U. S. Supreme Court. 201 U. S. 633.

[5] People ex rel. McAuley v. Wahle (1908) 124 A. D. 762 1st Dept. Section 26 Agriculture Law (L. 1893, Ch. 338); a later version of this law prohibiting the manufacture of oleomargarine so as to imitate dairy butter by the introduction of foreign substances was upheld in People v. Clark (1910) 140 A.D. 150 2nd Dept. (Cons. Laws, Ch. 1; L. 1909, Ch. 9, Sections 30, 38); also People v. Guiton (1912) 152 A. D. 614 3rd Dept.

milk cans before returning them;[6] an act forbidding the sale of coloring matter with oleomargarine;[7] a requirement that no one was to buy milk or cream for shipment to the city, as a business, without an office in the state and a license;[8] a provision for the quarantine of a herd of cattle untested for tuberculosis where ninety per cent of the herds in a town had been tested;[9] a prohibition against the use, without the consent of the owner, of any milk bottle having the name or initials of the owner stamped, marked or fastened inside the bottle;[10] a restriction against the operation of a station for the purchase of milk from producers, without a license and the posting of a bond to secure payment;[11] the establishment of a milk control board with the power to fix minimum wholesale and retail prices for milk within the state;[12] and two parts of the Agriculture and Markets Law, one of which provided that no license should be granted to any person not engaged in the business of a milk dealer when the act took effect, unless he became the owner of a then existing business, and the other of which stipulated that no license should be granted to authorize the extension of an existing business, unless the Com-

[6] People v. Frudenberg (1913) 155 A. D. 199 1st Dept. Ch. 608, L. 1911.

[7] People v. VonKampen (1914) 210 N. Y. 381, L. 1909, Ch. 357, Section 1.

[8] People v. Beakes Dairy Co. (1918) 222 N. Y. 416. Section 55 Agriculture Law (Cons. Laws, Ch. 1; amended L. 1915, Ch. 651).

[9] People v. Teussher (1928) 248 N. Y. 454. Section 76 Farms and Markets Law (Cons. Laws, Ch. 69; amended L. 1924, Ch. 267).

Sections 72 and 74 of the Agriculture and Markets Law pursuant to which cattle had been barred from the State, because a certificate was lacking that the herd from which they came were free of Bang's disease, were upheld by the United States Supreme Court in Mintz v. Baldwin (1933) (1933) 289 U. S. 346.

[10] People v. Ryan (1930) 230 A. D. 252 4th Dept. Section 70 Agriculture and Markets Law (as amended by L. 1928, Ch. 51).

[11] People v. Perretta (1930) 253 N. Y. 305. Section 252 Agriculture and Markets Law (Cons. Laws, Ch. 69).

[12] People v. Nebbia (1933) 262 N. Y. 259. Ch. 158, L. 1933 amending Agriculture and Markets Law (Cons. Laws, Ch. 69). Section 312 granted the power to fix prices.

missioner of Agriculture were satisfied as to certain particulars mentioned in the statute.[13]

The most famous of these cases was the law giving the Milk Control Board the power to fix prices of milk. When the decision of the Court of Appeals was passed upon by the United States Supreme Court, the latter divided five to four in the case of Nebbia v. New York (1934).[14] Justice Roberts, who wrote the majority opinion upholding the law, stated that the dairy industry was not a public utility in the accepted sense of the phrase. "But if," he asked, "as must be conceded, the industry is subject to regulation in the public interest, what constitutional principle bars the state from correcting existing maladjustments by legislation touching prices?" Stating that the majority thought that there was no such principle, he went on to declare:

> So far as the requirement of due process is concerned, and in the absence of other constitutional restriction, a state is free to adopt whatever economic policy may reasonably be deemed to promote public welfare, and to enforce that policy by legislation adapted to its purpose. The courts are without authority either to declare such policy, or, when it is declared by the legislature, to override it. If the laws passed are seen to have a reasonable relation to a proper legislative purpose, and are neither arbitrary nor discriminatory, the requirements of due process are satisfied, and judicial determination to that effect renders a court *functus officio* . . . The Constitution does not secure to anyone liberty to conduct his business in such fashion as to inflict injury upon the public at large, or upon any substantial group of the people. Price control, like any other form of regulation, is unconstitutional only if arbitrary, discriminatory, or demonstrably irrelevant to the policy the

---

[13] Matter of Elite Dairy Products v. Ten Eyck (1936) 247 A. D. 443 3rd Dept. Section 258-c of Article 21 of Agriculture and Markets Law (April 1, 1934).

[14] 291 U. S. 302.

legislature is free to adopt, and hence an unnecessary and unwarranted interference with individual liberty.[15]

Three laws dealing with meat and other food products were also sustained. The first of these was a section of the Agricultural Law prohibiting the sale or exposure of calves less than four weeks old and authorizing the seizure of calves under four weeks of age.[16] The second was a provision of the Public Health Law making it unlawful for anyone engaged in the cold storage warehouse or refrigeration business, or for any person placing food in such a warehouse to keep any article used for food longer than ten calendar months in storage, except butter products, which might be kept twelve months.[17] The third made it a misdemeanor to expose for sale, with intent to defraud, meat preparations falsely represented to be " kosher ".[18]

An amendment to the Agriculture and Markets Law, adopted in 1928, provided that a certificate by the Commissioner of Agriculture should be presumptive evidence of a claim by a consignor creditor against a commission merchant on a bond executed by the latter. In its opinion the Appellate Division noted that " In many cases the amount of the farmer's claim would be too small to justify the expense of prosecuting the claim to collect," but for this law.[19]

Though intended for human consumption like milk, meat and other food products, liquor has not been regarded in the

[15] " functus officio " translated from the Latin means " having performed its office or duty, hence out of office." *Ibid.*, quoted at pp. 537, 538-39.

[16] Williams v. Rivenburg (1911) 145 A. D. 93 4th Dept. Section 106 Agriculture Law (Cons. Laws, Ch. 1).

[17] People v. Finkelstein (1915) 167 A. D. 591 1st Dept. Section 337 Public Health Law as amended by Ch. 414, L. 1914.

[18] People v. Atlas (1918) 183 A. D. 595 1st Dept. Section 435 Penal Law, Subd. 4, L. 1915, Ch. 223. The United States Supreme Court held constitutional Chapters 580 and 581, L. 1922 containing the same regulation in Hygrade Provision Co. v. Sherman (1925) 266 U. S. 497.

[19] Baldwin v. Standard Accident Insurance Co. (1932) 237 A. D. 334 3rd Dept. Article 20 Agriculture and Markets Law amended by L. 1928, Ch. 454.

168   JUDICIAL REVIEW OF LEGISLATION IN N. Y.

same light by observers in and out of the legislature. It will be remembered that the outstanding case of Wynehamer v. People [20] resulted in the invalidation of a prohibition statute. Although no later act of the same nature was passed before the Eighteenth Amendment, excise regulations were put into effect and sustained by the courts.[21]

Only one law dealing with the regulation of liquor was found unconstitutional in these years. This was a section of the Alcoholic Beverage Control Law giving the Alcoholic Beverage Control Board the power to make a rule forbidding the sale of liquor on Sunday before 2 P. M. This was held to be a delegation of legislative power in violation of Article 3, Section 1.[22] The following were the laws treating of liquor which the courts held valid: a law of 1908 under which the legislature had changed the expiration of the excise year from April 30th to September 30th in a town which had voted against the issuance of a license under local option;[23] two subdivisions of the Liquor Tax Law allowing the seizure of liquors stored for the purpose of sale in violation of the law;[24] an act of 1917 authorizing the State Excise Commissioner to prohibit the sale of liquor near camps or barracks or munition factories;[25] a section of the Liquor Tax Law as amended in 1918 making it unlawful for a person to have liquors in any quantity in his possession in any city or town where trafficking in liquors was

20 See Chapter VIII, note 26 supra.

21 Metropolitan Board of Excise v. Barrie (1866) 34 N. Y. 657.

22 People v. Ryan (1935) 267 N. Y. 133. Subd. 4 Section 97 of Alcoholic Beverage Control Law, L. 1933, Ch. 180; People v. Grant (1935) 267 N. Y. 508. In this latter case the board had issued a rule forbidding the sale of beer or wine to minors under the age of sixteen.

23 People ex rel. McEachron v. Bashford (1908) 128 A. D. 351 4th Dept. Ch. 144, L. 1908.

24 Clement v. May (1909) 136 A. D. 199 3rd Dept. Subds. 1 and 2 of Section 31c Liquor Tax Law, L. 1896, Ch. 112 added by L. 1908, Ch. 350.

25 People ex rel. Doscher v. Sisson (1918) 222 N. Y. 387. L. 1917, Ch. 521.

prohibited;[26] a section of the Penal Law denominating a building in which intoxicating liquor was kept as a common nuisance, and empowering a court to order the building not to be used for a year;[27] a subdivision of the Alcoholic Beverage Control Law providing that a license for the sale of beer at retail to be consumed on the premises might be granted only to a *bona fide* hotel, restaurant, beer garden, club, railroad car or vessel;[28] a provision in the same law for the expiration of all licenses on June 1, 1934 and for the City of New York to make a pro rata refund for a temporary permit issued for the sale of beer and wine;[29] and another section of the same law stating that no common carrier or other person should bring liquors into the state.[30]

In 1923 the creation of the Emergency State Fuel Administration, set up by law to supervise the allotment and rationing of fuel to localities, dealers and consumers, the administrator of which was given power to adopt and enforce the rules and orders necessary to carry out the provisions of the statute passed in 1922 in anticipation of a coal strike, was sustained by a lower court.[31]

[26] People v. Willi (1919) 109 Misc. 79. County Court Delaware Co.; People v. Blanchard (1919) 110 Misc. 402. Supreme Court Franklin Special Term; People v. Fritzsche (1920) 111 Misc. 336. County Court Fulton Co. Section 30-P Liquor Tax Law as amended in 1918.

[27] Matter of Love (1923) 205 A. D. 363 4th Dept. Sections 1214-g and 1217 Penal Law, Ch. 155, L. 1921.

[28] Matter of Berger v. Quinn (1933) 149 Misc. 545. Supreme Court Albany Co. (Cons. Laws, Ch. 3-b, L. 1933, Ch. 180).

[29] Matter of Bushell v. City of New York (1934) 242 A. D. 366 1st Dept. Section 130 Alcoholic Beverage Control Law, L. 1933, Ch. 180. No conflict was found with Article 8, Section 10.

[30] People v. Ryan (1936) 248 A. D. 236 2nd Dept. Paragraph (d), Subd. 1, Section 102, Alcoholic Beverage Control Law. The commerce clause was not infringed upon by this paragraph, which was considered harmonious with the Twenty-first Amendment.

[31] People v. Moynihan (1923) 121 Misc. 34. County Court Chautauqua Co. Ch. 673, L. 1922.

170 JUDICIAL REVIEW OF LEGISLATION IN N. Y.

A large category of cases was that concerned with real estate and housing. The first law declared unconstitutional under this heading was a section of the Penal Code making people in cities of the first and second classes who offered for sale any real property without the written consent of the owner of the property guilty of a misdemeanor.[32] This was held to be an unreasonable exercise of the police power. An attempt to confine the business of insurance broker to those who made that their principal business, or to real estate agents or brokers, was declared to be invalid in 1912.[33] An act making it a misdemeanor to apply for a loan on real property without the written consent of the owner was ruled void by a lower court on the authority of the Fisher Company case.[34] The last enactment of this type held void was a subdivision of the Multiple Dwelling Law providing that the expense of making improvements in old law tenements directed by the Department of Housing and Building of New York City should, where the directions were not complied with, be assessed against the property, and that the lien of the assessment was to have priority over all other liens and encumbrances including previously recorded mortgages.[35]

The acts concerned with real estate and housing which were held constitutional were: a section of the New York City

[32] Fisher Co. v. Woods (1907) 187 N. Y. 90. Section 640d Penal Code, L. 1901, Ch. 128. The contract clause was also found to have been violated in this case. The same conclusion was previously reached in Tieck v. McKenna (1906) 115 A. D. 701 2nd Dept. The ruling of the Court of Appeals was followed in Harnett and Co. Inc. v. Englander (1907) 120 A. D. 351 1st Dept.

[33] Hauser v. North British and Mercantile Insurance Co. 206 N. Y. 455. Section 142 Insurance Law, first inserted in 1911 by Ch. 748, as amended by Ch. 1, L. 1912.

[34] Keller v. Jamaica Motor Service Corporation (1925) 115 Misc. 825. Supreme Court Appellate Term 2nd Dept. Section 2039 Penal Law.

[35] Central Savings Bank v. City of New York (1938) 279 N. Y. 266. Subd. 6, Section 309 Multiple Dwelling Law (Cons. Laws, Ch. 61-A, amended L. 1937, Ch. 353). A conflict with the contract as well as the due process clause was also noted by the court.

Building Code, which had been given the force of a legislative act through confirmation by the city charter and subsequent legislation, requiring all dumbwaiter shafts over three stories above the basement to be enclosed in fireproof walls, the requirement to apply to previously erected buildings; [36] a section of the Tenement House Law prohibiting the use of a tenement house for purposes of prostitution and declaring a violation of the law a misdemeanor without proof of guilty knowledge on the part of the owner of the real estate; [37] a statute suspending for two years in New York City the possessory remedies to gain possession of real property; [38] two requirements incorporated in the Labor Law, one that there should be fireproofing of stairways and passageways as well as exits in factory buildings,[39] and the other that a sprinkler system should be installed

[36] City of New York v. Foster (1911) 148 A. D. 258 1st Dept. Building Code (1899) confirmed by Section 407 New York City Charter (Ch. 466, L. 1901) amended by Ch. 602, L. 1904, Ch. 628, Section 2 L. 1904. Section 97 of the Building Code contained the requirement in question.

[37] People v. McKinley Realty and Construction Co. (1918) 182 A. D. 773 1st Dept. Section 109 Tenement House Law (Cons. Laws, Ch. 61, L. 1909, Ch. 99, as amended by L. 1913, Ch. 598).

[38] People ex rel. Durham Realty Corporation v. La Fetra (1921) 230 N. Y. 429. Chapters 942-953, L. 1920; Levy Leasing Co. v. Siegel (1921) 230 N. Y. 634. Ch. 944, L. 1920; Clenult Realty Co. v. Wood (1921) 230 N. Y. 646. Ch. 944, L. 1920; Guttag v. Shatzkin (1921) 230 N. Y. 647. Ch. 947, L. 1920; West End Avenue Inc. v. Stern (1921) 230 N. Y. 652. Ch. 947, L. 1920; People ex rel. Rayland Realty Co. v. Fagan (1921) 230 N. Y. 653 Ch. 942, L. 1920; People ex rel. H. D. H. Realty Corporation v. Murphy (1921) 230 N. Y. 654, Ch. 942, L. 1920; People ex rel. Ballin v. O'Connell (1921) 230 N. Y. 655, Ch. 942, L. 1920; All these decisions were handed down on the same date, March 8, 1921. Objection was brought against this act on the grounds of violating the due process, equal protection, the obligation of contracts and just compensation clauses. The Appellate Division had upheld the act in People ex rel. Brixton Operating Corporation v. La Fetra (1920) 194 A. D. 523 1st Dept., affirmed in 230 N. Y. 429 at the same time as People ex rel. Durham Realty Corporation v. La Fetra, above. The United States Supreme Court upheld this type of legislation in Marcus Brown Holding Co. v. Feldman (1921) 256 U. S. 170.

[39] Cockcroft v. Mitchel (1921) 230 N. Y. 630. Section 79b Labor Law. Definition of a factory had been given in Section 2 of the Labor Law as amended by L. 1915, Ch. 650.

in a building where inflammable materials were used;[40] the establishment of a system of licenses for real estate brokers with annual renewals;[41] the establishing of minimum standards of safety and sanitation for tenements to which buildings erected before 1901 were required to conform;[42] and an amendment to the Multiple Dwelling Law providing that, for failure to comply with its requirements, no rent was to be recovered except at the lowest rate charged for any month between September 30th, 1937 and March 1st, 1938.[43] A law of 1911 required fireproof booths for moving picture machines, and this too was sustained.[44]

Four statutes regulating cemeteries were upheld. The first of these forbade the founding of public cemeteries within one-half mile from any reservoir or pond forming a part of the water supply system of the former City of Brooklyn.[45] A provision that a cemetery corporation was not to be incorporated thereafter for the purpose of conducting its operations in the County of Nassau was held applicable only to cemeteries established after the passage of the law.[46] An enactment allowing the sale of unused cemetery land in satisfaction of a mechanic's

[40] People ex rel. Cockcroft v. Miller (1919) 187 A. D. 704 1st Dept. Section 83-b Labor Law, L. 1912, Ch. 332 as amended L. 1915, Ch. 347. The law was held applicable to a building occupied mainly by manufacturing jewelers who did not work with or upon inflammable materials.

[41] Roman v. Lobe (1926) 243 N. Y. 51. Article XII-A Real Property Law (Cons. Laws, Ch. 50).

[42] Adamec v. Post (1937) 273 N. Y. 250. Provisions of Multiple Dwelling Law.

[43] Mordred Realties Co. v. Langley (1938) 279 N. Y. 636. Ch. 675, L. 1938 amending Multiple Dwelling Law Section 302.

[44] Matter of Whitten (1912) 152 A. D. 506 2nd Dept. Ch. 756, L. 1911.

[45] City of New York v. Kelsey (1913) 158 A. D. 183 2nd Dept. L. 1868, Ch. 591.

[46] Baylis v. Van Nostrand (1917) 176 A. D. 396 2nd Dept. Section 85 Membership Corporations Law added by Ch. 139, L. 1913. The court stated that the legislature had the power to control the question of new and additional cemeteries.

lien was found unobjectionable in 1921.[47] In 1935 the Court of Appeals sustained a prohibition against the further extension of the right to use land for burial purposes within New York City, even if the consent of the Board of Aldermen were obtained.[48]

The selling of a variety of objects was subjected to regulations during this period. All were found satisfactory by the state courts, but one did not meet with the approval of the United States Supreme Court. The earliest of these was passed in 1909, and required a license of persons conducting a transient retail business in municipalities who advertised a sale of bankrupt or fire-damaged stock.[49] The second law imposed restrictions upon the business of reselling theatre tickets. The provisions requiring a license were upheld in 1924 by the Court of Appeals, and later by the United States Supreme Court.[50] The sections of the act, however, limiting the price at which the tickets could be resold to fifty cents above the original cost were held unconstitutional in the noted case of Tyson v. Banton (1927) by the United States Supreme Court.[51] The majority stated that theaters were not public utilities, and hence not subject to that form of regulation, but Justice Holmes, in a dissenting opinion, said that according to "fashionable conventions . . . theaters are as much devoted to public use

[47] Johnson v. Ocean View Cemetery (1921) 198 A. D. 854 2nd Dept. Amendment by L. 1918, Ch. 404 to Real Property Law Section 450.

[48] Moritz v. United Brethren's Church on Staten Island 269 N. Y. 175. Section 451 of Real Property Law (Cons. Laws, Ch. 51 and Section 1539-a of New York City Charter L. 1904, Ch. 618.

[49] People ex rel. Moskowitz v. Jenkins (1910) 140 A. D. 786 3rd Dept. Section 85 of the General Municipal Law (Cons. Laws, Ch. 24, L. 1909, Ch. 29). The cost of the license ranged from twenty-five to one hundred dollars.

[50] People v. Weller (1924) 237 N. Y. 316. General Business Law Sections 167-174, as amended by Ch. 590, L. 1922. Affirmed in Weller v. New York (1925) 268 U. S. 319.

[51] 273 U. S. 418. Section 167 declared that the price of admission to theaters was a matter affected with a public interest, while Section 172 contained the price limitation.

as anything well can be" and that, whether the law were wise or not, nothing in the United States Constitution could be discovered that would prevent the people of New York from having it if they so wished.[52] Auction sales of jewelry and similar merchandise at night, that is, between the hours of sunset and sunrise, were prohibited in 1918.[53] A "Blue Sky Law" was adopted in 1926 providing for an examination by the Attorney-General as to fraudulent practices in respect to the sale of stocks and other securities and commodities.[54] A section of the Penal Law, later repealed, which forbade the sale of articles falsely stamped "platinum" was held to refer to sales in the usual course of business, and not to occasional transactions such as a sale by an executor of an estate.[55]

It has generally been conceded that railroads, public ultilities and banks are affected with a public interest. Three laws dealing with the first of these activities were sustained. The first empowered the Public Service Commission to fix reasonable and just rates for commutation for the public convenience and welfare.[56] The second authorized a railroad to cross a street or

[52] *Ibid.*, at p. 447.

[53] Biddles Inc. v. Enright (1925) 239 N. Y. 354 Section 1991 Consolidation Act (L. 1882, Ch. 410, amended L. 1918, Ch. 179) made applicable to New York City by Section 1610 of its charter (L. 1901, Ch. 466). This law had been previously sustained in Alexander v. Enright (1924) 211 A. D. 146 1st Dept.

[54] Durham v. Ottinger (1926) 243 N. Y. 423.

[55] People v. Friedman (1928) 249 N. Y. 86. Section 1445 Penal Law. A law providing that dealers in junk or second hand materials, or their agents when receiving wire, cable, copper, lead, solder, iron or brass used by or belonging to a railroad, telephone, telegraph, gas or electric light company, should ascertain by diligent inquiry whether the person selling or delivering the property had a right to do so was upheld, when construed as only necessitating inquiry whether the property was stolen, in Rosenthal v. New York (1912) 226 U. S. 260. Ch. 326, L. 1903, amending Section 550 Penal Code; reenacted in Penal Code as Section 1308.

[56] People ex rel. New York, New Haven and Hartford Railroad Co. v. Public Service Commission (1914) 159 A. D. 531, 3rd Dept. Section 33, Subd. 4 Public Service Commission Law (Cons. Laws, Ch. 48, L. 1910, Ch. 460 as amended by L. 1911, Ch. 546).

highway without the consent of the local authorities.[57] The third gave power to the Public Service Commission to determine whether the public welfare required the elimination of a particular grade crossing.[58]

One act concerned with public utilities was invalidated. It fixed a rate of 80¢ per thousand cubic feet of gas throughout the Borough of Brooklyn, which was regarded as confiscatory.[59] Another act was partially upheld and partially invalidated. Passed in 1905, it authorized the Public Service Commission to determine the maximum price of service of gas and electric light companies on the complaint of municipal authorities. This provision was upheld, but it was considered a violation of the Fourteenth Amendment not to afford an opportunity for a petition for a new rate at the end of a term of three years.[60]

The remaining laws met with the approval of the judges as far as their validity was concerned. Laws of 1905 and 1906 regulating the price of gas were presumed by the Appellate Division to be valid in the latter year, and their operation could not be suspended in the absence of proof to the contrary.[61] The commissioners of water supply of New York City were

[57] People ex rel. New York, Westchester and Boston Railway Co. v. The Public Service Commission (1920) 193 A. D. 445 1st Dept. L. 1910, Ch. 481 as amended by L. 1918, Ch. 166. It was also valid to allow the Public Service Commission to regulate fares in order to secure efficiency. Sections 29 and 49 Public Service Commission Law.

[58] Matter of New York, Ontario and Western Railway Co. (1935) 244 A. D. 634 4th Dept. Subd. 5 Section 2 Grade Crossing Elimination Act, L. 1923, Ch. 678.

[59] Kings County Lighting Co v. Newton (1923) 235 N. Y. 599. Ch. 604, L. 1916 amending Ch. 125, L. 1906. The Appellate Division had previously come to the same conclusion in Public Service Commission v. Brooklyn Borough Gas. Co. (1919) 189 A. D. 62 2nd Dept.

[60] Matter of Trustees of Village of Saratoga Springs v. Saratoga Gas, Electric Light, Heat and Power Co. (1908) 191 N. Y. 123, L. 1905, Ch. 737.

[61] Richman v. Consolidated Gas Co. (1906) 114 A. D. 216 1st Dept. Ch. 125, L. 1906 and Ch. 736, L. 1905.

authorized by a section of that city's charter to place meters on the premises of consumers at the latter's expense, and the Appellate Division could see no violation of contract rights since the payment of water rates was not sonsidered as a contract.[62] Persons operating jitney bus lines in cities were required in 1915 to obtain a certificate of convenience and necessity from the Public Service Commission, and such lines were subjected to reasonable regulations imposed by the Commission.[63] The power of the legislature to establish a rate for the consumption of gas in one locality, without fixing it for all localities, was affirmed in 1919.[64] The next year it was ruled that power might be delegated by the legislature to municipal authorities to grant a franchise to a corporation for stringing wires on a highway crossing a railroad's right of way where no interference with the latter's operation resulted, and approval was secured from the Public Service Commission.[65] Another decision in 1920 confirmed the legislature's power to modify rates fixed by a local franchise.[66] Five years later another ruling allowed the Public Service Commission to regulate fares, notwithstanding that a higher rate might have been prescribed by statute, contract or in some other manner.[67] Finally, in 1935 the Appellate Division upheld provisions for the investigation by the Public Service Commission of the

[62] Swanberg v. The City of New York (1908) 123 A. D. 774 2nd Dept. Section 475 Charter of New York, L. 1901, Ch. 466.

[63] Public Service Commission v. Booth (1915) 170 A. D. 590 3rd Dept. Ch. 67, L. 1915 amending Section 25 Transportation Corporations Law.

[64] Bronx Gas and Electric Co. v. Public Service Commission 190 A. D. 13 1st Dept. Ch. 125, L. 1906.

[65] New York Central Railroad Co. v. Middleport Gas and Electric Light Co. (1920) 193 A. D. 273 4th Dept. General Corporation Law Section 320.

[66] Matter of Application of City of Niagara Falls (1920) 229 N. Y. 333. Section 181 Railroad Law 1910 read in conjunction with Section 49 Railroad Law.

[67] People ex rel. Village of Brownville v. Public Service Commission (1925) 240 N. Y. 586. Section 49 of Public Service Commission Law, as amended by Ch. 134 and Ch. 335, L. 1921, which had been repealed in 1923.

operations and records of public utilities, the latter to bear a portion of the expenses of the Commission which might be reasonably attributed to such investigation.[68]

One legislative act regulating banking was declared unconstitutional. This, a law of 1933, granted the State Banking Board the power to suspend the provisions of the Banking Law. The Board was allowed to "adopt, rescind, alter and amend rules and regulations inconsistent with and in contravention of any law" with respect to the interests of depositors and stockholders in corporations subject to the Banking Department. The Appellate Division considered this to be an improper delegation of legislative power in 1934.[69]

The stamp of judicial approval was placed upon acts which gave the Superintendent of Banks the authority to enforce the statutory liability of the stockholders of an insolvent bank,[70] which made a deposit in a savings bank in the form of a joint account conclusive evidence, in the absence of fraud or undue influence, of the intention of both depositors to vest title to the deposit and any additions to such deposit in the surviving depositor,[71] which created the Mortgage Commission to take

[68] Matter of Kings County Lighting Co. v. Maltbie (1935) 244 A. D. 475 3rd Dept. Sections 18-a and 18-b Public Service Law, added by Ch. 282, L. 1934. The law was not considered an improper delegation of legislative power because money was paid by the public utilities into a revolving fund from which appropriations were made.

[69] Moses v. Guaranteed Mortgage Co. of New York 239 A. D. 703 1st Dept. Ch. 41, L. 1933.

A decision of the United States Supreme Court held invalid a provision to the effect that in the event of a bank's insolvency, claims of creditors whose paper the bank had collected and for which it had not paid them should be preferred, as applied to a national bank in Old Company's Lehigh, Inc. v. Meeker (1935) 294 U. S. 227. Provision of Uniform Bank Collection Code; amendment of Negotiable Instruments Law (Cons. Laws, Ch. 38; Article 19A, Sections 350-350(1)).

[70] Van Tuyl v. Sullivan (1915) 173 A. D. 391 2nd Dept. Section 19 Banking Law as amended Ch. 452, L. 1910.

[71] Heiner v. Greenwich Savings Bank (1922) 118 Misc. 326. Supreme Court Kings Special Term. Last paragraph Subd. 3, Section 249 Banking Law added by L. 1914, Ch. 369.

over the duties previously performed as statutory receiver in certain cases, either by the Superintendent of Insurance or the Superintendent of Banks,[72] which provided that a transfer of stock, while a bank is solvent, to a resident of New York State relieved a stockholder from liability,[73] which prohibited engaging in the business of making loans of $300 or less and charging more than six per cent a year on those loans without a license, [74] and which made the stockholders of a bank liable " equally and ratably " for the unpaid debts of the bank and " not one for another," where formerly, one stockholder had been liable for the debts of another.[75]

In 1915 the Appellate Division affirmed the validity of a section of the Insurance Law requiring an agent of a life insurance company to have a certificate issued by the Superintendent of Insurance before a company could pay him a commission. Objection had been taken that the Superintendent of Insurance was thereby vested with the arbitrary power to prevent a person from pursuing a lawful calling, since he might

[72] Hutchinson v. Nassau County Trust Company (1935) 246 A. D. 628 2nd Dept. Ch. 19, L. 1935.

[73] Broderick v. Adamson (1936) 270 N. Y. 228 Section 120 of Banking Law (Cons. Laws, Ch. 2). No conflict was found with Article 8, Section 7, which at that time stated:

" The stockholders of every corporation and joint-stock association for banking purposes shall be individually responsible to the amount of their respective share or shares of stock in any such corporation or association, for all its debts and liabilities of every kind."

[74] People v. Blumenthal (alias Blumenfeld) (1936) 157 Misc. 943. Supreme Court New York County. Sections 340 and 357 Banking Law as added by L. 1932, Ch. 389.

[75] Broderick v. Weinsier (1938) 278 N. Y. 419. Section 120 (at the time of the decision 113-a) of Banking Law (Cons. Laws, Ch. 2). This law had been held unconstitutional by the Supreme Court at a Special Term in New York County in 1937, as a violation of Article 8, Section 7, which had been repealed in 1935, because it limited the stockholder's liability. 161 Misc. 820.

The view of the Court of Appeals was that the constitutional provision was not self-executing and that the legislature might define the procedure for enforcing liability.

"refuse to issue or renew such certificate in his discretion" but the court did not agree.[76]

Five acts regulating the qualifications for entering various occupations were held invalid by the courts. One required undertakers to be licensed as embalmers, and to have been employed as assistants to a licensed undertaker for three years. In addition, members of firms were to be licensed. Although undertaking was, in the court's opinion, subject to regulation because of its close relation to the health and general welfare of a community, this particular law was deemed arbitrary and unreasonable.[77] After this law had been invalidated, another law was passed requiring an apprenticeship to an undertaker for two years for the license. This, too, was thought unreasonable, since undertakers might acquire the knowledge necessary for their profession, by attending some type of school or by special training, without an apprenticeship.[78] The first-mentioned case served as a precedent when a requirement that an applicant for a license as motion picture operator should serve a six months apprenticeship under a licensed operator was ruled invalid in 1930.[79] So too was the requirement that a pharmacy should be owned and conducted by a licensed pharmacist, coupled with a prohibition of ownership by a licensed druggist.[80] Although it was considered proper to restrict the

[76] Stern v. Metropolitan Life Insurance Company 169 A. D. 217 1st Dept. Section 91 of the Insurance Law, L. 1909, Ch. 33 (Cons. Laws, Ch. 8, Section 91 as amended by L. 1909, Ch. 301).

[77] People v. Ringe (1910) 197 N. Y. 143. Section 6a of Ch. 512, L. 1905, Section 295 of the Public Health Law at the time of the decision.

[78] People v. Harrison (1915) 170 A. D. 802 1st Dept. Section 295 Public Health Law as amended by Ch. 71, L. 1913. As all the provisions of the section were considered interdependent, the whole section was held unconstitutional.

[79] People v. Kozanowski 136 Misc. 353. City Court of Buffalo. Section 18 General City Law added by L. 1911, Ch. 252 as amended by L. 1916, Ch. 184.

[80] Pratter v. Lascoff (1933) 261 N. Y. 509. Sections 1354 and 1362 of Education Law (Cons. Laws, Ch. 16).

vocation of master plumber to persons who had obtained licenses after demonstrating their competency, it was regarded as an arbitrary discrimination to provide that the Commissioner of Health of New York City or the Municipal Civil Service Commission might require an examination for the renewal of a plumber's license issued after January 1, 1920, and to leave to an administrative officer the power to determine who should take an examination and who should be exempt. This latter was viewed as an unlawful delegation of legislative power.[81] Despite the contention that the business of public dancing academies was such as to attract crowds and require police surveillance, the Court of Appeals considered it unreasonable to necessitate their being licensed.[82]

The professions of medicine, dentistry and pharmacy were all subjected to measures of control subsequently held valid. It was made a misdemeanor in 1907 to practice medicine without a license, and this applied to the laying on of hands and manipulation, such as is the method of chiropractors.[83] Making a professional education necessary as a condition for a license to practice dentistry was not regarded as a violation of Article 3, Section 18 of the State Constitution, forbidding the passage of a private or local bill granting an exclusive privilege, immunity or franchise to any private corporation, association or individual.[84] Later the practicing of dentistry under a false or assumed name was made illegal.[85] A law of 1900 prohibited

[81] Seignious v. Rice (1936) 273 N. Y. 44. Title 5 of Ch. 23 of New York City Charter (L. 1936, Ch. 610).

[82] People ex rel. Duryea v. Wilber (1910) 198 N. Y. 1. Ch. 400, L. 1909 amending New York Charter. The court did not regard the law as an intended protection to minors.

[83] People v. Mulford (1910) 140 A. D. 716 4th Dept. Ch. 344, L. 1907.

[84] People v. Griswold (1914) 213 N. Y. 92. Provisions Public Health Law (Cons. Laws, Ch. 45 Sections 194, 196, and 198). It was not considered a discrimination in favor of aliens or against the citizens of other states or a violation of the Federal Constitution.

[85] People v. Hewson (1917) 181 A. D. 202 3rd Dept. Section 205 Public Health Law Ch. 49, L. 1909 as amended Ch. 129, L. 1916 and Ch. 507, L. 1917.

POLICE POWER 181

the sale of "medicines or poisons" except in the presence of a licensed pharmacist. Provision was made, however, to permit the sale of poisonous domestic remedies by merchants or traders, in unincorporated villages or villages of the fourth class, three miles distant from a drug store. This was not thought arbitrary or unreasonable.[86] An authorization to the Board of Regents to determine the unfitness of a pharmacist was not an improper delegation of legislative power in the opinion of the Court of Appeals.[87] The same court also did not think it unreasonable to permit a licensed druggist to carry on the business of a pharmacist in a place of not more than one thousand inhabitants, and to be employed for dispensing drugs in a registered pharmacy, except in cities of over a million inhabitants.[88]

In 1901 an act was passed requiring a license to engage in the business of a private detective for hire. It was sustained by the Appellate Division,[89] as was a section of the Penal Law making it a misdemeanor "to make it a business to solicit employment for a lawyer, or to furnish attorneys or counsel."[90]

The growing use of the automobile proved a great stimulus to legislation. Compelling the operators of motor vehicles to secure licenses was sustained in 1913.[91] Laws authorizing the exclusion of motor vehicles from certain highways were also

[86] State Board of Pharmacy v. Matthews (1910) 197 N. Y. 353. Public Health Law (L. 1900, Ch. 667; Cons. Laws, Ch. 45). Sections 194, 199, 200 and 201.

[87] Matter of Madel v. The Board of Regents (1928) 200 N. Y. 173. Section 1362 Education Law (Cons. Laws, Ch. 16).

[88] Lutz v. Houck (1933) 263 N. Y. 116. Provisions of Education Law, Paragraph 4 of Section 1354 (Cons. Laws, Ch. 16).

[89] Fox v. Smith (1908) 123 A. D. 369 1st Dept. Ch. 422, L. 1898 as amended by Ch. 362, L. 1901.

[90] People v. Meola (1920) 193 A. D. 487 2nd Dept. Section 270 Penal Law. Litigation for litigations's sake was seen as a public evil.

[91] People v. Rosenheimer 209 N. Y. 115. Ch. 374, L. 1910 Section 290, Subd. 3 Highway Law. See People v. Rosenheimer referred to in Chapter III, note 33 supra.

182 JUDICIAL REVIEW OF LEGISLATION IN N. Y.

upheld on two occasions.[92] A later act compelled those engaged in carrying passengers for hire in motor vehicles in first class cities to file a bond or policy of insurance with the State Tax Commission. The Appellate Division did not approve the contention that it violated the due process clause.[93] The courts also confirmed the legislature's power to suspend the license of a driver, pending determination of a charge of operating a motor vehicle while intoxicated,[94] and to make every owner of an automobile liable for the negligence of an operator using the car with his permission.[95] Another law, challenged as violating the equal protection clause, but sustained by the Appellate Division, provided that the renter of an automobile from a corporation was to be insured by the corporation against any liability arising out of his negligence.[96]

In another area than the regulation of business activities and of occupations, the Appellate Division upheld the legislature when the latter forbade the levying of unlawful dues or assessments in fraternal associations. The law in question made it illegal for officers of such associations to collect dues unless

[92] People ex rel. Cavanagh v. Waldo (1911) 72 Misc. 416. Supreme Court Kings Special Term, Ch. 681, L. 1910 adding Section 612b to the Greater New York Charter. The Commissioner of Parks of the Boroughs of Brooklyn and Queens was given discretionary authority by this law to exclude bicycles and motor vehicles from the main driveway of Ocean Boulevard, in Brooklyn, from Twenty-second Avenue to King's Highway; Strauss v. Enright (1918) 105 Misc. 367. Supreme Court New York Special Term. L. 1900, Ch. 710, amending L. 1893, Ch. 102. This restricted the use of the " Harlem River Driveway," commonly known as the " Speedway," to the driving of horses attached to light carriages.

[93] People v. Martin (1922) 203 A. D. 423 1st Dept. Section 282-b Highway Law. Ch. 612, L. 1922.

[94] People v. Stryker (1924) 124 Misc. 1. Supreme Court Delaware Special Term. Section 290-a Highway Law (as added by L. 1924, Ch. 260).

[95] Dawley v. McRibbin (1927) 245 N. Y. 557. Section 282-e Highway Law.

[96] Atkins v. Hertz Driv-Urself Stations Inc. (1932) 237 A. D. 31 1st Dept. Section 59 Vehicle and Traffic Law, Ch. 54, L. 1929, as amended. Nor was this considered a special law in conflict with Article 3, Section 18.

elected by delegates to a convention.[97] No objection was found either to permitting municipal bodies to adopt standard daylight saving time.[98]

The legislature's authority was successfully challenged, however, in two cases bearing the same name, Gedney v. Marlton Realty Company, and involving the same act. In the first, it was ruled that power could not be devolved upon the Supreme Court to direct the sale of premises for the benefit of a life tenant of property, upon her petition, where there were five adults, under no disability, who would have been entitled to the property in the event of her death.[99] The second case involved an infant remainderman, for whose welfare the statute had not been enacted, as neither she nor her guardian could initiate the proceedings under the act to bring about the sale of the property.[100]

The apparent conclusions to be drawn from this collection of cases are that, in the main, legislative exercise of the police power was upheld, especially in those lines of endeavor where the necessity for its employment was generally accepted. The courts demurred on relatively minor questions of method and on regulations where there was greater doubt as to the need for intervention by the state. The total count reveals seventy-seven acts upheld as opposed to seventeen pronounced invalid. This would tend to support a statement that, on the whole, the legislature did not abuse its police powers, in the opinion of the judiciary.

[97] People ex rel. Moore v. Holmes (1912) 151 A. D. 257 4th Dept. Section 936a Penal Code Ch. 837, L. 1911.

[98] Briegel v. Day (1922) 202 A. D. 484 1st Dept. Ch. 70, 260, L. 1921 Section 91 General Municipal Act.

[99] (1932) 258 N. Y. 355. Ch. 154, L. 1865.

[100] (1934) 264 N. Y. 224.

CHAPTER XI
EDUCATION, CIVIL SERVICE AND CONSERVATION

ARTICLES in the State Constitution are devoted to the three subjects of Education, Civil Service and Conservation, though only part of Article 7 deals specifically with the latter topic. Article 9 of the 1894 Constitution, which dealt with education, provided for a system of free common schools to be supported by provision of the legislature, for a continuation of an earlier corporation which supervises the educational system under the name of The University of the State of New York, for certain funds for the support of the schools to be " preserved inviolate " and concluded with the following prohibition:

> Neither the state nor any subdivision thereof shall use its property or credit or any public money, or authorize or permit either to be used, directly or indirectly, in aid or maintenance, other than for examination or inspection, of any school or institution of learning wholly or in part under the control or direction of any religious denomination, or in which any denominational tenet or doctrine is taught.[1]

Discrimination between male and female teachers in the determination of salaries was forbidden in 1924. This prohibition was upheld in 1926.[2] It was under a section of the Constitution providing that appointments and promotions in the civil service of the state and of all its civil divisions should " be made according to merit and fitness to be ascertained, so far as practicable, by examinations, which so far as practicable, shall be competitive " that a section of the Education Law was held invalid in 1936.[3] This section had extended the term

[1] Article 9, Sections 1 to 4, Constitution of 1894.

[2] Matter of Moses v. Board of Education of Syracuse 127 Misc. 477. Supreme Court Onondaga County. Section 569 Education Law, as added by L. 1924, Ch. 614.

[3] Article 5, Section 6 which was the same as Article 5, Section 9 of the Constitution of 1894, but was renumbered in 1925; Amendments Proposed, *op. cit.*, pp. 342, 360-61.

of eligibility of persons whose names were on the eligible list for public school teacher in a city having a population of one million or more, which list had expired before the enactment of the statute.[4] In 1938 the Court of Appeals by a vote of four to three decided that, in so far as the Education Law authorized the use of public funds for the transportation of pupils to private or parochial schools, it violated Article 9, Section 4.[5]

Among the acts held constitutional were these: a section of the Education Law requiring a person, in order to be eligible for the office of district superintendent of schools (an office in rural districts), to possess a teacher's certificate and to pass an examination on the supervision of courses of study in agriculture and in the teaching of that subject;[6] an act of 1911 enabling the State Board of Trustees of the Teachers' Retirement Fund to dissolve a local organization, when two-thirds of the teachers in a district with a special retirement act peti-

[4] Hurley v. Board of Education (1936) 270 N. Y. 275. Section 871b of Education Law (Cons. Laws Ch. 16 amended L. 1933, Ch. 146); Ciaccia v. Board of Education (1936) 271 N. Y. 336. Same law as in preceding case; Carow v. Board of Education (1936) 272 N. Y. 341. Same law as in two preceding cases.

[5] Judd v. Board of Education 278 N. Y. 200. Section 206 of Education Law (Cons. Laws Ch. 16 amended L. 1936, Ch. 541). The majority rejected the argument that such transportation was furnished in aid of the pupils rather than in aid of the schools, since it induced attendance at the schools and so promoted the interests of the latter. The majority also held that the statute could not be sustained as an exercise of the police power, because of its repugnance to the Constitution. In 1938 the Constitutional Convention added the following words to Article 9, Section 4, which later became Article 11, Section 4, of the Constitution: "but the legislature may provide for the transportation of children to and from any school or institution of learning." *Record of the Constitutional Convention of the State of New York 1938* (Albany, 1938), p. 3509.

[6] People ex rel. Pintler v. Transue (1911) 174 Misc. 504. Supreme Court Wayne Special Term. Section 384 Paragraph 2 Education Law as amended in 1910. These qualifications were in addition to the requirement that the person be twenty-one, a citizen of the United States and a resident of the state. The bases for questioning the law were the Home Rule and Equal Protection clauses.

tion to come under the general act;[7] sections of the Education Law reorganizing rural school districts into a town school system with the exception of districts in Nassau County;[8] a law passed in 1919, after the repeal of the law just discussed in 1918, providing for the adjustment of accounts between the school districts by the district superintendent for the expense incurred during the year the Town Unit Law was in force;[9] the requirement that minors aged fourteen to eighteen attend continuation school if not attending full-time day school or at work;[10] the authorization given the Commissioner of Education to lay out central school districts in any territory of the state exclusive of city school districts;[11] and the provision that no individual or corporation should advertise or transact business under the name " school of law,*** unless the right to do so shall have been granted by the Regents in writing under their seal."[12]

Article 5, Section 9 of the Constitution of 1894, which was renumbered in 1925 as Article 5, Section 6 without any change in text, read:

[7] Matter of Bristol v. Board of Trustees (1916) 173 A. D. 545 3rd Dept. Article 43b Education Law, as added by Ch. 449, L. 1911.

[8] Brown v. Bunselmeyer (1917) 101 Misc. 625, Supreme Court Westchester Special Term; Education Law Article XI-A, Sections 330-365, added by Ch. 328, L. 1917. Section 331 excluded the districts in Nassau County. This was not looked upon as an unlawful discrimination against the citizens of Westchester County. After Ch. 328, L. 1917 had been repealed in 1918 (Ch. 199, L. 1918) it was held constitutional in Wadsworth v. Menzie (1919) 105 Misc. 697, Supreme Court Livingston Equity Term.

[9] Matter of Pardee v. Rayfield (1920) 230 N. Y. 543. Ch. 561, L. 1919. The period referred to started with the enactment of Ch. 328, L. 1917 and ended with the passage of Ch. 199, L. 1918, referred to in the previous note, by which the old system of school units was restored.

[10] People v. Braunstein (1928) 248 N. Y. 308. Section 601 Education Law (Cons. Laws Ch. 16).

[11] Gardner v. Ginther (1931) 232 A. D. 246 4th Dept. Section 180 Education Law (as added by Ch. 55, L. 1914).

[12] Institute of the Metropolis Inc. v. University of State (1936) 249 A. D. 33 3rd Dept. Section 66 Education Law.

Appointments and promotions in the civil service of the State, and of all the civil divisions thereof, including cities and villages, shall be made according to merit and fitness to be ascertained, so far as practicable, by examinations, which, so far as practicable, shall be competitive; provided however, that honorably discharged soldiers and sailors from the army and navy of the United States in the late civil war, who are citizens and residents of this state, shall be entitled to preference in appointment and promotion, without regard to their standing on any list from which such appointment or promotion may be made. Laws shall be made to provide for the enforcement of this section.[13]

The laws held to be in conflict with this section were: an act of 1920 providing that entrance into the military or naval service of the United States was to give preference in promotion in the civil service;[14] a section of the General Business Law empowering the Attorney-General to employ such deputies as he might think necessary without examination;[15] a section of the General City Law authorizing promotions in the New York City Police Department by the Police Commissioner;[16] a section of the New York City Charter permitting the Police

---

[13] Amendments Proposed, *op. cit.*, pp. 342, 360-61. See note 2 supra.

[14] Matter of Barthelmess v. Cukor (1921) 231 N. Y. 435. Ch. 282, L. 1920. In 1929 Article 5, Section 6 was amended by omitting the words "that honorably discharged soldiers and sailors from the army and navy of the United States in the late civil war" and inserting "any honorably discharged soldiers, sailors, marines or nurses of the army, navy or marine corps of the United States disabled in the actual performance of duty in any war, to an extent recognized by the United States Veterans' Bureau" before the words "who are citizens and residents of this state" and adding immediately after this last quoted phrase "and were at the time of their entrance into the military or naval service of the United States, and whose disability exists at the time of his or her application for such appointment or promotion." Amendments Proposed, *op. cit.*, p. 364.

[15] Matter of Ottinger (1925) 240 N. Y. 435. Section 359a General Business Law.

[16] Schieffelin v. Kelliher (1925) 125 Misc. 305. Supreme Court New York Special Term. Affirmed 275 A. D. 770. Section 15-a General City Law as added by L. 1924, Ch. 643.

Commissioner to promote to the rank of captain a lieutenant who had been a member of the force thirty-five years, a lieutenant twenty years, an acting captain seven years and on an eligible list of the civil service for promotion to captain on January 1, 1923;[17] a section of the Civil Service Law extending the term of eligibility of candidates for appointment as assistant deputy or record clerk of the Court of General Sessions of the County of New York after the expiration of the terms of eligibility fixed for certain eligible lists;[18] and an article of the Executive Law, in so far as it placed the whole state police force in the non-competitive or unclassified service, exempting them all from competitive examination and leaving their selection to the Superintendent of Police.[19]

Laws concerned with civil service held constitutional included these fifteen: a prohibition against the removal of veterans by the Superintendent of Public Works except for incompetency or misconduct shown after a hearing and notice;[20] a provision in the Civil Service Law requiring the appointment of a village street commissioner from the three persons standing highest on an eligible list certified by the Civil Service Commission;[21] an exemption of Union veterans from removal from office " except for incompetency or misconduct shown after a hearing upon due notice upon stated charges and with

[17] Barlow v. Berry (1927) 245 N. Y. 500. Section 288a New York City Charter L. 1923, Ch. 778.

[18] Matter of Kornbluth v. Rice (1937) 250 A. D. 654 3rd Dept. Section 14-b Civil Service Law as added by Ch. 884, L. 1936.

[19] Matter of Andreson v. Rice (1938) 277 N. Y. 271. Article 9-A Executive Law (Cons. Laws Ch. 18).

[20] Matter of Seeley (1907) 190 N. Y. 158. L. 1899, Ch. 370 Section 21. The Court of Appeals held that this law was not in conflict with Article 5, Section 3 giving the powers of the Superintendent of Public Works, including that of appointment and removal of most of the persons employed in the care and management of the canals.

[21] People ex rel. Qua v. Gaffney (1911) 142 A. D. 122 3rd Dept. (Cons. Laws Ch. 7, L. 1909, Ch. 15) One objection was on grounds of violating the constitutional provision granting villages the power to elect their own officials.

EDUCATION, CIVIL SERVICE

the right to such employee or appointee to a review by a writ of certiorari;"[22] a classification of probation officers as confidential officers and hence exempt from competitive examination;[23] an amendment to the New York City Charter providing that every member in the city service who had attained the age of seventy should be retired forthwith, except that, with the approval of the head of his department, a member who had reached that age might request the Board of Estimate and Apportionment to be continued in public service for a period of two years;[24] an amendment to the Civil Service Law authorizing a payment by the city to Civil War veterans employed ten years in the state civil service;[25] a section of the Farms and Markets Law under which appointment of supervisors and assistant supervisors of public markets was to be made after competitive examinations for such positions pursuant to the Civil Service Law;[26] a subdivision of the Buffalo Charter granting pensions to members of the police department superior to captain, who had served ten years on the force and one year in a position superior to captain;[27] an amendment to the Civil

---

[22] People ex rel. Long v. Whitney (1911) 143 A. D. 17 1st Dept. L. 1909, Ch. 15, as amended by L. 1910, Ch. 264.

[23] Matter of Simons v. McGuire (1911) 145 A. D. 471 2nd Dept. Ch. 639 Section 96, L. 1910.

[24] Haag v. City of New York (1921) 130 Misc. 124. Supreme Court New York Special Term. There was no constitutional objection to the fact that all city employees were not included immediately in the retirement system.

[25] Matter of Wright v. Craig (1922) 202 A. D. 684 1st Dept. Section 21-a Civil Service Law, L. 1916, Ch. 438 and amendment by L. 1921, Ch. 54. Objection had been raised because of Article 8, Section 10 forbidding a city to give money to or in aid of any individual. Quoted in Chapter VII supra.

[26] Murray v. Kaplan (1923) 206 A. D. 202 1st Dept. Section 260-a Farms and Markets Law as added by L. 1922, Ch. 633. The court held it was not necessary to say why such positions should be placed in the competitive class.

[27] Matter of Carr v. Roesch (1930) 231 A. D. 19 4th Dept. Subd. 3 Section 464 Buffalo Charter. Affirmed 255 N. Y. 614. The constitutional objection here was based on Article 3, Section 28 quoted in Chapter II supra, and Article 8, Section 10 quoted in Chapter VII supra.

Service Law giving preference to disabled war veterans, who were citizens and residents of this state at the time of their entry into service; [28] a section of the Civil Service Law giving the power to any person placed on a preferred list since January 1, 1934 to maintain mandamus proceedings for reinstatement to the position from which he had been suspended, where another person, not appointed in accordance with the provisions of the chapter, had been employed in the same or a similar position or assigned to similar duties; [29] a section of the New York City Charter providing that employees of directors of the counting of votes for councilmen must pass a non-competitive civil service examination; [30] an amendment to the previous New York City Charter requiring competitive examinations for New York City firemen so far as practicable; [31] a section of the same charter suspending the pension of a retired employee of New York City during his incumbency of any city or state office; [32] an amendment to the Public Welfare

[28] Matter of Gianastasio v. Kaplan (1931) 142 Misc. 611. Supreme Court New York County. Section 21 Civil Service Law as amended by L. 1930, Ch. 374. This law and Article 5, Section 6 of the State Constitution were questioned as conflicting with the Privileges and Immunities Clause of the Federal Constitution, but the decision was affirmed in 257 N. Y. 531 and by the United States Supreme Court, 284 U. S. 595; the same conclusion was reached in Matter of Potts v. Kaplan (1934) 264 N. Y. 110.

[29] Matter of Liebowitz v. Goldwater (1936) 161 Misc. 115. Section 31-b Civil Service Law. The section was objected to as being in conflict with Article 8, Section 10 quoted in Chapter VII supra and Article 12, Section 3 quoted in Chapter VI supra. The fact that a person on "Federal work relief" was holding the position, or that no funds were available to pay the one to be reinstated, was not to deprive the latter of being reemployed, as the city was not without control of the personnel on the type of project involved.

[30] Matter of Finegan v. Cohen (1937) 275 N. Y. 432. Section 1006 New York City Charter Ch. 867, L. 1934 and Ch. 292, L. 1935. Article 2, Section 6 providing for equal representation of the two political parties in the counting of votes was not violated by these laws.

[31] Matter of Sullivan v. Finegan (1937) 275 N. Y. 479. Section 722 New York City Charter L. 1901, Ch. 466 amended L. 1904, Ch. 700.

[32] Cox v. McElligott (1937) 163 Misc. 619. Supreme Court New York County Special Term. Section 1560 Greater New York Charter. This sec-

EDUCATION, CIVIL SERVICE 191

Law giving an exemption to persons employed in a public welfare department or emergency relief bureau, so as to make such persons eligible for examinations for positions in the particular department of bureau without being high school graduates;[33] and the law conferring upon the Municipal Civil Service Commission the power to examine applicants for plumbers' licenses and requiring ten years experience in the plumbing industry in the United States, or three years experience and a technical degree from a college or university approved by the New York Board of Regents.[34]

The conservation of natural resources has its place in the constitutional history of the state. Article 7, Section 7 of the Constitution of 1894 provides:

> The lands of the state, now owned or hereafter acquired, constituting the forest preserve as now fixed by law, shall be forever kept as wild forest land. They shall not be leased, sold, or exchanged, or be taken by any corporation, public or private, nor shall the timber thereon be sold, removed, or destroyed.[35]

---

tion was also held valid in Jones v. Valentine (1937) 164 Misc. 443. Supreme Court Queens County. In the opinion of the judges no contractual relationship was involved and Article 1, Section 1, quoted supra, was not considered violated.

[33] Matter of O'Callaghan v. Finegan (1937) 166 Misc. 556. Supreme Court New York County Special Term. Affirmed without opinion, 276 N. Y. 587. Livingston Act (L. 1937, Ch. 358) Section 6, amending Public Welfare Law by adding Sections 3-j and 3-k. The court considered the constitutional provision violated by the declaration in the same statute that experience in the department or bureau must be regarded as having greater weight than experience obtained in any other department or agency.

[34] Matter of Bendetto v. Kern (1938) 167 Misc. 831. Supreme Court New York. Ch. 610, L. 1936. The provisions authorizing the Municipal Service Commission to call upon the plumbing industry for assistance in the preparation, conduct and rating on the practical and written examinations were held invalid.

[35] Amendments Proposed, *op. cit.*, p. 564.
In 1913 this section was amended by adding the following:
> But the legislature may by general laws provide for the use of not exceeding three per centum of such lands for the construction and main-

The authorization given the Conservation Commission in 1929 to remove trees to construct a bob-sleigh run was held unconstitutional, because of this provision.[36] In 1898 the legislature authorized Cornell University to take title to lands purchased by the state for its Department of Forestry to hold for thirty years and then to be part of the forest preserve. This was held constitutional by the Court of Appeals.[37] The courts also sustained acts abandoning portions of the canal system of the state, despite Article 7, Section 8 forbidding the disposal of the Erie, Oswego, Champlain, Cayuga and Seneca, or Black

tenance of reservoirs for municipal water supply, for the canals of the state and to regulate the flow of streams. Such reservoirs shall be constructed, owned and controlled by the state, but such work shall not be undertaken until after the boundaries and high flow lines thereof shall have been accurately surveyed and fixed, and after public notice, hearing and determination that such lands are required for such public use. The expense of any such improvements shall be apportioned on the public and private property and municipalities benefited to the extent of the benefits received. Any such reservoir shall always be operated by the state and the legislature shall provide for a charge upon the property and municipalities benefited for a reasonable return to the state upon the value of the rights and property of the state used and the services of the state rendered, which shall be fixed for terms of not exceeding ten years and be readjustable at the end of any term. Unsanitary conditions shall not be created or continued by any such public works. A violation of any of the provisions of this section may be restrained at the suit of the people or, with consent of the supreme court in appellate division, on notice to the attorney-general at the suit of any citizen. *Ibid.*, pp. 574-75.
In 1918 the following sentence was added after the first two sentences:
Nothing contained in this section shall prevent the state from constructing a state highway from Saranac Lake in Franklin county to Long Lake in Hamilton county and thence to Old Forge in Herkimer county by way of Blue Mountain Lake and Racquette Lake. *Ibid.*, p. 579.
In 1927 there were added to this last sentence the words:
and nothing shall prevent the state from constructing a state highway in Essex county from Wilmington to the top of Whiteface mountain. *Ibid.*, p. 590.

36 Association for the Protection of the Adirondacks v. MacDonald (1930) 253 N. Y. 234. Ch. 417, L. 1929.

37 People v. Brooklyn Cooperage Company (1907) 187 N. Y. 142. Ch. 122, L. 1898. Besides Article 7, Section 7, Article 8, Section 9 quoted in Chapter II above was at issue.

River canals;[38] and providing for river regulation by storage reservoirs.[39] A prohibition against the depletion by pumping of a subterranean supply of percolating waters or natural carbonic acid gas by the surface owner was sustained by both the Court of Appeals and the United States Supreme Court.[40]

Although the cases mentioned have little in common in subject matter, a lowest common denominator of relationship may be found in that they represent different aspects of obligations imposed upon the legislature in the course of time, namely: to support an adequate educational system, to maintain an efficient civil service and to conserve the state's natural resources, particularly its forests. A record of twenty-seven statutes sustained in the courts, against nine condemned as violations of the Constitution, demonstrates that the judges and the legislature saw eye to eye on the meaning of the clauses adjudicated in three-fourths of the cases to reach the courts.

[38] Pelo v. Stevens (1909) 66 Misc. 35. Supreme Court Monroe Special Term. Barge Canal Law (L. 1903, Ch. 147). Other provisions objected to in this case included a tax to pay bonds issued for an improvement in the canals, only until the bonds were due and not until they were paid. Ch 302, L. 1906. The legislature had the right, in the court's opinion, to assume that a substantial increase in the valuation of the property to be taxed would continue in the future as in the past; in Kibbee v. Lyons (1922) 202 A. D. 562 3rd Dept., Ch. 687, L. 1921 amending Section 3 of the Barge Canal Act, abandoning a portion of the old Erie Canal in the lumber district of the City of Albany, without submitting the act to a referendum, was passed upon and found valid by the Appellate Division because no debt was considered contracted which would have required a referendum under Article 7, Section 4, and because Section 5 of the Barge Canal Act allowed useless lands to be abandoned.

[39] Board of Black River Regulating District v. Ogdensburg (1922) 203 A. D. 43 4th Dept. Article VI-A Conservation Law, Ch. 662, L. 1915.

[40] Hathorn v. Natural Carbonic Gas Company (1909) 194 N. Y. 326. Ch. 429, L. 1908; Lindsley v. Natural Carbonic Gas Company (1911) 220 U. S. 61.

CHAPTER XII
TAXATION

THE importance of taxation as a means for maintaining the government of the state was realized so strongly by the judges that it was relatively late before statutes on that subject were questioned on a large scale.[1] Even after the courts began to declare some of the statutes unconstitutional, their opinions bore witness to the fact that they appreciated the role that this power occupied, then and now, in the functioning of the body politic. The general tendency has been to approach this class of legislation with a respect not always accorded to other regulations of economic activity within the state.

The objections to which this kind of enactment was subject resembled strongly those which were raised against the laws discussed in the previous chapters. There was no example in this period of a tax challenged as an encroachment on the judicial power, but if a very high imposition had been laid upon the salaries of the judges, such a case might have arisen. The single instance in which a tax was overturned as an infringement on civil liberties has already been discussed.[2]

Arguments against the validity of the taxes were frequently founded on clauses of the Federal Constitution, particularly the commerce, privileges, due process and equal protection clauses. Three acts were questioned without success as placing an undue burden on interstate commerce. The first of these, the Stock Transfer Stamp Tax Law, placed a uniform tax on all sales, agreements or memoranda of sales of stock certificates made within the state. The tax on transfers was distinguished from one on property.[3] A franchise tax which New York imposed

[1] E. S. Corwin, The Extension of Judicial Review in New York, *op. cit.*, pp. 298, 305.

[2] See People ex rel. Lemon v. Elmore, Chapter III note 20 supra.

[3] People ex rel. Hatch v. Reardon (1906) 110 A. D. 821 1st Dept. Ch. 241, L. 1905. Affirmed 184 N. Y. 431. Affirmed in 1907, 204 U. S. 152.

on foreign corporations doing business here was upheld by the Appellate Division in 1908.[4] A later tax was sustained as applied to freighting which was a continuation of carriage from without the state.[5]

In 1937 a law authorizing New York City to tax the proceeds of special orders obtained in that city for goods to be manufactured in a foreign state, and shipped from there in packages designated for particular customers, was held to violate the commerce clause.[6] The privileged character of the national banks was an issue in two cases. In the first, a law providing in effect for the taxation at the rate of one per cent of certain moneyed capital coming into competition with the business of national banks, and for exemption from other taxes, was sustained.[7] In the second, sections of the Tax Law which

[4] People ex rel. Union Sulphur Co. v. Glynn (1908) 125 A. D. 328 3rd Dept. L. 1896, Ch. 908 Sections 181, 182, amended L. 1901, Ch. 558; later L. 1906, Ch. 474, L. 1907, Ch. 734.
A franchise tax on property which allowed no deduction from the capital stock, unless some specific portion of the corporate property were outside of the state during the whole tax year, was sustained by the United States Supreme Court in 1906 in New York Central Railroad v. Miller. 202 U. S. 584. Ch. 908, L. 1896 Section 182. The allegations against the tax were based on the due process and commerce clauses.

[5] People ex rel. New York and Albany Lighterage Co. v. Lynch (1932) 259 N. Y. 638. Section 184 Tax Law (Cons. Laws, Ch. 60). Objection was also voiced on the ground that the Fourteenth Amendment was violated. In 1915 the United States Supreme Court had passed on the validity of this law. It imposed a tax on transmission and transportation corporations of the state, for the privilege of carrying on business in a corporate capacity within the state bounds, on the gross earnings on transportation originating and terminating within the state, expressly excluding earnings derived in business of an interstate character. The Supreme Court decided the law was constitutional. Cornell Steamboat Co. v. Sohmer (1915) 235 U. S. 549.

[6] National Cash Register Co. v. Taylor (1937) 276 N. Y. 208. Ch. 873, L. 1934.

[7] People ex rel. Pratt v. Goldfogle (1926) 242 N. Y. 277. Ch. 897, L. 1923. The United States Supreme Court decided in 1913 that under Section 5219 of the Revised Statutes, passed by Congress, granting the authority to the state to tax "all the shares of national banking associations located within the state" with the restriction that "the taxation shall not be at a greater rate than is assessed upon other moneyed capital in the hands of in-

included interest on United States bonds and dividends from national banks and affiliated corporations among the assets upon which franchise taxes were assessed were upheld by the Court of Appeals.[8]

Under Article 4, Section 2, Clause 3, the privilege clause, seven statutes were held unconstitutional. In order to determine the Franchise Tax on foreign corporations the legislature had established a complicated formula. According to this, the tax was to be imposed on a portion of the total net income of the corporation for the last preceding year, to be determined by the ratio between the value of the assets of the corporation of certain classes—such as real and tangible personal property, and bills and accounts receivable—located in New York, and the value of all its assets of those classes. Under one provision of this law, the dividends from investments in stocks of other corporations were to be included in the income for computation, but the principal was to be disregarded in the allocation of the assets. This was considered a violation of the privileges clause by the Court of Appeals.[9] Placing a tax on transfers by

---

dividual citizens of such state." Chapter 12 of the Laws of 1909 (Cons. Laws, Ch. 60) was constitutional. Section 24 of this law provided that the owners of bank stock (state or national) should not be entitled to deduction from the taxable value of their shares, because of their personal indebtedness, while Section 21 permitted all persons to deduct their debts from their other taxable personal property, including, as was claimed, other moneyed capital. According to the court, the same system of taxation was not required, providing there was no injustice, inequality or unfriendly discrimination. Amoskeag Savings Bank v. Purdy 231 U. S. 373.

[8] People ex rel. Northern Finance Corporation v. Lynch (1933) 262 N. Y. 477. Sections 208 and 209 Tax Law.

[9] People ex rel. Alpha Portland Cement Co. v. Knapp (1920) 230 N. Y. 48. Amendment to Subds. 3 and 6 of Section 214, Article 9-A Tax Law, L. 1918, Ch. 417. In 1924 the United States Supreme Court declared valid a later version of this tax which included the shares held by a foreign corporation in other corporations among the assets to be allocated for the determination of the tax. Bass, Ratcliff and Gretton Ltd. v. State Tax Commission 266 U. S. 271. Article 9-A Tax Law (Cons. Laws, 1909, Ch. 60) as amended by L. 1917, Ch. 726 and L. 1918, Chapters 271, 276 and 417. In 1929 the same court sustained the imposition of a tax on every foreign corporation doing business in New York, computed upon the basis of the capital stock

TAXATION 197

will or intestate succession of property of non-residents within the state, which was sometimes heavier and sometimes lighter than the amount imposed on residents, also infringed upon the privileges clause.[10] It was held in 1928 that a license tax on foreign corporations with stock of no par value, of six cents on each share employed in the state, was not applicable to those already doing business here, but was otherwise valid.[11] In so far as a law of 1928 attempted to revoke the exemption of non-resident estates for the period for July 1, 1925 to March 12, 1928 by stating that there should be no refund of taxes collected during that period, unless the laws of the state of the non-resident transferees made provision for the refund of like taxes collected upon transfers by residents of this state, and declared non-residents, in such circumstances, to have lost any privilege of its reciprocal exemption, and to be subject to the tax, it was in conflict with the Constitution. However, the remainder of the law, exempting estates of non-residents from the transfer tax where the state in which they resided extended a similar exemption to residents of this state, was upheld.[12] The legislature attempted in 1929 to validate the ruling of an administrative board under the statute held unconstitutional in

---

employed by the corporation within the state during the first year it did business there, the amount of the stock so employed being that proportion of its total issued capital stock which its gross assets employed within the state bore to its gross assets wherever employed. New York v. Latrobe 279 U. S. 421. Section 181, Article 9 Tax Law. Ch. 62, L. 1909 as amended.

[10] Smith v. Loughman (1937) 245 N. Y. 486. Article 10-A Tax Law L. 1925, Ch. 143, Section 9 (Cons. Laws, Ch. 60); to the same effect was the decision in People ex rel. Nash v. Loughman (1927) 245 N. Y. 649.

A provision in the Inheritance Tax Statute imposing a transfer tax on property within the state belonging to a non-resident at time of death was held to apply to promissory notes the makers of which were non-residents of New York. This interpretation did not violate the due process clause. Wheeler v. New York (1914) 233 U. S. 434.

[11] People ex rel. Griffith Inc. v. Loughman 249 N. Y. 369. Section 181 Tax Law (Cons. Laws, Ch. 60) amended L. 1921, Ch. 705.

[12] City Bank Farmers' Trust Co. v. New York Central Railroad Co. (1930) 253 N. Y. 49. Section 248-p Tax Law (Cons. Laws, Ch. 60) amended L. 1925, Ch. 143.

the Alpha Portland Cement Company case, but was forestalled by the Appellate Division.[13] In 1936 the Appellate Division decided that the state was without power to tax a resident on account of rents or income received from land located beyond its borders, but this decision was reversed by the United States Supreme Court in the following year.[14] Another section of the Tax Law which included intangible property wherever situated within the gross estate of a decedent, without reference to the fact that it might have acquired an actual or business situs outside the state, was held invalid in 1937.[15]

Laws held consistent with the privileges clause included the following: provisions of the charter of the City of Niagara Falls concerning the assessment of lands within the city which were held applicable to the lands of non-resident owners;[16] the taxation under the Transfer Tax Laws of a grant of property to others from which the grantor was to receive income until her death, at which time the transfer was to become fully effective, at a higher rate than other types

[13] People ex rel. International Salt Co. v. Graves (1934) 242 A. D. 124 3rd Dept. L. 1929, Ch. 218.

[14] People ex rel. Cohn v. Graves (1936) 246 A. D. 335 3rd Dept. Affirmed 271 N. Y. 353. This decision was, however, reversed in New York ex rel. Cohn v. Graves (1937) 300 U. S. 308 when the United States Supreme Court held the tax valid. Section 359 Tax Law, as amended by L. 1935, Ch. 933. The United States Supreme Court had held unconstitutional in 1920 a general tax on the income of both residents and non-residents, which allowed exemptions to residents with increases for married persons and for dependents, but gave no equivalent exemptions to non-residents. Travis v. Yale and Towne Manufacturing Co. 252 U. S. 60. Ch. 627, L. 1919. In 1937 a tax imposed upon the profits realized by a non-resident upon the sale of a right appurtenent to membership in the New York Stock Exchange was sustained in New York ex rel. Whitney v. Graves 299 U. S. 366 by the United States Supreme Court. Sections 351 and 351-a Tax Law.

[15] Matter of Brown 274 N. Y. 10. Section 249-r Tax Law. (Cons. Laws, Ch. 60). This section, in so far as it imposed an estate tax on real property held by a husband and wife, as tenants by the entirety, upon the death of one of them, had earlier been held constitutional in Matter of Weiden (1933) 263 N. Y. 107.

[16] Clinton v. Krull (1908) 125 A. D. 157 4th Dept. Ch. 143, L. 1892. The lands assessed were located with reasonable definiteness.

of transfers of property;[17] a tax on the transfer of the shares of stock owned by a non-resident in a foreign corporation owning real estate within the State of New York, which fixed the tax as the proportion of the value of the decedent's stock that the real estate bore to the value of the entire property of the corporation;[18] a tax on the income from business carried on in the state by non-residents;[19] a provision that shares without par value should be deemed to have a face value of one hundred dollars in determining the franchise tax on foreign corporations;[20] a transfer tax on the estates of both resident and non-resident decedents dying between July 1, 1925 and March 12, 1928;[21] and a tax on the exercise of the power of appointment of a resident, as though the property to which such appointment referred belonged absolutely to the donee of the power, except that where the donor was a resident, and the donee, at the time the appointment was effective, was a non-resident, the property was taxable as having been transferred in the estate of the donor.[22]

[17] Matter of Patterson 146 A. D. 286 4th Dept. L. 1896, Ch. 908 and L. 1909, Ch. 12.

[18] Matter of McMullen (1921) 114 Misc. 505. Surrogate's Court New York County. Section 2, Subd. 2 Tax Law. Ch. 664, L. 1915.

[19] People ex rel. Stafford v. Travis (1921) 231 N. Y. 339. Tax Law as amended by Ch. 627, L. 1919. An assessment on income, under this law, from bonds and debts secured by mortgages, upon which latter a mortgage recording tax had been paid, was upheld by the United States Supreme Court in Clyde v. Gilchrist (1923) 262 U. S. 94, since no exemption from the taxation of income was obtained by the payment of that tax.

[20] People ex rel. Terminal and Town Taxi Corporation v. Walsh (1922) 202 A. D. 651 3rd Dept. Ch. 640, L. 1920. Section 214 Tax Law.

[21] Matter of Caulfield (1930) 136 Misc. 685. Surrogate's Court New York County. Article 10 Tax Law as amended by L. 1925, Ch. 143.

[22] Matter of Davison (1930) 137 Misc. 852. Surrogate's Court Kings County. Subd. 4, Section 220 Tax Law. The claims against this act based on the due process and the privileges clauses were without merit, in the opinion of the surrogate, for the statute, fairly interpreted, required a construction equalizing the taxes paid upon the exercise of a power of appointment by a resident and by a non-resident.

The contract clause was urged to no avail against several statutes. One such statute provided the calculation of the franchise tax on foreign insurance corporations might be computed upon the premiums received during the past year, and not merely upon those received from new business, but the tax was not to be retroactive.[23] In 1908 the Appellate Division upheld an act of 1896 repealing the exemption from taxes granted a hospital by a special charter as far as the lands leased to tenants were concerned.[24] The next year the revocation and cancellation of a liquor tax certificate, on the ground that a disorderly house was being maintained upon the licensed premises, was likewise declared to be valid.[25] A tax, which was not retroactive, on the transfer of the one-half interest of a decedent in a jointly held mortgage was adjudged constitutional in

[23] People ex rel. Connecticut Mutual Life Insurance Co. v. Kelsey (1906) 116 A. D. 97 3rd Dept. Amendment to Subd. 5, Section 189 Tax Law by Ch. 94, L. 1905.

[24] People ex rel. Roosevelt Hospital v. Raymond (1908) 126 A. D. 720 1st Dept. General Tax Law Ch. 908, L. 1896. A tax exemption granted one corporation was not transferred to another corporation when the first corporation lost its identity by being merged in the second, which acquired its property. This was the gist of the decision in Rochester Railway Co. v. City of Rochester (1907) 205 U. S. 236. Ch. 252, L. 1884 imposed the tax to which objection had been made. In Interborough Rapid Transit Co. v. Sohmer (1915) 237 U. S. 276 the United States Supreme Court held that a law giving exemption from taxation to a person or persons constructing and operating a railroad, in respect to his or their interest under the contract for the construction, and in respect to the rolling stock and other equipment of the railroad, need not extend to a tax on the privilege to operate as a corporation in case the parties decide to operate the road in a corporate form. Exemption under Ch. 752, Section 35 and Ch. 729, Section 4, L. 1896, reenacted L. 1900, Ch. 616, Section 4. Tax Laws 1907-1910, Section 184. Giving tax exemption as to city and county taxes to a railroad company was a repealable privilege in the view of the United States Supreme Court in Troy Union Railroad Co. v. Mealy (1920) 254 U. S. 47. Ch. 201, L. 1909.

[25] Matter of Clement (Siemens Certificate) (1910) 136 A. D. 199 2nd Dept. Chapters 144 and 350, L. 1908 and Subd. 8, Section 15, Liquor Tax Law (L. 1909, Ch. 281, later amended by L. 1910, Chapters 485, 503).

1917,[26] as was the taxation of estates by the entirety which, at the enactment of the particular statute, had already vested.[27] A case of significance was decided in 1918 when the Court of Appeals confirmed the validity of the tax on transfers of property by authority of the power of appointment given by a deed or will. This device of appointment had been used to circumvent the inheritance taxes.[28] A part of the Tax Law, which had granted a corporation credit toward the annual franchise tax for the amount of taxes paid on capital stock or personal property assessed in any tax district in 1917, was amended because the original act was unfair to those municipalities whose fiscal year was not co-terminous with the tax calendar year. In such districts credit was only allowed locally in the ratio that the portion of the year 1918 bore to the calendar year. This amendment, which was retroactive, satisfied the Appellate Division as to its constitutionality in 1919.[29] It was permissible as well to tax a voting trust agreement of stock where the redelivery of the stock was taxable.[30] Finally, a tax on the

[26] Matter of Teller 178 A. D. 450 1st Dept. Subd. 7 Section 220 Tax Law, as added by Ch. 664, L. 1915.

[27] Matter of Moebus (1917) 178 A. D. 709 2nd Dept. Subd. 7 Section 220 Tax Law, as amended by L. 1916, Ch. 223.

[28] Matter of Wendel 223 N. Y. 433. (Cons. Laws, Ch. 20) Section 220 Subd. 6 Tax Law L. 1910, Ch. 706. The United States Supreme Court had upheld a transfer tax on the exercise of the power of appointment, in the same manner as though the estate passing thereby belonged absolutely to the person exercising the power, in Chanler v. Kelsey (1907) 205 U. S. 466. Ch. 284, L. 1897.
In 1912 the United States Supreme Court upheld, against charges of violating the due process and equal protection clauses, a tax on the transfer of property, passing under a deed, to take effect at the grantor's death, which included personal property with a situs in the state when the deed was made. Keeney v. Comptroller (1912) 222 U. S. 525. Ch. 908, L. 1896, Section 220, Subds. 1, 3.

[29] People ex rel. Iroquois Door Co. v. Knapp 186 A. D. 172 3rd Dept. Ch. 271, L. 1918, amending Section 219-j Tax Law.

[30] Chicago Great Western Railroad Co. v. State of New York (1921) 197 A. D. 742 3rd Dept. Section 270 Tax Law, as amended by L. 1911, Ch. 352.

gross income of utilities in New York City, by local laws passed pursuant to state laws of 1934 and 1935, was ruled not in conflict with the contract or the due process clauses.[31]

Conflict with the due process clause was frequently charged against the tax laws. The Court of Appeals upheld a provision for the taxation of debts secured by mortgages, the proceeds of which were to belong one-half to the state and one-half to the locality in which the tax was collected, despite contentions that the equal protection and due process clauses were violated.[32] A law of 1909 attempting to complete an imperfect assessment was held constitutional, except for the effect of permitting a correction of assessments in New York City, because notice was not given. Another objection was the prohibition against the court giving relief in pending actions.[33] Another law failed to provide for notice to a landowner of a proposed reassessment, and charged the land with the unpaid and rejected tax, but was upheld in a lower court.[34] An authorization given the Board of Taxes and Assessments to correct the tax roll in a ten-day period while the books were open, adding the names of owners or valuations which might have been omitted, was considered constitutional by the Appellate Divi-

[31] New York Rapid Transit Corporation v. City of New York (1937) 275 N. Y. 258; Brooklyn and Queens Transit Corporation v. City of New York 275 N. Y. 454. Ch. 873, L. 1934 and Ch. 601, L. 1935.

[32] People ex rel. Eisman v. Ronner (1906) 185 N. Y. 285. Ch. 729, L. 1905.

[33] People ex rel. American Exchange National Bank v. Purdy (1909) 196 N. Y. 270. The same law was involved in a case of the same name occurring in the following year, when it was held valid as providing for taking necessary and jurisdictional steps at a later stage than usual in assessment proceedings. 199 N. Y. 51.

In 1908 the United States Supreme Court had held that land subject to a mortgage might be taxed for its full value without deduction of the mortgage debt from the valuation either of the land or of the owner's personal property. Paddell v. City of New York 211 U. S. 446. L. 1902, Ch. 171, Section 1.

[34] People ex rel. Consolidated Water Co. v. Barrett (1910) 68 Misc. 59. Supreme Court Westchester Special Term. Ch. 193, L. 1877.

sion.[35] So, too, were laws providing that failure to pay a stock transfer tax at the time of transfer would bar an action by the vendor to enforce the contract of sale,[36] requiring that no person should sell a stamp issued to be placed on stock transfers without the written consent of the Comptroller and making a violation of the provision a misdemeanor,[37] and allowing a person to exercise the common-law right of acting judicially to have a review of an assessment by a common council.[38] Estates in expectancy were required by a section of the Tax Law to be appraised at their full undiminished value, without diminution on account of any valuation previously made of the particular estates, for the purpose of taxation.[39] The Appellate Division asserted in 1916 that a law could not transfer title to land by taking away rights previously vested, in a case in which the county seal had been omitted on a tax warrant issued to the receiver of taxes.[40] The Statute of Limitations could apply to a person claiming land which had been sold under an invalid tax sale, in the opinion of the Appellate Division, however.[41] In 1916 Surrogate Fowler stated that an amendment to the Tax Law making taxable intangible property held in the joint names of two or more persons, either as tenants by the entirety or as joint tenants, upon the death of one, could

35 People ex rel. Stebbins v. Purdy (1931) 144 A. D. 361 1st Dept. L. 1906, Ch. 207 Section 894a New York City Charter.

36 Sheridan v. Tucker (1911) 145 A. D. 145 4th Dept. L. 1906, Ch. 414.

37 People ex rel. Isaacs v. Moran (1912) 150 A. D. 226 1st Dept. Section 271a Tax Law (Cons. Laws, Ch. 60) L. 1909, Ch. 62 as added by L. 1911, Ch. 12.

38 People ex rel. Empie v. Smith (1915) 166 A. D. 406 3rd Dept. Section 135 Charter of Johnstown, L. 1905, Ch. 593. The opposite construction would have been unconstitutional.

39 Matter of Whitewright (1915) 89 Misc. 97. Surrogate's Court New York County. Section 230 Tax Law.

40 People ex rel. Boenig v. Hegeman (1916) 172 A. D. 94 2nd Dept. Ch. 470, L. 1911.

41 Doud v. The Huntington Hebrew Congregation (1917) 178 A. D. 748 2nd Dept. General Laws Ch. 24.

not be given a retroactive effect so as to tax an interest vested prior to its enactment, since such a construction would in effect impose a tax upon property and not upon the succession to property, thus violating the due process clause.[42] The Court of Appeals held in 1919 that a gift by deed of trust, to take effect in enjoyment upon the death of the donor, with the reservation of intermediate use and with complete power of revocation, was so near a gift by will, that it might be declared substantially identical for the purpose of taxation.[43] In 1926 the Court of Appeals ruled that in a situation where the distribution of income was in the discretion of a fiduciary, a provision that the income tax was to be imposed upon an estate or trust, or otherwise on each beneficiary, did not imply that the choice as to which should be taxed need be arbitrary.[44] The imposition of a graduated tax on the transfer of contingent remainders, this tax to be measured by the value at the testator's death of the estate transferred, undiminished by the value of the intervening life estate, by a law requiring the executor to deposit security for the payment of the tax, but postponing the definitive assessment and the payment of the tax until after the death of the life tenant, was considered consistent with the due process clause by both the Court of Appeals and the United States Supreme Court.[45] The Appellate Division sustained a law which authorized the town of Caroga to reassess certain property in 1924 for the year 1923, the latter assessment

[42] Matter of Horler (1916) 97 Misc. 587. Surrogate's Court New York County. Amendment (L. 1915, Ch. 864) to Section 220 Tax Law.

[43] Matter of Schmidlapp (1923) 236 N. Y. 278. The act involved was the amendment to the Tax Law by L. 1919, Ch. 626.

[44] People ex rel. Bank of America v. State Tax Commission 244 N. Y. 56; Matter of Minnick v. Newmann 244 N. Y. 530; Matter of Nugent v. Fitzgerald 246 N. Y. 531; Matter of Van Ness v. Abrams 246 N. Y. 532. Subd. 4 Section 365 Tax Law (Cons. Laws, Ch. 60) amended L. 1922, Ch. 466.

[45] Matter of Simonson (1927) 246 N. Y. 601; Matter of Hecht 246 N. Y. 602; affirmed in Salomon v. State Tax Commission (1929) 278 U. S. 484. Amendments to Section 230 Tax Law made by Ch. 144, L. 1925.

having been stricken from the 1923 rolls on the ground of indefiniteness of description of the property to be assessed.[46]

In the last five years of the period under examination, the following tax laws challenged under the due process clause were held constitutional: a tax on the transfers of real property belonging to the estates of decedents, which had been held unconstitutional by the surrogate, who thought that the act discriminated against citizens of New York;[47] the inclusion in the tax base for the purpose of determining the minimum tax on a corporation, of a percentage of the salaries and compensation paid to officers and stockholders owning over five per cent of the issued capital stock;[48] the curing of an administrative defect in an existing law so as to prevent the evasion of the franchise tax by the transfer of assets or franchises from one corporation to another, a law considered retroactive but not arbitrary;[49] the taxation of employers in order to raise funds for the relief of the unemployed;[50] a tax at a stated rate per share on the sales, deliveries or transfers of stock shares or certificates;[51] a transfer tax on the estates of non-resident decendents, not invalid because of the direction that intangible personal property not within the state was to be used as a measure of the tax on property here;[52] the inclusion of a fund subject to a limited power of appointment over the principal

[46] People ex rel. Adirondack Power and Light Corporation v. Durey (1927) 221 A. D. 294 3rd Dept. Ch. 504, L. 1924.

[47] Matter of Cole (1934) 263 N. Y. 643. Articles 10 and 10-A Tax Law.

[48] People ex rel. Presbrey Co. v. Lynch (1934) 265 N. Y. 454. Subd. 10, Section 214 Tax Law.

[49] People ex rel. Best and Co. v. Graves (1934) 265 N. Y. 431. Ch. 323, L. 1925 amending Section 214-a Tax Law.

[50] Chamberlin Inc. v. Andrews (1936) 271 N. Y. 1. Labor Law, Art. 18; L. 1935, Ch. 468.

[51] Vaughan v State of New York (1936) 272 N. Y. 102. (Cons. Laws, Ch. 60) amended L. 1933, Ch. 643, Sections 270 and 270-a Tax Law; followed in Williams v. State of New York (1936) 273 N. Y. 458.

[52] Matter of Lagergren (1937) 276 N. Y. 184. Section 249-p. Tax Law.

as part of a decedent's gross estate for the purpose of taxation;[53] and a tax on the undiminished remainder of an appointive fund, imposed though an heir refused to accept the share of the fund and elected to take under the will of the original donor.[54]

An amendment to the Charter of Long Beach was held unconstitutional in so far as it attempted to discharge that city from its liability to the county for uncollected taxes certified to it prior to the date of the relieving statute. The indebtedness and cause of action constituted property in the opinion of the Court of Appeals.[55]

Claims that the classifications made in tax laws were arbitrary were a frequent source of criticism. The following laws were sustained in the face of these allegations: the exemption of crossings outside a city or incorporated villages and the authorization of assessments upon crossings in cities or villages;[56] the assignment of a definite portion of the cost of an

[53] Matter of Vanderbilt (1937) 163 Misc. 667. Surrogate's Court New York County. Subd. 7-a, Section 249-r Tax Law. The tax was on the privilege of transmitting an appointed fund by will.

[54] Matter of Lathers (1938) 167 Misc. 186. Surrogate's Court Westchester County. Tax Law, Section 220, Subd. 5, as amended by L. 1897, Ch. 284.

[55] County of Nassau v. Long Beach (1936) 272 N. Y. 260. Ch. 594, L. 1933, amending L. 1922, Ch. 635.

[56] People ex rel. New York Central and Hudson River Railroad Co. v. Woodbury (1910) 74 Misc. 131. Supreme Court Albany Special Term. Ch. 720, L. 1907. The reasoning given for this decision was that every railroad company was assessed in the same way upon the same class of property, and the burden fell upon each alike. In addition the court upheld a provision authorizing the assessment of special franchises by a state board instead of by the local assessors, since this type of taxable property was considered a new species never before assessed, so that the right of home rule was not impaired. The court also remarked that a special term should not declare a law unconstitutional unless clearly so.

A provision of the Inheritance Tax Law taxing the personalty of non-resident decedents who owned realty in New York, but not taxing the personalty of that group if they did not own realty, was thought consistent with both the equal protection and due process clauses by the United States Supreme Court in Beers v. Glynn (1909) 211 U. S. 477, Ch. 713, L. 1887 amending Ch. 483, L. 1887.

improvement in New York City to be paid proportionately to the assessed values of the real property of certain boroughs, when another portion was to be paid by the owners of property peculiarly and directly benefited by the improvement;[57] a five per cent tax placed on transfers of investments, unless a stamp tax of 75¢ per hundred dollars face value had been paid, or unless the personal property tax had been paid, or unless the decedent had been engaged in the purchase and sale of investments as a business;[58] the defining of the method for the collection of a tax and the maintenance of a sewer, despite the claim that the property assessed had no use for the trunk part of the sewer;[59] the exemption from taxation for ten years of new buildings planned exclusively for dwelling purposes in New York City;[60] the taxing of every corporation subject to the franchise tax acquiring the major portion of the assets or the franchise of another corporation exercising the franchise or doing business in this state on its net income for the ensuing year except for the part used in measuring the franchise tax;[61] the classification of forest and reforested lands for taxa-

[57] Goodale v. City of New York (1914) 85 Misc. 603. Supreme Court New York Special Term. Ch. 679, L. 1911. A distinction was made between an assessment levied for a benefit received and a tax imposed to meet the necessary cost of carrying on the city government.

[58] Matter of Watson (1919) 226 N. Y. 384. Article 15 as amended and Section 221-b Tax Law as added by Ch. 700, L. 1917; affirmed in Watson v. The State Comptroller (1920) 254 U. S. 122 by the United States Supreme Court.

[59] Valley Farms Co. v. Yonkers (1921), 231 N. Y. 558. Ch. 646, L. 1917; affirmed in Valley Farms Co. v. County of Westchester (1923) 261 U. S. 155 by the United States Supreme Court. No notice had been given of the valuation of the property for this special assessment, since the valuation for general taxation had been used.

[60] Moberg Co. v. Mohr (1923) 236 N. Y. 553; Hermitage Co. v. Goldfogle (1923) 236 N. Y. 554. Ch. 949, L. 1920 and Ch. 444, L. 1921.

[61] Matter of French Co. v. Lynch (1931) 233 A. D. 178 3rd Dept.; People ex rel. Salisbury Axle Co. v. Lynch (1932) 259 N. Y. 228. Section 214-a Tax Law. L. 1918, Ch. 292 as amended by L. 1925, Ch. 323, in Matter of French Co.; as amended by L. 1919, Ch. 628 in People ex rel. Salisbury Axle Co. v. Lynch.

tion and the direction that so long as the forest growth was to remain uncut, such lands were to be assessed at no higher valuation than at the time of the filing of the application for classification;[62] and the exemptions of a private limited dividend corporation from taxes by virtue of the State Housing Law,[63] and of the Home Owners Loan Corporation from the payment of a mortgage recording tax.[64]

The one tax law which the courts branded as an example of arbitrary classification was an amendment to the Stock Transfer Act of 1906 which imposed a tax of 2¢ " on each share of $100 of face value or fraction thereof " instead of " on each $100 of face value or fraction thereof " as in 1905. This would have meant a $2 tax on a sale of one hundred shares of a face value of $10, while only a 20¢ tax on the sale of ten shares of a face value of $100.[65]

In 1920 a section of the Liquor Tax Law was found in partial violation of the Eighteenth Amendment, in so far as it permitted traffic in liquor having a percentage of alcohol greater than defined by that act as intoxicating, on the payment of a tax. The portions of it were considered valid, however, that made it a crime to traffic in liquor having an alcoholic content of 2.75 per cent.[66]

The Court of Appeals held invalid in 1928 a tax upon an alleged interest under a contract with the United States to purchase the structures and fixed equipment erected and owned

[62] People ex rel. Luther v. McDermott (1934) 265 N. Y. 47. Section 13 Tax Law (Cons. Laws, Ch. 60).

[63] People ex rel. Academy Housing Corporation v. Miller (1937) 163 Misc. 500. Supreme Court Special Term Bronx County. State Housing Law, L. 1926, Ch. 823 as amended.

[64] H.O.L.C. v. Barone (1937) 164 Misc. 187. Supreme Court Onondaga County. Section 252 Tax Law.

[65] People ex rel Farrington v. Mensching (1907) 187 N. Y. 8. Section 1, Ch. 414, L. 1906 amending Stock Transfer Tax Act. Section 315 Tax Law, as amended by Ch. 241, L. 1905.

[66] People v. Cook (1921) 197 A. D. 155 4th Dept. Liquor Tax Law as amended by Ch. 911, L. 1920.

by the United States upon land of the relator in the case in the City of Buffalo, as it would tend to impede the government in disposing of the plant.[67]

Turning from the Federal Constitution [68] to the State Constitution, one law was held to violate the home rule provisions of the latter document. The provision for the establishment by the Board of Aldermen of Syracuse of a Board of Review appointed by Supreme Court justices resident in the city, for appeals from aggrieved assessees before review under another section of the statute, was judged invalid because it attempted to transfer to a board, to be appointed by state officers, essential functions previously belonging to the assessors of the City of Syracuse.[69]

The prohibition against gifts of money or credit to private individuals was the basis for Surrogate Foley's decision in 1924 that an amendment to the Tax Law, to the extent that it directed the cancellation or refund of taxes under a section

[67] People ex rel. Donner-Hanna Coke Corporation v. Burke 248 N. Y. 507, affirming 222 A. D. 790 4th Dept. Section 4 Tax Law as amended by Ch. 99, L. 1925 and Ch. 99, L. 1926.

[68] Two other state laws were upheld by the United States Supreme Court.

A tax law of 1903 had been questioned on the ground that the required three-fifths of the membership of the legislature had not voted for it. It had been validated when the legislature, by a retroactive act of 1906, declared printed copies to be the original journals of the two houses, and making them or copies of them competent evidence of votes of the legislature, when certified by the respective clerks of the Senate and Assembly. This evidence was sufficient to prove the validity of the law of 1903. The United States Supreme Court refused to interfere when a case was appealed on the ground that the legislature had violated the due process clause. Stickney v. Kelsey (1908) 209 U. S. 419. Ch. 240, L. 1906.

The inclusion of income derived in part as copyright royalties in measuring the annual franchise tax on domestic corporations did not violate the United States Constitution according to the decision in Educational Films Corporation v. Ward (1930) 282 U. S. 379. Section 209, Article 9-A Tax Law. L. 1929, Ch. 384.

[69] Prescott v. Ferris (1937) 251 A. D. 113, 4th Dept.; Brown-Lipe Gear Co. v. Ferris (1937) 275 N. Y. 148 Ch. 449, L. 1935 amending Ch. 75, L. 1906.

of the Tax Law which had been repealed, violated the Constitution.[70]

The various provisions forbidding the state and localities to give or loan money or credit to private individuals, and regulating claims, were adduced without success in opposition to the following seven laws: a provision for the refund of an excessive school tax, which was retroactive and allowed interest;[71] provisions in the amended New York City Charter for the sale of tax liens by that city and for foreclosure by the purchaser;[72] an act entitling the purchaser of a tax sale certificate to recover the money paid for the certificate by bringing an action to foreclose the lien against the land, given by the statute in the same manner as though the lien were a mortgage;[73] an authorization given the common council of Auburn to create lighting districts within the city, with full power to order such construction and installation of lighting or additional lighting as it might prescribe, the cost of which was to be fixed and collected as determined by the common council;[74]

[70] Matter of Guiteras (1924) 122 Misc. 523. L. 1920, Ch. 765, amending Section 221 Tax Law. The taxes to be refunded had been collected under Section 221-b Tax Law which had been repealed by Ch. 644, L. 1920.

[71] People ex rel. Eckerson v. Board of Education of Haverstraw (1908) 126 A. D. 414 2nd Dept. Section 256 Tax Law as amended by Ch. 721, L. 1907. In the opinion of the court, taxes were not debts, and even if an excess were returned, it was not a donation or a gift. Furthermore, the law was not considered obnoxious to Article 7, Section 6, prohibiting the allowance of state claims against the state.

[72] Gautier v. Ditmar (1912) 204 N. Y. 20. Sections 1027, 1045 Greater New York Charter as amended by Ch. 490, L. 1908.

[73] City of Schenectady v. Kalteux (1937) 275 N. Y. 610 affirming 251 A. D. 631. Article 7-A Tax Law (Cons. Laws, Ch. 60). No particular constitutional provision was brought forward against this act, but the preceding case, Gautier v. Ditmar, was cited as an authority by counsel seeking its overturning, according to the opinion of Justice Bliss of the Appellate Division.

[74] Parker v. Wallace (1913) 80 Misc. 425. Supreme Court Cayuga Trial Term. L. 1910, Ch. 678, Section 131. It had been urged that this law violated Article 12, Section 1, the relevant part of which read:

a retroactive statute declaring that stock dividends allocated by a trustee to the beneficiary of a trust were received by the beneficiary as a shareholder and were not subject to the income tax;[75] an article of the Tax Law under which a county, by foreclosing a lien on lands bid in at a tax sale, met the full amount of unpaid taxes plus expenses for the benefit of a town, which might, in the court's opinion, have an incidental interest, thus assuring that the money would be used for governmental purposes;[76] and the act, with its amendments, creating the Port District of Albany, part of the expenses for which were to be paid by Rensselaer County.[77]

In 1907 the Bronx Parkway Commission was created in order to preserve the waters of the Bronx River from pollution. The lands acquired by the commission were to constitute a public parkway. In 1913 it was provided that these lands were to be exempt from taxes and assessments. This provision was not regarded by the Supreme Court as a violation of Article 3, Section 18 which prohibited a private or local bill granting tax exemption to any " person, association, firm or corporation " since the commission was considered a public

It shall be the duty of the legislature to provide for the organization of cities and incorporated villages, and to restrict their power of taxation, assessment, borrowing money, contracting debts, and loaning their credit, so as to prevent abuses in assessments and in contracting debt by such municipal corporations.

The court, however, followed the decision of the Court of Appeals in Bank of Rome v. Village of Rome (1858) in which this provision was held to have no mandatory affect.

[75] People ex rel. Clark v. Gilchrist (1926) 243 N. Y. 173. Ch. 543, L. 1926 amending Sections 350 and 359 Tax Law (Cons. Laws, Ch. 60). The basis for the challenge to these laws was Article 7, Section 1 and Article 8, Section 9 of the State Constitution quoted supra.

[76] Whaley v. County of Monroe (1932) 235 A. D. 334 4th Dept. Article 7-A Tax Law added by L. 1930, Ch. 809 as amended. The objection to the law was taken under Article 8, Section 10.

[77] Wright v. Albany Port District Commission (1938) 254 A. D. 915 3rd Dept. L. 1925, Ch. 192 as amended by L. 1927, Ch. 523 and L. 1929, Ch. 293.

body.[78] In 1932, however, an act of 1868 which had provided for the improvement of the hydraulic power of the Great Chazy River, and for the checking of freshets, was held constitutional without the necessity of tax exemption being extended to the property acquired by the Board of Commissioners for improvements on the river, because such property was not used exclusively for a public purpose.[79]

A group of cases remains, not easily classified in any of the aforementioned categories. A requirement that delinquent taxes should bear interest from the time such delinquency commenced was upheld in 1914.[80] The Society for the Prevention of Cruelty to Animals, a private corporation, was given the power by another law to collect the money for dog licenses which it issued, and use the receipts to support its various activities. Both the Court of Appeals and the United States Supreme Court pronounced it valid.[81] A section of the Education Law permitted a town to recover from a county the difference between the amount collected by the town collector for the purposes of education and the amount necessary to fulfill those purposes.[82] Finally, in 1937 an amendment to the Tax Law which repealed the requirement that the holder of a mortgage

[78] Matter of Bronx Parkway Commission v. Common Council of Yonkers (1919) 106 Misc. 579. Supreme Court Westchester Special Term. Ch. 594, L. 1907 created the commission and Ch. 757, L. 1913 granted the exemption.

[79] People ex rel. Board of Commissioners for Improvement on the Great Chazy River v. Sancomb (1932) 259 N. Y. 1. Ch. 289, L. 1868 providing for the above mentioned improvements. Subd. 3-a Section 4 Tax Law (Cons. Laws, Ch. 60).

[80] People v. Park Row Realty Co. (1914) 88 Misc. 254. Supreme Court Albany Special Term. Sections 265 and 266 Tax Law added by L. 1909, Ch. 412.

[81] People v. Nicchia (1918) 224 N. Y. 637; affirmed in Nicchia v. New York (1920) 254 U. S. 228. Ch. 115, L. 1894 as amended by L. 1895, Ch. 412 and L. 1902, Ch. 495. It was not considered an improper delegation of the legislative power.

[82] Common School District No. 3 v. County of Chemung (1936) 160 Misc. 477. Supreme Court Trial and Special Term Chemung County. Section 435 Education Law.

on land which had been sold at a tax sale must file a notice describing the property and giving his name and address, in order to be entitled to give notification if he wished to redeem the land, was declared not to infringe on the vested rights of the purchaser at the tax sale.[83]

The most important taxes which the state sought to impose, such as income, inheritance and franchise taxes, all survived the judicial tests without much change in their major outlines. The difficulties in determining the division of authority between one state and that of another, or of the Federal government, over an estate or a business were a source of trouble, but it was an infrequent occurrence for a tax law to be invalidated because of conflict with a provision occurring only in the State Constitution. The attitude of the courts in these matters may be illustrated by the remark of Chief Judge Crane on the unemployment relief tax mentioned above. This tax placed a three per cent levy on the payrolls of employers, but certain groups, such as those with less than four employees, were exempted. Not all of the latter were eligible for benefits, either. Those receiving a salary of over fifty dollars a week and those engaged in a number of occupations, such as domestic service and educational work, were exempted. Replying to strictures against the law for these reasons and others, the Chief Judge stated:

> It is said that this is taxation for the benefit of a special class, not the public at large, and thus the purpose is essentially private. The Legislature, after investigation, has found the facts to be that those who are to receive benefits under the act are the ones most likely to be out of employment in times of depression. The courts cannot investigate these facts and should not attempt to do so. The briefs submitted show that the classification or selection made by the Legislature has followed investigation and has sought to reach the weakest spot. Experience may show this to be a mistake. No law can act

[83] Lowe v. Sheldon 276 N. Y. 1. Ch. 179, L. 1931 amending Section 139 Tax Law (Cons. Laws, Ch. 60).

with certainty; it measures reasonable probabilities. " Judicial inquiry does not concern itself with the accuracy of a legislative finding, but only with the question whether it so lacks any reasonable basis as to be arbitrary (Standard Oil Co. v. Marysville, 279 U. S. 582, 586, 587) " (Mr. J. Roberts in Borden's Farm Products Co. v. Ten Eyck, 297 U. S. 251, 263) 84.

The propensity of the courts to be in unison with the legislature on tax laws is further substantiated by the enumeration of cases, which shows sixty-three declarations of constitutionality and sixteen with the reverse effect.

84 Chamberlin Inc v. Andrews 271 N. Y. 1, at p. 14. See note 50, *supra*.

CHAPTER XIII
THE LEGISLATURE AS A BRANCH OF GOVERNMENT

THE relations of the legislature to the judiciary have been discussed in Chapter II. In this chapter it is sufficient to note that an act of 1921 allowing the courts to establish certain rules regarding their own practice was decided not to be an unlawful delegation of legislative power.[1] Legislation affecting the other branches of the government, the executive, the administration and the electorate, remains for examination.

The principal case in which the relations between the governor and the legislature were at issue was People v. Tremaine (1929). The Republican-dominated legislature had passed a provision designating the chairmen of the Senate Finance Committee and of the Assembly Ways and Means Committee to approve the segregation of lump sum appropriations, made by the governor under the Executive Budget system adopted by the state in 1927. The governor, a Democrat, had vetoed it but the legislature had repassed it over his veto. The Court of Appeals held that the law was invalid as conferring administrative functions on legislative officers.[2]

The case of Darweger v. Staats (1935) has been covered in Chapter VI. There it was noted that the act providing that the codes promulgated by the President under the National Industrial Recovery Act to apply to industries engaged in interstate commerce should be the law of the state for intrastate commerce violated Article 3, Section 17. The law was

[1] General Investment Co. v. I.R.T.Co. (1923) 235 N. Y. 532; Hanna v. Mitchell (1923) 235 N. Y. 534. Ch. 370, L. 1921 under which Rule 113 of Rules of Civil Practice had been established.

[2] 252 N. Y. 27 Section 139 State Finance Law (Cons. Laws, Ch. 56), the vetoed Section 11 of Ch. 593, L. 1929 and a similar provision in L. 1929, Chs. 364, 405, 458. At the same time Ch. 93, L. 1929, appropriating money for the erection of public buildings to the State Office Site and Building Commission, created by Ch. 5, L. 1926, a majority of the members being legislative officers acting ex officio, was likewise held invalid.

also held to delegate the legislative power in violation of Article 3, Section 1 under which that power was vested in the Senate and Assembly.[3] Other cases in which the legislature was held to have delegated its power unconstitutionally have been treated in previous chapters. Among them were such cases as People v. Ryan (1935)[4] and Seignious v. Rice (1936).[5] The act establishing the State Labor Relations Board was upheld against the contention that in giving the board the power to fix the unit for collective bargaining the legislature had unconstitutionally delegated its power, because the units to be chosen from were vested in the act.[6]

A frequent source of controversy has been the apportionment of the senate and assembly districts by the legislature. Constitutional restrictions operate to prevent a division of the state into districts exactly or nearly exactly equal in population. New York City has been underrepresented on the basis of population since 1894 when these restrictions were adopted. As the city has been predominantly Democratic and upstate New York has been correspondingly Republican, antagonism has developed between the two parts of the state. Nearly all the apportionment acts of the legislature since 1894 have been

[3] See Chapter VI, note 11 supra. In several of the lower courts this act was also held unconstitutional: Cline v. Consumers Cooperative Gas and Oil Co., Inc. (1934) 152 Misc. 653. Supreme Court Jefferson Co.; DeAgostina v. Parkshire Ridge Amusements Inc. (1935) 155 Misc. 518. Supreme Court Kings Co.; following the Darweger case and agreeing with it were Gross v. Jamaica Auction Galleries Inc. (1935) 267 N. Y. 555 and People v. Princeton Inc. (1935) 154 Misc. 811. City Magistrates' Court of New York, Commercial Frauds Court.

[4] See Chapter X, note 22 supra.

[5] See Chapter X, note 81 supra.

[6] Matter of Metropolitan Life Insurance Co. v. New York State Labor Relations Board (1938) 168 Misc. 948. Supreme Court Special Term New York County. L. 1937, Ch. 413. In a case earlier in that year, Nevins Inc. v. Boland (1938) 167 Misc. 428, it had been decided that in view of the provision for judicial protection against possible illegal action on the part of the board, there could be no doubt about the constitutionality of the conclusive fact-finding power vested in the board. Supreme Court Special Term New York Co.

challenged in the courts. In 1907 the Court of Appeals declared such an act passed in 1903 wholly unconstitutional and void, because of two violations of the stipulations as to a proper apportionment laid down by the Constitution. Under this act Richmond and Queens Counties had been joined to form a senatorial district. Article 3, Section 4 provided that the senate district should "at all times consist of contiguous territory" and these two counties are separated by water and intervening Kings County. Article 3, Section 4 also required that each senate district should contain "as nearly as may be, an equal number of inhabitants, excluding aliens, and be in as compact form as practicable," and that "no county shall be divided in the formation of a senate district except to make two or more senate districts wholly in such county." Thus the legislature had a difficult problem in satisfying all the requirements at the same time. A second violation of this section was found because one of the senatorial districts, the thirteenth, was not as compact as possible.[7]

An act of 1907 which placed Richmond and Rockland Counties, widely separated by land and water, in the same senatorial district was held constitutional in 1911 by the Court of Appeals because the legislature had complied as nearly as possible with the constitutional provisions.[8]

In 1916 the apportionment act of the same year was held wholly unconstitutional because it violated another requirement of Article 3, Section 4, that no district should contain a greater excess in population over an adjoining district than the population of a town or block therein adjoining such district.[9]

An attempt to reapportion the Congressional districts within the state made in 1931 by joint resolution of the Senate and

[7] Sherrill v. O'Brien 188 N. Y. 185. L. 1903, Ch. 431. The legislature, however, elected under the invalid Apportionment Act was regarded as a de facto body and its acts as valid.

[8] Matter of Reynolds 202 N. Y. 430, Ch. 727, L. 1907. Several legislatures had been elected under the act challenged.

[9] Matter of Dowling 219 N. Y. 44, Ch. 373, L. 1916.

Assembly without being submitted to the governor was adjudged null and void as a violation of both the Federal and State Constitutions. The Court of Appeals held that the word "legislature" used in these documents meant the lawmaking body including the governor. The United States Supreme Court affirmed the state court's decision.[10]

Two other joint resolutions of the legislature were held unconstitutional. One of these, Matter of Doyle, has been discussed in Chapter III, Civil Liberties.[11] In the other the legislature tried to declare a law no longer operative by passing a resolution stating that the emergency created by that law was at an end.[12]

An attempt to have the statute by which the legislature called for the election of delegates to the Constitutional Convenion of 1915 held unconstitutional on the grounds that the proceedings for registering voters were not in accord with constitutional provisions was defeated by the Court of Appeals. It ruled that a court of equity had no power to declare a statute unconstitutional except in an actual controversy, and that the taxpayer who had brought the suit in the case before it, had no such interest as to entitle him to do so.[13]

In 1926 the power of the legislature to submit the question to the voters at an election as to whether Congress should modify a Federal act, in the instance at hand the Volstead Act, was upheld by the Court of Appeals.[14]

A somewhat unusual case occurred in 1910. In that year, a section of the Public Health Law under which the State Board of Pharmacy was established, to be "elected" by the licensed

[10] Koenig v. Flynn (1932) 258 N. Y. 292. Affirmed 285 U. S. 375 (1932). Concurrent resolution of Senate and Assembly adopted April 10, 1931.

[11] See Chapter III, note 28 supra.

[12] Moran v. City of New York (1936) 270 N. Y. 650. Resolutions of April 12, 1935 applying to Ch. 637, L. 1932.

[13] Schieffelin v. Komfort (1914) 212 N. Y. 520. L. 1913, Ch. 819; Section 605 Code of Civil Procedure.

[14] People ex rel. Peaks v. Voorhis 243 N. Y. 420. Ch. 850, L. 1926.

pharmacists of the state, was sustained. The Appellate Division considered that the word "elected" amounted to appointment by a restricted electorate. Hence, the law did not violate Article 10, Section 2, the relevant provision of which read:

> All other officers whose election or appointment is not provided for by this Constitution, and all officers whose offices may hereafter be created by law, shall be elected by the people, or appointed, as the legislature may direct.[15]

Although five of the eleven acts covered for the first time in this chapter were held unconstitutional, the proportion of statutes declared invalid is much less when it is recalled how many of the acts dealt with in preceding chapters, such as those on Police Power, have involved the delegation of the functions of administration to boards or commissions. The joint resolutions held invalid were exceptions in that they were instances where the legislature was acting in opposition to the executive, thus introducing the complications of a three-cornered struggle, the ramifications of which constitute a subject for separate treatment. The clash between the legislature and the executive was also involved in People v. Tremaine. As the concern throughout these chapters has been the relation between the legislature and the judiciary, the topic will not be pursued further. It seems sufficient to say that examples of legislative encroachment in the form of legislation which reached the courts for decision were exceptional, and the sore spots in the relationships thus brought up might, if probed, reveal the necessity for institutions to achieve greater collaboration between the governor and the lawmakers. At any rate, it does not appear that judicial review would have been the remedy for the clashes, if long continued, as one side or the other might have retaliated at the courts, which would then have been dragged into the midst of the struggle.

[15] New York State Constitution Annotated, *op. cit.*, p. 172. State Board of Pharmacy v. Bellinger 138 A. D. 12 2nd Dept. Art. 11, Public Health Law, re-enacting Ch. 667, L. 1900, as amended.

Some of the difficulties in the relationship between the governor and the legislature might be traced to the fact that the governor was elected by the people at large while the legislators were elected from districts, established under constitutional requirements which discriminated against New York City and favored the upstate districts. For years the governor and legislature were of opposite parties. It is due to these same constitutional restrictions that the legislature was unable to apportion the state fairly according to population. As has been indicated, the restrictions were so worded that it was difficult for the legislature, with the best intentions, to comply with them. Even conceding that the legislature deliberately violated the Constitution in the two cases where the courts so ruled, the latter could only declare the offending apportionment unconstitutional. They could not compel the legislature to act in accordance with the Constitution. This meant that the apportionment preceding the one declared unconstitutional came into force, and this was not a satisfactory solution to the problem. Thus, judical review of itself could not have bettered the situation.

SUMMARY AND CONCLUSIONS

The decline of the legislature in power and prestige has been one of the most outstanding phenomena in the history of American state government since the ratification of the Constitution. The causes of this development may be partly traced to the corruption and extravagance which marked a large share of legislative activity in the last century. The pernicious influence of land speculators, of railroad magnates and of industrialists on the moral fiber of the lawmakers has been depicted by many writers. The prodigal expenditures on canals and railroads in the first half of the nineteenth century contributed to the growing distrust of men in government. The sordid spectacle of the post-Civil War era, with both jobbery and dissipation of public funds rampant in all levels of government throughout the nation, greatly heightened the dissatisfaction. Episodes of venality and wastefulness which have come to light since then, culminating in the revelations of the muckrakers at the beginning of the twentieth century, have kept reenforcing the impression of baseness on the part of those in authority, until the stereotype of the corrupt politician has become part of the American intellectual heritage.

Simultanously, influential writers and publicists were advancing theories which justified the suspicions of the legislators derived from everyday political life. To the advocates of laissez-faire, legislative interference with the economic activities of the state was bound to be harmful. The combination of theoretical belief and practical experience led to the introduction of restrictions on the power of that branch of government which passed the laws and thus was deemed responsible for both acts which resulted in corruption and extravagance, and injurious intrusions into the economic life of the state. New York did not adopt the two features common to many of the states, the biennial session and the limitation on the number of days the legislature could meet. Nor did it adopt the much later innovations, the initiative and the referendum, which were so strenuously debated at the beginning of this century. The Constitution of New York does require popular assent to certain expenditures by the legislature. Ever since the demise of the Council of Revision, the governor of New York has possessed the veto power, one of the most important limitations on the legislature in New York. To override the governor's veto, a vote of two-thirds of those elected, not merely present, in both houses has been required, thus further strengthening the power of the executive.

More important than any of these devices was the incorporation of specific restrictions on the powers of the legislature in the state constitutions, which have been made more or less difficult to amend, by the constitutional conventions, with reliance for the enforcement of these curbs placed on the judicial branch of the government. Examples of such restrictions have been noted in New York, such as Article 3, Sections 16 and 18, treated respectively in Chapters VI and VIII. Although the institution of judical review has now become deeply rooted in American thinking, it has been subject to sporadic attacks which have taken the form of demands for various alterations mentioned in Chapter I. The fundamental nature of the problem has frequently been overlooked in the concentration of attention on specific cases. Factual material on the workings of this institution throughout the forty-eight states has been compiled to only a limited extent. The study of judicial review in these thirty-three years in the most populous state of the Union constitutes but one segment of a greater work that remains to be done.

Attempting, however, to draw some tentative conclusions based on what has been done, it can be seen that most of the laws whose constitutionality has been questioned have not been challenged as violating unmistakable meanings of words, about which there could be little disagreement among rational people. In each chapter, the questions that have arisen have been concerned with constructions of words which would admit of opposite meanings. If a court's jurisdiction is defined in the Constitution, does this prevent the legislature from adding to its jurisdiction? What is interstate and what is intra-state commerce? When does a law affect the remedy only and when the contract? At what point has legislative power been improperly delegated? When does the title of an act express its contents adequately? Where is the line between a general and a local bill? Not to continue further, one may end this list by a reminder of the oft-mentioned difficulties associated with interpreting the due process and equal protection clauses. It takes more than legal acumen to decide these questions. Because of the necessity of legislation on a great number of subjects, those who have phrased the restrictions have either intentionally left some ambiguous word or words in the restriction to allow for unforeseeable exigencies, or the courts themselves have so interpreted some word or phrase as to confirm the legislature's power. Attention has been called to the fairly loose interpretation of the section on titles in Chapter VI. A similar development occurred with legislation in regard to the affairs of cities, described in Chapter VII on Home Rule. In both instances those responsible for the constitutional provisions might not have approved of the outcome.

If it is true that the courts have had a tendency to sustain the legislature where doubt has existed, and the statistics showing that the courts have held 451 acts constitutional as against 136 unconstitutional would so seem to demonstrate, one can begin to understand why the institution has managed to survive. It has not stood as an absolute barrier to legislation. Even in those instances where the courts have held acts unconstitutional, their decisions have not prevented eventual enactment of the desired laws, either by reenactment in slightly different form, by amendment of the Constitution or by judicial reversal. The delay, though, incident to the success of these laws has been frequently criticized as harmful. Defenders of this lengthy process retort that the legislators might act without sober reflection and that the people are thereby given a chance to show whether the legislation at issue is actually desired. The critics rejoin that every act has to pass through a bicameral legislature with its committee system and secure either the governor's approval or a two-thirds vote in the face of his opposition. This, of course, is in addition to the preliminary necessity of procuring the assent of the legislators themselves.

Another question, of perhaps greater moment, is that of divided responsibility. The legislators may pass an act which, to their own minds, is of doubtful constitutionality, feeling that it is for the courts to decide. Unscrupulous legislators might vote for the passage of acts ardently desired by one set of constituents but repugnant to another group, in such form that the judges would hold them invalid, thus preventing the correct assignment of responsibility, considered so essential by many political scientists.

The point has also been raised that the anxiety as to the future action of the courts on a proposed bill introduces a criterion into the discussion of the bill other than that of its merits. Since it is known that the bill will be tested as to its constitutionality, it is examined with respect to its harmony with the actual clauses of the Constitution. Because these are subject to more than one interpretation, the legislators will not examine the bill as to whether they themselves think it constitutional, but whether the judges then in office will. As these judges cannot determine the meaning of the clauses involved by legal knowledge alone, they will decide the question on the basis of beliefs and outlook partly influenced by such conditions as their earlier legal training, including the schools at which they studied, and the commentaries and treatises which they have read. They may also be swayed by the arguments and briefs of counsel. In as much as the constitutionality of laws is only decided when an actual case arises, a party to a suit who has the abler counsel and who desires a law to be declared unconstitutional may have an advantage, which some have thought unwise, especially as in many of these cases in the past the state has not been represented in the defense of the acts of its own lawmaking body.

In actual practice, as has been noted, the great majority of laws challenged have been sustained. There do not appear to have been any laws passed for which some rational justification could not have been offered. Some of the important laws declared unconstitutional have been later repassed and upheld through the use of the means mentioned above. On the other hand, the courts have confirmed legislative acts when the latter were under heavy fire. Gitlow v. New York, Adler v. Deegan and People v. Nebbia are three examples of the last-mentioned kind of action. The tendency has been, particularly with labor legislation, for the courts to acquiesce eventually to enactments if the legislative determination to pass them is persistent enough. In short, neither the hopes of its advocates that judicial review would be the cure for legislative misbehavior, nor the fears of its opponents that it would act as an insuperable obstacle to essential laws, have been realized.

TABLE OF CASES CITED

		PAGE
Abbye Employment Agency Inc. v. Robinson	1938 166 Misc. 820	161
Abell v. Clarkson	1923 237 N. Y. 85	126
Adamec v. Post	1937 273 N. Y. 250	172
Addiss v. Selig	1934 264 N. Y. 274	94
Adkins v. Children's Hospital	1923 261 U. S. 525	158
Adler v. Deegan	1914 251 N. Y. 467	125, 131, 225
Admiral Realty Co. v. The City of N. Y.	1912 206 N. Y. 110	139
Agnew v. State	1938 166 Misc. 602	54
Akely v. Kinnicutt	1924 238 N. Y. 471	76
Alexander v. Enright	1924 211 A. D. 146	174
Alpren v. Consolidated Edison Co. of N. Y. Inc.	1938 168 Misc. 381	96
American Historical Society v. Glenn	1928 248 N. Y. 445	45
Amoskeag Savings Bank v. Purdy	1913 231 U. S. 373	196
Appleby v. City of New York	1926 271 U. S. 364	102
Appleby v. Delaney	1926 271 U. S. 403	102
Arbetter Inc. v. Isabel Inc.	1933 147 Misc. 54	46
Associated Indemnity Corp. v. Chais	1936 161 Misc. 763	96
Association for the Protection of the Adirondacks v. MacDonald	1930 253 N. Y. 234	192
Atkins v. Hertz Driv-Urself Stations Inc.	1932 237 A. D. 31	182
Atkin v. Kansas	1903 191 U. S. 207	151
Ausable Chasm Co. v. State	1935 266 N. Y. 326	53
Babcock v. State	1919 190 A. D. 147	53
Baird v. Erie Railroad Co.	1911 148 A. D. 452	90
Baldwin v. Seelig	1935 294 U. S. 511	163
Baldwin v. Standard Accident Insurance Co.	1932 237 A. D. 334	167
Bank of Rome v. Village of Rome	1858 18 N. Y. 38	211
Barlow v. Berry	1927 245 N. Y. 500	188
Barnes v. Dairymen's League Cooperative Association Inc.	1927 220 A. D. 624	160
Barr and Co. v. State	1926 127 Misc. 75	55
Bass, Ratcliff and Gretton Ltd. v. State Tax Commission	1924 266 U. S. 271	196
Baylis v. Van Nostrand	1917 176 A. D. 396	172
Beers v. Glynn	1909 211 U. S. 477	206
Biddles Inc. v. Enright	1925 239 N. Y. 354	174
Blank v. Walker	1930 253 N. Y. 513	140
Board of Black River Regulating District v. Ogdensburg	1922 203 A. D. 43	193
Bonagur v. Orlandi	1906 51 Misc. 582	108

TABLE OF CASES CITED

		PAGE
Borden's Farm Product Company Inc. v. Ten Eyck	1936 297 U.S. 251, 263	164, 214
Bosley v. McLaughlin	1915 236 U. S. 385	155
Boswell v. Security Mutual Life Ins. Co.	1908 193 N. Y. 465	90
Bourjois Sales Corporation v. Dorfman	1937 273 N. Y. 167	161
Bradstreet's Collection Bureau v. Dayler's Brass Works	1917 188 A. D. 511	46
Brayman v. Grant	1909 130 A. D. 272	70
Brearley School Limited v. Ward	1911 201 N. Y. 358	91
Briegel v. Day	1922 202 A. D. 484	183
Broderick v. Adamson	1936 270 N. Y. 228	178
Broderick v. Weinsier	1938 278 N. Y. 419	178
Bronx Gas and Electric Co. v. Public Service Commission	1919 190 A. D. 13	176
Brood en Beschnit Fabrick v. Aluminum Co. of America	1931 231 A. D. 693	79
Brooklyn and Queens Transit Corporation v. City of New York	1937 275 N. Y. 454	202
Brown v. Bunselmeyer	1917 101 Misc. 625	186
Brown v. City of Ithaca	1911 148 A. D. 477	103
Brown-Lipe Gear Co. v. Ferris	1937 275 N. Y. 148	209
Browne v. City of New York	1925 213 A. D. 206	121
Bull v. State	1931 231 A. D. 313	54
Bullock v. Cooley	1919 225 N. Y. 566	49
Bunting v. Oregon	1917 243 U. S. 426	158
Bush Jewelry Co. v. United Retail Employees' Union, Local 830	1938 168 Misc. 224	48
Bush v. N. Y. Life Ins. Co.	1909 135 A. D. 447	111
Campbell v. City of New York	1927 244 N. Y. 317	159
Carow v. Board of Education	1936 272 N. Y. 341	185
Cascade Automatic Sprinkler Corp. v. State	1938 277 N. Y. 612	54
Cauldwell-Wingate Co. v. State	1937 249 A. D. 892	54
Central Savings Bank v. City of New York	1938 279 N. Y. 266	170
Central Union Gas Co. v. Browning	1911 146 A. D. 783	91
Chaloner v. Sherman	1917 242 U. S. 455	70
Chamberlin Inc. v. Andrews	1936 271 N. Y. 1	205, 214
Chanler v. Kelsey	1907 205 U. S. 466	201
Chappell v. Chappell	1906 116 A. D. 573	67
Charles River Bridge v. Warren Bridge	1837 11 Pet. 420	86
Chicago Great Western Railroad Co. v. State of New York	1921 197 A. D. 742	201
Ciaccia v. Board of Education	1936 271 N. Y. 336	185
City Bank Farmers' Trust Co. v. New York Central Railroad Co.	1930 253 N. Y. 49	197

		PAGE
City of Buffalo v. Hawks	1929 226 A. D. 480	150
City of Elmira v. Seymour	1906 111 A. D. 199	110
City of N. Y. v. Fifth Ave. Coach Co.	1933 262 N. Y. 481	114
City of New York v. Foster	1911 148 A. D. 258	171
City of New York v. Kelsey	1913 158 A. D. 183	172
City of New York v. Village of Lawrence	1929 250 N. Y. 429	133
City of New York v. Willcox	1921 115 Misc. 351	81
City of New York v. Wright	1926 243 N. Y. 80	149
City of Rochester v. Gray	1909 133 A. D. 852	139
City of Rochester v. Holder	1918 224 N. Y. 386	101
City of Schenectady v. Kalteux	1937 275 N. Y. 610	210
Clarke v. Carlisle Foundry Co.	1934 150 Misc. 710	46
Clement v. May	1909 136 A. D. 199	168
Clenult Realty Co. v. Wood	1921 230 N. Y. 646	171
Cleveland v. City of Watertown	1917 222 N. Y. 159	118, 131
Clinton v. Krull	1908 125 A. D. 157	198
Cline v. Consumers Cooperative Gas and Oil Co. Inc.	1934 152 Misc. 653	216
Clydè v. Gilchrist	1923 262 U. S. 94	199
Cockcroft v. Mitchel	1921 230 N. Y. 630	171
Coler v. Brooklyn Daily Eagle	1909 133 A. D. 300	138
Coler v. The Corn Exchange Bank	1928 250 N. Y. 136	149
Commissioner of Public Welfare v. Jackson	1934 265 N. Y. 469	160
Common School District No. 3 v. County of Chemung	1936 160 Misc. 477	212
Commonwealth of Massachusetts v. Klaus	1911 145 A. D. 798	84
Compton and Co. v. Williams	1936 248 A. D. 545	95
Cookman v. Stoddard	1909 132 A. D. 480	90
Cooley v. The Board of Wardens	1852 12 Howard 299	79
Corlesi v. New York	1914 233 U. S. 51	72
Cornell Steamboat Co. v. Sohmer	1915 235 U. S. 549	195
Corrigan v. State	1932 260 N. Y. 645	53
County of Nassau v. Long Beach	1936 272 N. Y. 260	206
County of Niagara v. City of Lockport	1934 264 N. Y. 423	144
Cox v. McElligott	1937 163 Misc. 619	190
Crane v. Hablo	1922 258 U. S. 142	105
Crane v. Voorhis	1931 257 N. Y. 298	75
Cuvillier v. State of New York	1929 250 N. Y. 258	53
Dairy Sealed Inc. v. Ten Eyck	1936 159 Misc. 716	48
Darling v. White	1910 67 Misc. 366	45
Dartmouth College v. Woodward	1819 4 Wheat. 518	86
Darweger v. Staats	1935 267 N. Y. 290	110, 215, 216
Dawley v. McRibbin	1927 245 N. Y. 557	182
De Agostina v. Parkshire Ridge Amusements Inc.	1935 155 Misc. 518	216

TABLE OF CASES CITED

		PAGE
Debusto v. Dupont Denemours and Co., Inc.	1938 167 Misc. 920	157
Decker v. Pouvailsmith Corporation	1929 252 N. Y. 1	158
Demuth v. Kemp	1909 130 A. D. 546	91
Dodge v. Cornelius	1901 168 N. Y. 242	32
Dollar Co. v. Canadian Car and Foundry Co.	1917 220 N. Y. 270	84
Dornhoefer v. Farley	1914 161 A. D. 600	48
Doubleday Doran and Company v. Macy and Company	1936 269 N. Y. 272	160
Doud v. The Huntington Hebrew Congregation	1917 178 A. D. 748	203
Douglas v. New York, New Haven and Hartford Railroad Co.	1929 279 U. S. 577	84
Doyle v. Gleason	1934 152 Misc. 641	88
Drew v. Thaw	1914 235 U. S. 432	70
Durham v. Ottinger	1926 243 N. Y. 423	174
Economic Power and Construction Co. v. Buffalo	1909 195 N. Y. 286	108
Educational Films Corporation v. Ward	1930 282 U. S. 379	209
Erie Railroad Co. v. New York	1914 233 U. S. 671	82
Erie Railroad Co. v. Williams	1914 233 U. S. 685	81
Failing v. Grounds	1914 160 A. D. 71	46
Farrington v. State	1928 248 N. Y. 112	54
Fawcett v. Andrews	1922 203 A. D. 591	76
Fearon v. Treanor	1936 272 N. Y. 268	95
First Construction Co. of Brooklyn v. N. Y.	1917 221 N. Y. 295	104, 108
Fisher Co. v. Woods	1907 187 N. Y. 90	170
Fletcher v. Peck	1810 6 Cranch 87	86
Flood Abatement Commission v. Merritt	1916 94 Misc. 388	112
Foster v. New York Central and Hudson River Railroad Co.	1907 118 A. D. 143	103
Fox v. Smith	1908 123 A. D. 369	181
Funkhouser v. Preston Co.	1933 290 U. S. 163	94
Gardner v. Ginther	1931 232 A. D. 246	186
Gardner v. Newburgh	1816 2 Johnson Chancery 162	86, 99
Garfield v. N. Y. Telephone Co.	1935 268 N. Y. 549	132
Gautier v. Ditmar	1912 204 N. Y. 20	210
Gaynor v. Marohn	1935 268 N. Y. 417	126, 134
Gaynor v. Village of Port Chester	1920 230 N. Y. 210	109
Gaynor v. Village of Port Chester	1921 231 N. Y. 451	143
Geary v. Geary	1936 272 N. Y. 390	149
Gedney v. Marlton Realty Company	1932 258 N. Y. 355	183
Gedney v. Marlton Realty Company	1934 264 N. Y. 244	183
Gehagin v. Fairbanks	1933 147 Misc. 685	45
General Investment Co. v. I.R.T. Co.	1923 235 N. Y. 532	215

		PAGE
Gersman v. Levy	1908 126 A. D. 83	44
Gibbons v. Ogden	1824 9 Wheaton 1	79
Gitlow v. New York	1925 268 U. S. 652	61, 225
Goldberg v. People's Security Co.	1914 162 A. D. 385	92
Goodale v. City of New York	1914 85 Misc. 603	207
Gordon v. State	1922 233 N. Y. 1	55
Gould v. Bennett	1934 153 Misc. 818	62
Grant v. Cananea Consolidated Copper Company	1907 189 N. Y. 241	84
Greenspan v. Olivier	1914 164 A. D. 535	92
Gross v. Jamaica Auction Galleries Inc.	1935 267 N. Y. 555	216
Gubner v. McClellan	1909 130 A. D. 716	111
Guttag v. Shatzkin	1921 230 N. Y. 647	171
Gwynne v. Board of Education of Union Free School District No. 3	1931 234 A. D. 629	128
Haag v. City of New York	1921 130 Misc. 124	189
Halfmoon Bridge Co. v. The Canal Board	1915 91 Misc. 600	102
Hall v. House of St. Giles the Cripple	1915 91 Misc. 122	104
Hammitt v. Gaynor	1913 82 Misc. 196	118
Hanfgarn v. Mark	1936 274 N. Y. 22	95
Hanna v. Mitchell	1923 235 N. Y. 534	215
Hanower v. Candide	1935 269 N. Y. 593	51
Harnett and Co. Inc. v. Englander	1907 120 A. D. 351	170
Hathorn v. Natural Carbonic Gas Company	1909 194 N. Y. 326	193
Hauser v. North British and Mercantile Insurance Co.	1912 206 N. Y. 455	170
Hawley v. Walker	1914 232 U. S. 718	155
Heiner v. Greenwich Savings Bank	1922 118 Misc. 326	177
Helme v. Buckalew	1920 191 A. D. 59	149
Hermitage Co. v. Goldfogle	1923 236 N. Y. 554	207
Hesse v. Roth	1928 249 N. Y. 436	144
Hollender v. Rochester Food Products Corp.	1924 124 Misc. 130	93
H.O.L.C. v. Barone	1937 164 Misc. 187	208
Honeyman v. Clark	1938 278 N. Y. 467	96
Honeyman v. Hanan	1937 275 N. Y. 382	94
Hopper v. Britt	1911 203 N. Y. 144	75
Hopper v. Willcox	1913 155 A. D. 213	139
Horton v. Andras	1908 191 N. Y. 231	142
House v. Bodour	1938 168 Misc. 766	117
Hovey v. The DeLong Hook and Eye Co.	1911 147 A. D. 881	80
Hurley v. Board of Education	1936 270 N. Y. 275	185
Hutchinson v. Nassau County Trust Company	1935 246 A. D. 628	178
Hygrade Provision Co. v. Sherman	1925 266 U. S. 497	167
In Re Callahan	1910 200 N. Y. 59	74
In Re Galvin's Estate	1934 153 Misc. 11	148
In Re Jacobs	1881 98 N. Y. 98	147, 151

TABLE OF CASES CITED

		PAGE
Institute of the Metropolis Inc. v. University of State	1936 249 A. D. 33	186
Interborough Rapid Transit Co. v. Sohmer	1915 237 U. S. 276	200
Ives v. South Buffalo Railway Company	1911 201 N. Y. 271	9, 39, 145, 153, 155
Jackson v. State	1933 261 N. Y. 134	54
Jacobson v. Baltimore and Ohio Railroad Co.	1936 161 Misc. 268	81
Jamaica Water Supply Co. v. City of N. Y.	1908 57 Misc. 475	90
Jemison v. The Bell Telephone Co. of Buffalo	1906 186 N. Y. 493	80
Jimeson v. Lehley	1906 51 Misc. 352	111
Johnson v. Flynn	1936 248 A. D. 649	51
Johnson v. Lasser	1936 159 Misc. 340	47
Johnson v. Ocean View Cemetery	1921 198 A. D. 854	173
Johnson v. Victoria Chief Copper Mining and Smelting Co.	1912 150 A. D. 653	84
Jones v. Valentine	1937 164 Misc. 443	191
Judd v. Board of Education	1938 278 N. Y. 200	185
Juilliard v. Greenman	1883 110 U. S. 421	8
Kane v. Bowers, Brennan and Ricoro Estates Inc.	1938 276 N. Y. 665	96
Keeney v. Comptroller	1912 222 U. S. 525	201
Keller v. Jamaica Motor Service Corporation	1925 115 Misc. 825	170
Kenmore v. Erie	1930 252 N. Y. 437	141
Kibbee v. Lyons	1922 202 A. D. 562	193
Kings Co. Lighting Co. v. The City of N. Y.	1916 176 A. D. 175	92
Kings County Lighting Co. v. Newton	1923 235 N. Y. 599	175
Kline v. Imperial Coal and Coke Co.	1910 66 Misc. 616	45
Klinke v. Samuels	1934 264 N. Y. 144	94
Klotz v. Angle	1917 220 N. Y. 347	85
Koenig v. Flynn	1932 258 N. Y. 292	218
Koster v. Coyne	1906 110 A. D. 742	132
Knickerbocker Ice Co. v. Stewart	1920 253 U. S. 149	82
Krauss v. Krauss No. 1	1908 127 A. D. 740	91
Kranowitz v. Schlansky	1935 156 Misc. 717	67
Kuhn v. Knight	1906 115 A. D. 837	138
La Rocca v. La Rocca	1932 144 Misc. 737	47
Leach v. Anwell	1912 154 A. D. 170	44
Lewis v. State	1921 234 N. Y. 587	53
Lewkowicz v. Queen Aeroplane Co.	1913 207 N. Y. 290	44
Leffman v. Long Island Railroad Co.	1907 120 A. D. 528	111
Levy Leasing Co. v. Siegel	1921 230 N. Y. 634	171
Lindenmuller v. the People	1861 33 Barb. 548	64
Lindsley v. Natural Carbonic Gas Co.	1911 220 U. S. 61	193
Lissner v. Cohen	1906 49 Misc. 272	147

		PAGE
Litchfield v. Bond	1906 186 N. Y. 66	100
Livingston v. Van Ingen	1812 9 Johns. 507	31
Lochner v. New York	1905 198 U. S. 45	152
Long Island Railroad Co. v. Jones	1912 151 A. D. 407	103
Lord v. Equitable Life Ass. Co. of U. S.	1909 194 N. Y. 212	90
Lotz v. Standard Vulcanite Pan Co.	1917 102 Misc. 68	48
Lowe v. Sheldon	1937 276 N. Y. 1	213
Lutz v. Houck	1933 263 N. Y. 116	181
Lynn v. Nichols	1930 254 N. Y. 630	76
MacMullen v. Middletown	1907 187 N. Y. 37	148
Magrum v. Village of Williamsville	1934 241 A. D. 55	126
Marbury v. Madison	1 Cranch 137	28
Marcus Brown Holding Co. v. Feldman	1921 256 U. S. 170	171
Markland v. Scully	1911 203 N. Y. 158	75
Mass. Nat. Bank v. Shinn	1900 18 A. D. 276 Aff. 163 N. Y. 360	32
Matter of Ahern	1909 195 N. Y. 493	73
Matter of Andreson v. Rice	1938 277 N. Y. 271	188
Matter of Application of City of Niagara Falls	1920 299 N. Y. 333	176
Matter of Bareham v. the Board of Supervisors of the County of Monroe	1936 247 A. D. 534	140
Matter of Barnes	1912 204 N. Y. 108	68
Matter of Barthelmess v. Cukor	1921 231 N. Y. 435	187
Matter of Becker v. Eisner	1938 277 N. Y. 143	110
Matter of Bendetto v. Kern	1938 167 Misc. 831	191
Matter of Berger v. Quinn	1933 149 Misc. 545	169
Matter of Berkowitz v. Arbid and Houlberg Inc.	1921 230 N. Y. 261	93
Matter of Birdsall	1906 49 Misc. 53	67
Matter of Board of Aldermen	1910 68 Misc. 478	68
Matter of Bond and Mortgage Guarantee Co.	1936 249 A. D. 25	141
Matter of Bristol v. Board of Trustees	1916 173 A. D. 545	186
Matter of Brock	1935 245 A. D. 5	43
Matter of Bronx Parkway Commission v. Common Council of Yonkers	1919 106 Misc. 579	212
Matter of Brown	1937 274 N. Y. 10	198
Matter of Brown v. Sisti	1936 160 Misc. 332	129
Matter of Buoneto v. Buoneto	1938 278 N. Y. 284	48
Matter of Buffalo Library v. Wanamaker	1937 162 Misc. 26	114
Matter of Burke	1911 203 N. Y. 293	74
Matter of Burke v. Krug	1936 272 N. Y. 575	125
Matter of Bushell v. City of New York	1934 242 A. D. 366	169
Matter of Callahan	1929 252 N. Y. 14	76
Matter of Capozolli v. Cruise	1927 244 N. Y. 529	50
Matter of Carey v. Cruise	1927 246 N. Y. 237	50
Matter of Carr v. Roesch	1930 231 A. D. 19	144, 189

TABLE OF CASES CITED 233

		PAGE
Matter of Casper	1936 161 Misc. 199	95
Matter of Caulfield	1930 136 Misc. 685	199
Matter of City of New York	1927 246 N. Y. 72	132
Matter of City of New York (Brooklyn Ferry)	1910 140 A. D. 238	105
Matter of City of New York (North River Waterfront)	1907 190 N. Y. 350	100
Matter of City of New York (Tibbett Ave.)	1914 162 A. D. 398	105
Matter of Claim of Anttonen v. Lakso Builders Inc.	1933 261 N. Y. 545	157
Matter of Claim of Boscarino v. Miller Cabinet Co.	1933 263 N. Y. 581, 608	157
Matter of Claim of Dalberth v. Iuppa and Battle Company	1933 262 N. Y. 537, 564	157
Matter of Claim of McNamara v. New York State Railways	1922 233 N. Y. 681	157
Matter of Clement (Siemens Certificate)	1910 136 A. D. 199	200
Matter of Cole	1934 263 N. Y. 643	205
Matter of Common Council of Lackawanna	1913 158 A. D. 263	42
Matter of County of Suffolk v. Water Power and Control Commission	1935 269 N. Y. 158	144
Matter of Davison	1930 137 Misc. 852	199
Matter of Dean	1920 230 N. Y. 1	109
Matter of Deuel	1906 112 A. D. 99	51
Matter of Donnelly v. Roosevelt (In Re Walker)	1932 144 Misc. 525	127
Matter of Dowling	1916 219 N. Y. 44	217
Matter of Doyle	1931 257 N. Y. 244	68, 218
Matter of Elite Dairy Products v. Ten Eyck	1936 247 A. D. 443	166
Matter of Ellard	1909 62 Misc. 374	87
Matter of Erlanger	1934 153 Misc. 573	95
Matter of Evans v. Berry	1933 262 N. Y. 61	134
Matter of Fenton	1908 58 Misc. 303	68
Matter of Finegan v. Cohen	1937 275 N. Y. 432	190
Matter of Finsilver, Still and Morse Inc. v. Goldberg, Maas and Company Inc.	1930 253 N. Y. 382	150
Matter of Frame	1910 69 Misc. 568	127
Matter of Fraser v. Brown	1911 203 N. Y. 136	73
Matter of French Co. v. Lynch	1931 233 A. D. 178	207
Matter of General Footwear Corp.	1931 140 Misc. 791	67
Matter of Gerling v. Nichols	1924 123 Misc. 811	76
Matter of Gianastasio v. Kaplan	1931 142 Misc. 611	190
Matter of Gilfillan v. Commissioners of Elections	1924 124 Misc. 628	75, 76
Matter of Goldberg	1935 157 Misc. 49	94
Matter of Gresser v. O'Brien	1934 263 N. Y. 622	50

			PAGE
Matter of Guiteras	1924	122 Misc. 523	210
Matter of Handler v. Berry	1931	138 Misc. 584	50
Matter of Hecht	1927	246 N. Y. 602	204
Matter of Hertle	1907	120 A. D. 717	42
Matter of Hopper v. Britt	1912	204 N. Y. 524	75
Matter of Horler	1916	97 Misc. 587	204
Matter of Howe v. Cohen	1935	268 N. Y. 706	75
Matter of Independent Certificate (Aldermen of Cohoes)	1912	78 Misc. 87	74
Matter of Jensen v. Southern Pacific Company	1915	215 N. Y. 514	156
Matter of Joiner St. (City of Rochester)	1917	177 A. D. 361	139
Matter of Jordan v. Smith	1930	137 Misc. 341	114
	1930	254 N. Y. 585	41
Matter of Kane	1911	71 Misc. 163	129
Matter of Kings County Lighting Co. v. Maltbie	1935	244 A. D. 475	177
Matter of Knob v. Cheshire	1927	246 N. Y. 533	140
Matter of Kornbluth v. Rice	1937	250 A. D. 654	188
Matter of Lagergren	1937	276 N. Y. 184	205
Matter of La Guardia v. Cohen	1933	149 Misc. 110	76
Matter of Lance	1907	55 Misc. 13	147
Matter of Lathers	1938	167 Misc. 186	206
Matter of Lawton v. City of New Rochelle	1908	123 A. D. 832	91
Matter of Levinson v. Rice	1934	152 Misc. 813	134
Matter of Levy	1920	192 A. D. 550	46
Matter of Liebowitz v. Goldwater	1936	161 Misc. 115	190
Matter of Littleton	1927	129 Misc. 845	148
Matter of Lockitt	1908	58 Misc. 5	111
Matter of Long Island Railroad Co.	1907	189 N. Y. 428	138
Matter of Long Sault Development Co.	1914	212 N. Y. 1	101
Matter of Long Sault Development Co. v. Kennedy	1913	158 A. D. 398	112
Matter of Love	1923	205 A. D. 363	169
Matter of Madel v. The Board of Regents	1928	250 N. Y. 173	181
Matter of McAneny v. Board of Estimate	1922	232 N. Y. 377	140
Matter of McCoy	1925	241 N. Y. 71	127
Matter of McMullen	1921	114 Misc. 505	199
Matter of McQueeney v. Sutphen and Myer	1915	167 A. D. 528	149
Matter of Metropolitan Life Insurance Co. v. New York State Labor Relations Board	1938	168 Misc. 948	216
Matter of Minnick v. Newmann	1926	244 N. Y. 530	204
Matter of Mitchel v. Cropsey	1917	177 A. D. 663	42
Matter of Moebus	1917	178 A. D. 709	201
Matter of Mooney v. Cohen	1936	272 N. Y. 33	133
Matter of Morgan	1906	186 N. Y. 202	127
	1906	114 A. D. 45	73

TABLE OF CASES CITED

		PAGE
Matter of Morse	1928 247 N. Y. 290	93
Matter of Mortgage Commission (1175 Evergreen Ave.)	1936 270 N. Y. 436	96
Matter of Moses v. Board of Education of Syracuse	1926 127 Misc. 477	184
Matter of Mount Sinai Hospital	1928 250 N. Y. 103	93
Matter of Neubert v. Butler	1933 146 Misc. 467	43
Matter of Newkirk	1931 144 Misc. 765	74
Matter of New York City Housing Authority v. Muller	1936 270 N. Y. 333	105
Matter of New York City and Hudson River Railroad Co. (Village of Ossining)	1910 136 A. D. 760	143
Matter of New York County	1911 72 Misc. 620	30
Matter of New York, Ontario and Western Railway Co.	1935 244 A. D. 634	175
Matter of Niagara, Lockport and Ontario Power Co.	1906 111 A. D. 686	102
Matter of Nugent v. Fitzgerald	1926 246 N. Y. 531	204
Matter of O'Brien	1912 152 A. D. 356	74
Matter of O'Brien v. Boyle	1916 219 N. Y. 195	128
Matter of O'Callaghan v. Finegan	1937 166 Misc. 556	191
Matter of O'Neill v. Cruise	1927 244 N. Y. 528	50
Matter of Osborne	1909 62 Misc. 575	65
Matter of Ottinger	1925 240 N. Y. 435	187
Matter of Pardee v. Rayfield	1920 230 N. Y. 543	186
Matter of Patterson	1911 146 A. D. 286	199
Matter of Potts v. Kaplan	1934 264 N. Y. 110	190
Matter of Reynolds	1911 202 N. Y. 430	217
Matter of Richards	1917 221 N. Y. 684	74
Matter of Richmond Railways Inc. v. Gilchrist	1929 225 A. D. 371	128
Matter of Rogers v. Craig	1921 231 N. Y. 186	42
Matter of Rosenthal	1935 269 N. Y. 584	140
Matter of Ruppert v. Rees	1914 212 N. Y. 514	73
Matter of Sacks	1935 155 Misc. 233	94
Matter of Schmidlapp	1923 236 N. Y. 278	204
Matter of Scott	1936 158 Misc. 401	95
Matter of Seeley	1907 190 N. Y. 158	188
Matter of Senior v. Boyle	1917 221 N. Y. 414	128
Matter of Simons v. McGuire	1911 145 A. D. 471	189
Matter of Simonson	1927 246 N. Y. 601	204
Matter of Stewart v. Knickerbocker Ice Co.	1919 226 N. Y. 302	82
Matter of Sullivan v. Finegan	1937 275 N. Y. 479	190
Matter of Supervisors of Ontario Co. v. Water Power and Control Commission	1929 227 A. D. 345	113
Matter of Teller	1917 178 A. D. 450	201

			PAGE
Matter of Thomas v. Cohen	1933	146 Misc. 836	76
Matter of Thompson v. Elliott	1934	152 Misc. 188	47
Matter of Thornburgh	1911	72 Misc. 619	48
Matter of Town of Tonawanda	1926	127 Misc. 852	113
Matter of Towne v. Porter	1908	128 A. D. 717	129
Matter of Troy v. Cruise	1927	244 N. Y. 529	50
Matter of Trustees of Village of Saratoga Springs v. Saratoga Gas, Electric Light, Heat and Power Co.	1908	191 N. Y. 123	175
Matter of Union Bank No. 2	1911	147 A. D. 593	148
Matter of Vanderbilt	1937	163 Misc. 667	206
Matter of VanNess v. Abrams	1926	246 N. Y. 532	204
Matter of Walsh v. Boyle	1917	179 A. D. 582	76
Matter of Walsh v. Walsh	1933	146 Misc. 604	45
Matter of Watson	1919	226 N. Y. 384	207
Matter of Weiden	1933	263 N. Y. 107	198
Matter of Wendel	1918	223 N. Y. 433	201
Matter of Wheeler	1909	62 Misc. 37	87
Matter of Whitewright	1915	89 Misc. 97	203
Matter of Whitten	1912	152 A. D. 506	172
Matter of Wolff v. Cruise	1927	246 N. Y. 537	50
Matter of Wright v. Craig	1922	202 A. D. 684	189
Matthews v. Matthews	1925	240 N. Y. 28	149
Mayflower Farms v. Ten Eyck	1936	297 U. S. 266	164
McCabe v. Gross	1937	274 N. Y. 39	142
McEwan v. The City of New York	1934	242 A. D. 559	105
McGovern v. City of New York	1923	234 N. Y. 377	55
McGuire and Co. v. Lent and Lent	1938	277 N. Y. 694	96
McMaster v. Gould	1925	240 N. Y. 379	147
McNamara v. Keene	1906	49 Misc. 452	90
Mead v. Turner	1909	134 A. D. 691	130
Mendelson v. State	1930	254 N. Y. 530	53
Metropolitan Board of Excise v. Barrie	1866	34 N. Y. 657	168
Metz v. Maddox	1907	189 N. Y. 460	41
Miele v. Chicago, Milwaukee, St. Paul and Pacific Rd. Co.	1934	151 Misc. 137	80
Miller v. Wilson	1915	236 U. S. 373	155
Mills Co. v. State of New York	1906	110 A. D. 843	89
Mintz v. Baldwin	1933	289 U. S. 346	165
Moberg Co. v. Mohr	1923	236 N. Y. 553	207
Moore v. Barker	1936	270 N. Y. 648	96
Moran v. City of New York	1936	270 N. Y. 650	218
Mordred Realities Co. v. Langley	1938	279 N. Y. 636	172
Morehead v. New York	1936	298 U. S. 587	159
Moritz v. United Brethren's Church on Staten Island	1935	269 N. Y. 175	173

TABLE OF CASES CITED

		PAGE
Mortgage Commission v. Daly	1937 165 Misc. 666	96
Moses v. Guaranteed Mortgage Co. of N. Y.	1934 239 A. D. 703	177
Mott v. Krug	1938 278 N. Y. 457	130
Muhlker v. Harlem Railroad Co.	1905 197 U. S. 544	103
Mullane v. McKenzie	1936 269 N. Y. 369	141
Muller v. Oregon	1908 208 U. S. 412	155
Munro v. State	1918 223 N. Y. 208	53
Murnan v. Wabash Railway Co.	1927 220 A. D. 218	81
Murray v. Kaplan	1923 206 A. D. 202	189
Musco v. United Security Co.	1909 186 N. Y. 459	80, 83
Myers v. Moran	1906 113 A. D. 427	89
National Cash Register Co. v. Taylor	1937 276 N. Y. 208	195
Nebbia v. New York	1934 291 U. S. 302	166
Needleman v. Voorhis	1930 254 N. Y. 339	130
Nevins Inc. v. Boland	1938 167 Misc. 428	216
New York v. Latrobe	1929 279 U. S. 421	197
New York Central Railroad Co. v. Bionc	1919 250 U. S. 596	157
New York Central Railroad Co. v. Middleport Gas and Electric Light Co.	1920 193 A. D. 273	176
New York Central Railroad v. Miller	1906 202 U. S. 584	195
New York Central Railroad Co. v. White	1917 243 U. S. 188	156
New York Central and Hudson Railroad Co. v. Williams	1910 199 N. Y. 108	81
New York ex rel. Cohn v. Graves	1937 300 U. S. 308	198
New York ex rel. Silz v. Hesterberg	1908 211 U. S. 31	84
New York ex rel. Whitney v. Graves	1937 299 U. S. 366	198
New York Rapid Transit Corporation v. City of New York	1937 275 N. Y. 258	202
New York Steam Corporation v. City of N. Y.	1935 268 N. Y. 137	132
Niagara County Irrigation and Water Supply Co. v. College Heights Land Co.	1906 111 A. D. 770	104
Nicchia v. New York	1920 254 U. S. 228	212
Noble State Bank v. Haskell	1911 219 U. S. 104	155
Oneonta Light and Power Co. v. Schwarzenbach	1914 164 A. D. 548	112
Old Company's Lehigh Inc. v. Meeker	1935 294 U. S. 227	177
Old Dearborn Distributing Co. v. Seagram Distillers Corporation	1936 299 U. S. 183	160
Osborn v. Cohen	1936 272 N. Y. 55	132
Paddell v. City of New York	1908 211 U. S. 446	202
Parker v. Wallace	1913 80 Misc. 425	210
Pathe Exchange Inc. v. Cobb	1923 236 N. Y. 539	63
Patti v. The United Surety Co.	1908 61 Misc. 445	83

			PAGE
Pauchogue Land Corporation v. Long Island Park Commission	1926	243 N. Y. 15	100
Pelletreau v. Greene Consolidated Gold Mining Co.	1906	49 Misc. 233	83
Pelo v. Stevens	1909	66 Misc. 35	193
Pennington Furniture Co. v. Miller Furniture Co.	1934	153 Misc. 669	46
People ex rel. Academy Housing Corporation v. Miller	1937	163 Misc. 500	208
People ex rel. Adirondack Power and Light Corporation v. Durey	1927	221 A. D. 294	205
People ex rel. Alpha Portland Cement Co. v. Knapp	1920	230 N. Y. 48	196, 198
People ex rel. American Exchange National Bank v. Purdy	1909	196 N. Y. 270	202
People ex rel. American Exchange National Bank v. Purdy	1910	199 N. Y. 51	202
People ex rel. Ammon v. Johnson	1906	114 A. D. 876	71
People ex rel. Andrews v. Zacker	1908	126 A. D. 744	70
People ex rel. Ballin v. O'Connell	1921	230 N. Y. 655	171
People ex rel. Bank of America v. State Tax Commission	1926	244 N. Y. 56	204
People ex rel. Battista v. Christian	1928	249 N. Y. 314	64
People ex rel. Berger v. The Warden	1917	176 A. D. 602	71
People ex rel. Best and Co. v. Graves	1934	265 N. Y. 431	205
People ex rel. Board of Commissioners for Improvement on the Great Chazy River v. Sancomb	1932	259 N. Y. 1	212
People ex rel. Boenig v. Hegeman	1916	172 A. D. 94	203
People ex rel. Borowick v. Hunt	1913	157 A. D. 818	46
People ex rel. Boyle v. Cruise	1921	231 N. Y. 639	116
People ex rel. Brixton Operating Corporation v. La Fetra	1920	194 A. D. 523	171
People ex rel. Bryant v. Zimmerman	1926	241 N. Y. 405	62, 63
People ex rel. Buffalo and Fort Erie Public Bridge Authority v Davis	1938	277 N. Y. 292	141
People ex rel. Burns v. Flaherty	1907	119 A. D. 462	65
People ex rel. Carmody v. Luce	1912	204 N. Y. 478	52
People ex rel. Carnerale v. Brophy	1938	277 N. Y. 667	72
People ex rel. Cavanagh v. Waldo	1911	72 Misc. 416	182
People ex rel. Central Trust Co. v. Prendergast	1911	202 N. Y. 188	143
People ex rel. Cerzosie v. The Warden	1918	224 N. Y. 307	71
People ex rel. Chadbourne v. Voorhis	1923	236 N. Y. 437	73
People ex rel. City of Geneva v. Geneva, Waterloo, Seneca Falls and Cayuga Lake Traction Co.	1906	112 A. D. 581	89

TABLE OF CASES CITED 239

		PAGE
People ex rel. City of Middletown v. McBride	1936 272 N. Y. 563	134
People ex rel. City of New York v. Neville	1918 183 A. D. 799	130
People ex rel. City of New York v. Stillings	1909 134 A. D 480	141
People ex rel. Clark v. Gilchrist	1926 243 N. Y. 173	211
People ex rel. Cockcroft v. Miller	1919 187 A. D. 704	172
People ex rel. Cohn v. Graves	1936 246 A. D. 335	198
People ex rel. Cohoes Railway Co. v. The Public Service Commission	1911 143 A. D. 769	90
People ex rel. Connecticut Mutual Life Insurance Co. v. Kelsey	1906 116 A. D. 97	200
People ex rel. Consolidated Water Co. v. Barrett	1910 68 Misc. 59	202
People ex rel. Cossey v. Grout	1904 179 N. Y. 417	151
People ex rel. Cotte v. Gilbert	1919 226 N. Y. 103	139
People ex rel. Crane v. Hablo	1920 228 N. Y. 309	49
People ex rel. Dare v. Howell	1916 174 A. D. 118	128
People ex rel. Delaware and Hudson Co. v. The Public Service Commission	1910 140 A. D. 839	90
People ex rel. Dixon v. Lewis	1937 249 A. D. 464	69
People ex rel. Donner-Hanna Coke Corporation v. Burke	1928 248 N. Y. 507	209
People ex rel. Doscher v. Sisson	1918 222 N. Y. 387	168
People ex rel. Doyle v. Atwell	1921 232 N. Y. 96	62
People ex rel. Durham Realty Corporation v. LaFetra	1921 230 N. Y. 429	171
People ex rel. Duryea v. Wilber	1910 198 N. Y. 1	180
People ex rel. Eckerson v. Board of Education of Haverstraw	1908 126 A. D. 414	210
People ex rel. Eisman v. Ronner	1906 185 N. Y. 285	202
People ex rel. Empie v. Smith	1915 166 A. D. 406	203
People ex rel. Enright v. Meyers	1911 71 Misc. 77	65
People ex rel. Equitable Life Ass. Society v. Pierce	1918 104 Misc. 343	92
People ex rel. Farrington v. Mensching	1907 187 N. Y. 8	208
People ex rel. Ferguson v. Reardon	1910 197 N. Y. 236	67
People ex rel. Fish v. Sandstrom	1938 167 Misc. 436	63
People ex rel. Frank v. McCann	1930 253 N. Y. 221	47
People ex rel. Griffith Inc. v. Loughman	1928 249 N. Y. 369	197
People ex rel. Haight v. Brown	1915 216 N. Y. 674	143
People ex rel. Hatch v. Reardon	1906 110 A. D. 821	194
People ex rel. Heminway v. Bostleman	1913 82 Misc. 629	46
People ex rel. Hill v. Hesterberg	1906 184 N. Y. 126	84
People ex rel. Hon Yost v. Becker	1911 203 N. Y. 201	125
People ex rel. Horton v. Prendergast	1928 248 N. Y. 215	104
People ex rel. Hotchkiss v. Smith	1912 206 N. Y. 231	74
People ex rel. Hubert v. Kaiser	1912 150 A. D. 541	64
People ex rel. Hunt v. Lane	1909 132 A. D. 406	69

		PAGE
People ex rel. H. D. H. Realty Corporation v. Murphy	1921 230 N. Y. 654	171
People ex rel. International Salt Co. v. Graves	1934 242 A. D. 124	198
People ex rel. Iroquois Door Co. v. Knapp	1919 186 A. D. 172	201
People ex rel. Isaacs v. Moran	1912 150 A. D. 226	203
People ex rel. Kipnis v. McCann	1921 199 A. D. 30	46
People ex rel. Kleinger v. Wilson	1938 254 A. D. 406	71
People ex rel. Krohn v. The Warden	1915 215 N. Y. 201	153
People ex rel. Lemon v. Elmore	1931 256 N. Y. 489	66, 194
People ex rel. Levy Dairy Co. v. Wilson	1917 179 A. D. 416	163
People ex rel. Liebowitz v. The Warden	1919 186 A. D. 730	71
People ex rel. Long v. Whitney	1911 143 A. D. 17	189
People ex rel. Luciano v. Murphy	1937 249 A. D. 879	66
People ex rel. Luther v. McDermott	1934 265 N. Y. 47	208
People ex rel. Luyster v. Cocks	1916 219 N. Y. 628	50
People ex rel. Mayo v. Hanley	1919 108 Misc. 591	65
People ex rel. McAuley v. Wahle	1908 124 A. D. 762	164
People ex rel. McEachron v. Bashford	1908 128 A. D. 351	168
People ex rel. Moore v. Holmes	1912 151 A. D. 257	183
People ex rel. Moskowitz v. Jenkins	1910 140 A. D. 786	173
People ex rel. Mount v. Chapter General of America, Knights of St. John of Malta	1909 132 A. D. 410	91
People ex rel. Nash v. Loughman	1927 245 N. Y. 649	197
People ex rel. New York and Albany Lighterage Co. v. Lynch	1932 259 N. Y. 639	195
People ex rel. New York Central and Hudson River Railroad Co. v. Woodbury	1910 74 Misc. 131	206
People ex rel. New York Electric Lines Co. v. Ellison	1906 115 A. D. 254	89
People ex rel. New York, New Haven and Hartford Railroad Co. v. Public Service Commission	1914 159 A. D. 531	174
People ex rel. New York, Westchester and Boston Railway Co. v. The Public Service Commission	1920 193 A. D. 445	175
People ex rel. Noble v. Mitchel	1917 220 N. Y. 86	50
People ex rel. Northern Finance Corporation v. Lynch	1933 262 N. Y. 477	196
People ex rel. Olin v. Hennessy	1912 206 N. Y. 33	112
People ex rel. Patrick v. Frost	1909 133 A. D. 179	64
People ex rel. Peabody v. Chanler	1909 133 A. D. 159	70
People ex rel. Peaks v. Voorhis	1926 243 N. Y. 420	218
People ex rel. Pelham v. Village of Pelham	1915 215 N. Y. 374	129
People ex rel. Pintler v. Transue	1911 174 Misc. 504	185
People ex rel. Pratt v. Goldfogle	1926 242 N. Y. 277	195

TABLE OF CASES CITED

		PAGE
People ex rel. Presbrey Co. v. Lynch	1934 265 N. Y. 454	205
People ex rel. Qua v. Gaffney	1911 142 A. D. 122	188
People ex rel. Rayland Realty Co. v. Fagan	1921 230 N. Y. 653	171
People ex rel. Rodgers v. Coler	1901 166 N. Y. 1	151
People ex rel. Roosevelt Hospital v. Raymond	1908 126 A. D. 720	200
People ex rel. Ross v. Wilson	1937 250 A. D. 143	72
People ex rel. Salisbury Axle Co. v. Lynch	1932 259 N. Y. 228	207
People ex rel. Sanford v. Thayer	1923 120 Misc. 571	66
People ex rel. Saranac Land and Timber Co. v. The Extraordinary Term of the Supreme Court	1917 220 N. Y. 487	43
People ex rel. Simpson Company v. Kempner	1913 154 A. D. 674	149
People ex rel. Slade v. Boice	1909 63 Misc. 357	45
People ex rel. Squires v. Hand	1913 158 A. D. 510	112
People ex rel. Stafford v. Travis	1921 231 N. Y. 339	199
People ex rel. Stebbins v. Purdy	1931 144 A. D. 361	203
People ex rel. Studwell v. Archer	1910 142 A. D. 71	139
People ex rel. Terminal and Town Taxi Corporation v. Walsh	1922 202 A. D. 651	199
People ex rel. Tipaldo v. Morehead	1936 270 N. Y. 233	159
People ex rel. Treat v. Coler	1901 166 N. Y. 144	151
People ex rel. Union Sulphur Co. v. Glynn	1908 125 A. D. 328	195
People ex rel. Veteran Volunteer Firemen v. Metz	1907 128 A. D. 565	142
People ex rel. Village of Brownville v. Public Service Commission	1925 240 N. Y. 586	176
People ex rel. Wagstaff v. Matthews	1938 168 Misc. 188	47
People ex rel. Welch v. Bard	1913 209 N. Y. 304	42
People ex rel. Welch v. Dunn	1915 168 A. D. 678	133
People ex rel. Whitman v. Woodward	1912 150 A. D. 770	64
People ex rel. Williams Engineering and Contracting Co. v. Metz	1908 193 N. Y. 148	152
People ex rel. Wogan v. Rafferty	1913 208 N. Y. 451	55
	1912 77 Misc. 258	30
People ex rel. Wood v. Draper	1857 15 N. Y. 532	115
People ex rel. Woronoff v. Mallon	1918 222 N. Y. 456	70
People v. Ahearn	1909 196 N. Y. 221	127
People v. Altman	1933 241 A. D. 858	63
People v. American Socialist Society	1922 202 A. D. 640	62
People v. Arcidiaco	1935 156 Misc. 461	68
People v. Arensberg	1887 105 N. Y. 123	163
People v. Ashley	1918 184 A. D. 520	63
People v. Atlas	1918 183 A. D. 595	167
People v. Beakes Dairy Co.	1918 222 N. Y. 416	165
People v. Berman	1935 156 Misc. 463	68
People v. Blanchard	1919 110 Misc. 402	169

		PAGE
People v. Blumenthal (alias Blumenfeld)	1936 157 Misc. 943	178
People v. Braunstein	1928 248 N. Y. 308	186
People v. Brooklyn Cooperage Company	1907 187 N. Y. 142	192
People v. Buffalo Cold Storage Co.	1920 113 Misc. 479	114
People v. Cahill	1908 126 A. D. 391	69
People v. Charles Schweinler Press	1915 214 N. Y. 395	152, 155
People v. Clark	1910 139 A. D. 687	49
People v. Clark	1910 140 A. D. 150	164
People v. Cook	1921 197 A. D. 155	208
People v. Crane	1915 214 N. Y. 154	62
People v. Desowitz (Complaint of Rabinowitz)	1938 166 Misc. 1	161
People v. Erie Railroad Co.	1910 198 N. Y. 369	82
People v. Finkelstein	1915 167 A. D. 591	114, 167
People v. Friedman	1928 249 N. Y. 86	174
People v. Fritzsche	1920 111 Misc. 336	169
People v. Frudenberg	1913 155 A. D. 199	165
People v. Gillson	1889 109 N. Y. 389	151
People v. Gitlow	1992 234 N. Y. 132	60, 61
People v. Gowasky	1927 244 N. Y. 451	72
People v. Grant	1935 267 N. Y. 508	168
People v. Griswold	1914 213 N. Y. 92	180
People v. Guiton	1912 152 A. D. 614	164
People v. Harrison	1915 170 A. D. 802	179
People v. Heron	1926 127 Misc. 141	72
People v. Hewson	1917 181 A. D. 202	180
People v. Hopkins	1924 208 A. D. 438	45
People v. Hudson River Connecting Railway	1920 228 N. Y. 203	79
People v. International Bridge Co.	1918 223 N. Y. 137	81
People v. Ireland Realty Co.	1916 96 Misc. 18	108
People v. Kassis	1931 145 Misc. 493	67
People v. Klinck Packing Company	1915 214 N. Y. 121	159
People v. Koster	1907 121 A. D. 852	164
People v. Kozanowski	1930 136 Misc. 353	179
People v. Lipschitz	1923 120 Misc. 633	65
People v. Lochner	1904 177 N. Y. 145	152
People v. Madden	1907 120 A. D. 338	71
People v. Marcus	1906 185 N. Y. 257	153
People v. Martin	1922 203 A. D. 423	182
People v. Marx	1885 99 N. Y. 377	151, 163
People v. McClellan	1907 56 Misc. 123	49
People v. McKinley Realty and Construction Co.	1918 182 A. D. 773	171
People v. Meola	1920 193 A. D. 487	181
People v. Mitchell	1934 266 N. Y. 15	66
People v. Moynihan	1923 121 Misc. 34	169
People v. Mulford	1910 140 A. D. 716	180

TABLE OF CASES CITED 243

		PAGE
People v. Nebbia	1933 262 N. Y. 259	165, 225
People v. Neff	1907 122 A. D. 135	43
People v. Nicchia	1918 224 N. Y. 637	212
People v. Orange County Road Construction Company	1903 175 N. Y. 84	151
People v. Park Row Realty Co.	1914 88 Misc. 254	212
People v. Parve	1918 181 A. D. 499	44
People v. Perretta	1930 253 N. Y. 305	165
People v. Persce	1912 204 N. Y. 397	69
People v. Platt	1819 17 Johnson 195	99, 100
People v. Princeton Inc.	1935 154 Misc. 811	216
People v. Qualey	1914 210 N. Y. 202	70
People v. Reiss	1938 255 A. D. 509	69
People v. Ringe	1910 197 N. Y. 143	179
People v. Rosenheimer	1913 209 N. Y. 115	69, 181
People v. Ryan	1930 230 A. D. 252	165
People v. Ryan	1935 267 N. Y. 133	168, 216
People v. Ryan	1936 248 A. D. 236	169
People v. Sanger	1918 222 N. Y. 192	62
People v. Santa Clara Lumber Co.	1914 213 N. Y. 61	101
People v. Schade	1936 161 Misc. 212	69
People v. Stein	1903 80 A. D. 457	65
People v. Stryker	1924 124 Misc. 1	182
People v. Tremaine	1929 252 N. Y. 27	215, 219
People v. Teussher	1928 248 N. Y. 454	165
People v. Vitusky	1914 155 A. D. 139	70
People v. Von Kampen	1914 210 N. Y. 381	165
People v. Waldorf-Astoria Hotel Co.	1907 118 A. D. 723	84
People v. Weller	1924 237 N. Y. 316	173
People v. Willi	1919 109 Misc. 79	169
People v. Williams	1907 189 N. Y. 131	152
People v. Yarbrough	1938 168 Misc. 769	82
People's Gas and Electric Co. v. The City of Oswego	1924 238 N. Y. 606	143
Pomeroy v. Hocking Valley Railway Co.	1917 220 N. Y. 645	84
Power v. Pennsylvania	188 127 U. S. 678	151
Pratter v. Lascoff	1933 261 N. Y. 509	179
Prescott v. Ferris	1937 251 A. D. 113	209
Preston Co. v. Funkhouser	1933 261 N. Y. 140	94
Public Service Commission v Booth	1915 170 A. D. 590	176
Public Service Commission v. Brooklyn Borough Gas Co.	1919 189 A. D. 62	175
Ralph v. Cronk	1934 150 Misc. 69	88
Ramapo Water Co. v. City of New York	1915 236 U. S. 579	102
Raphael v. Goldman Furniture Co.	1935 246 A. D. 548	88

			PAGE
Red Cross Line v. Atlantic Fruit Co.	1924	264 U. S. 109	93
Reid v. Stevens	1910	70 Misc. 177	127
Reis v. City of New York	1906	113 A. D. 464	102
Richardson v. Scudder	1928	247 N. Y. 401	41
Richman v. Consolidated Gas Co.	1906	114 A. D. 216	175
Riley v. Massachusetts	1914	232 U. S. 671	155
Roberts v. New York City	1935	295 U.S. 264	103
Robertson v. Zimmerman	1935	268 N. Y. 352	125, 134
Robia Holding Corp. v. Walker	1930	230 A. D. 666	113
Rochester Exposition Assoc. v. Bogorad	1932	149 Misc. 200	46
Rochester Railway Co. v. City of Rochester	1907	205 U. S. 236	200
Rojzenblitt v. Polish Trans-Atlantic Shipping Co.	1936	162 Misc. 251	80
Roman v. Lobe	1926	243 N. Y. 51	172
Roosevelt Memorial Association of Oyster Bay v. Jones	1926	244 N. Y. 538	105
Rosalsky v. State of New York	1930	254 N. Y. 117	53
Rosenthal v. New York	1912	226 U. S. 260	174
Rosa v. State	1919	186 A. D. 156	53
Rueffer v. Dept. of Agriculture and Markets	1938	279 N. Y. 16	81
Ruland v. Tuthill	1919	187 A. D. 20	113
Russo v. Illinois Surety Co.	1910	141 A. D. 690	92
Sakolski v. Schenkel	1906	50 Misc. 151	44
Saint John v. New York	1906	201 U.S. 633	164
Salomon v. State Tax Commission	1929	278 U.S. 484	204
Sammis v. Huntington	1919	186 A. D. 463	128
Saratoga State Waters Corp. v. Pratt	1920	227 N. Y. 429	87
Schafran and Finkel Inc. v. Lowenstein and Sons Inc.	1938	254 A. D. 218	150
Schieffelin v. Goldsmith	1930	253 N. Y. 243	50
Schieffelin v. Hylan	1923	236 N. Y. 254	143
Schieffelin v. Kelliher	1925	125 Misc. 305	187
Schieffelin v. Komfort	1914	212 N. Y. 520	218
Schieffelin v. Warren	1929	250 N. Y. 396	110
Seeck and Kade Inc. v. Tomshinsky	1935	269 N. Y. 613	160
Seglin Construction Co. v. State	1937	249 A. D. 476	54
Seignious v. Rice	1936	273 N. Y. 44	180, 216
Sheridan v. Tucker	1911	145 A. D. 145	203
Sherrill v. O'Brien	1907	188 N. Y. 185	217
Silberberg Bros. v. Douglas	1909	62 Misc. 340	64
Simson v. Parker	1907	190 N. Y. 19	142
Skinner v. Schwab	1919	188 A. D. 457	93
Sliosberg v. New York Life Ins. Co.	1927	244 N. Y. 482	88
Smith v. City of Buffalo	1906	51 Misc. 244	111
Smith v. Endicott Johnson Corp.	1921	199 A. D. 198	91

TABLE OF CASES CITED

		PAGE
Smith v. Loughman	1927 245 N. Y. 486	197
Smith v. Smith	1916 174 A. D. 473	127
Smith v. Smythe	1910 197 N. Y. 457	141
Smith v. The Western Railway Co.	1911 203 N. Y. 499	66
Smith v. Zimmerman	1935 268 N. Y. 491	125
Sommer v. Lorsch and Co.	1930 254 N. Y. 146	49
Southern Pacific Co. v. Jensen	1917 244 U. S. 205	156
Sperduto v. New York City Interborough Railroad Co.	1919 186 A. D. 145	158
Sporza v. The German Savings Bank	1908 192 N. Y. 8	66
Sprintz v. Sexton	1908 126 A. D. 421	55
Standard Oil Co. v. Marysville	279 U. S. 582, 586, 587	214
Stanton v. The Board of Supervisors of the County of Essex	1906 112 A. D. 877	138
State Board of Pharmacy v. Bellinger	1910 138 A. D. 12	219
State Board of Pharmacy v. Matthews	1910 197 N. Y. 353	181
State Water Supply Commission v. Curtis	1908 192 N. Y. 319	103
Stern v. Metropolitan Life Ins. Co.	1915 169 A. D. 217	179
Stewart and Co. v. Rivara	1927 274 U. S. 64	93
Stickney v. Kelsey	1908 209 U. S. 419	209
Strauss v. Enright	1918 105 Misc. 367	182
Stromberg v. California	1931 283 U. S. 359	63
Sturges and Burn Mfg. Co. v. Beauchamp	1913 231 U. S. 320	155
Swan v. Woolworth Co.	1927 129 Misc. 500	157
Swanberg v. The City of New York	1908 123 A. D. 774	176
Sweet v. Miller	1933 147 Misc. 806	81
Taggart's Paper Co. v. State of N. Y.	1919 187 A. D. 843	104
Taylor v. Porter	1843 4 Hill 140	101
The Miami Valley Gas and Fuel Co. v. Mills	1913 157 A. D. 542	92
Thomann v. City of Rochester	1930 230 A. D. 612	150
Tieck v. McKenna	1906 115 A. D. 701	170
Tommasi v. Archibald	1906 114 A. D. 838	107
Travis v. Yale and Towne Manufacturing Co.	1920 252 U. S. 60	198
Troy Union Railroad Co. v. Mealy	1920 254 U. S. 47	200
Tyson v. Banton	1927 273 U. S. 418	173
Valley Farms Co. v. County of Westchester	1923 261 U. S. 155	207
Valley Farms Co. v. Yonkers	1921 231 N.Y. 558	207
Van Tuyl v. Sullivan	1915 173 A. D. 391	177
Vaughn v. State of New York	1936 272 N. Y. 102	205
Vroman v. Fish	1919 224 N. Y. 540	139
Wadsworth v. Menzie	1919 105 Misc. 697	186
Ward and Gow v. Krinsky	1922 259 U.S. 503	157
Watson v. The State Comptroller	1920 254 U. S. 122	207
Weisberg v. Weisberg	1906 112 A. D. 231	89

		PAGE
Weller v. New York	1925 268 U. S. 319	173
Wendell v. Lavin	1927 246 N. Y. 115	129
West Coast Hotel Co. v. Parrish	1937 300 U. S. 379	159
West End Avenue Inc. v. Stern	1921 230 N. Y. 652	171
Weston v. State	1933 262 N. Y. 46	55
West Virginia Pulp and Paper Co. of Delaware v. Peck	1918 104 Misc. 172	109
Whaley v. County of Monroe	1932 235 A. D. 334	211
Wheeler v. New York	1914 233 U. S. 434	197
Wheeler v. State	1907 190 N. Y. 406	53
White v. Sparkill Realty Co.	1930 280 U. S. 500	103
White v. White	1912 154 A. D. 250	92
Williams v. Quill	1938 277 N. Y. 1	159
Williams v. Rivenburg	1911 145 A. D. 93	167
Williams v. State of New York	1936 273 N. Y. 458	205
Williamsburgh Savings Bank v. State	1926 243 N. Y. 231	54
Wolff v. Mortgage Commission	1936 270 N. Y. 428	96
Wright v. Albany Port District Commission	1938 254 A. D. 915	211
Wright v Hart	1905 182 N. Y. 330	55
Wynehamer v. People	1856 13 N. Y. 378	150, 168
Zambrotto v. Jeannette	1936 160 Misc. 558	47

SELECTED BIBLIOGRAPHY

Primary Sources

PRINTED

Appellate Division Reports, Volumes 110 to 235 (Albany, 1906-1939).
Documents of the Constitutional Convention of the State of New York (Albany, 1915).
Hoadly, George H., *The Constitutional Guarantees of the Right of Property as Affected by Recent Decisions* (Saratoga Springs, 1889).
Johnson, *Reports of Cases Argued and Determined in the Supreme Court of Judicature, and in the Court for the Trial of Impeachments and the Correction of Errors in the State of New York*, by William Johnson, Counsellor at Law, Volume 17, 3rd edition; with additional notes and references (Philadelphia, 1839).
Johnson Chancery, *Reports of Cases Argued in the Courts of Chancery of New York*, Volume 2, 2nd edition, Revised and Corrected (Philadelphia, 1837).
Miscellaneous Reports, Volumes 49 to 169 (Albany, 1906-1939).
New York Red Book, An illustrated state manual, Volumes for 1905, 1913, 1926, 1927, 1938 (Albany).
New York Reports, Volumes 183 to 279 (Albany, 1906-1939).
Outlook, The, Volume 98 (New York, 1911).
Roosevelt, Theodore, *Progressive Principles* (New York, 1913).
United States Supreme Court Reports, Volumes 110, 191, 201 to 305, Government Printing Office (Washington, D. C., 1884, 1904, 1906 to 1938).

Secondary Sources

BOOKS

Association of American Law Schools, ed., *Selected Essays in Constitutional Law*, Volumes I-V (New York, 1938).
Aumann, Francis R., *The Changing American Legal System: Some Selected Phases* (Columbus, Ohio, 1940).
Bancroft, George, *A Plea for the Constitution of the United States of America Wounded in the House of Its Guardians* (New York, 1886).
Beard, Charles A., *Supreme Court and the Constitution* (New York, 1912).
Boudin, Louis B., *Government by Judiciary* (New York, 1932).
Cardozo, Benjamin N., *The Jurisdiction of the Court of Appeals of the State of New York*, 2nd Edition (Albany, 1909).
Carr, Robert K., *The Supreme Court and Judicial Review* (New York, 1942).
Chafee, Zechariah, *Free Speech in the United States* (New York, 1934).
Cohen, Henry, *The Powers of the Court of Appeals* (New York, 1934).
Commons, John R. and Andrews, John B., *Principles of Labor Legislation*, 4th Revised Edition (New York, 1936).
Corwin, Edward S., *Court over Constitution; a Study of Judicial Review as an Instrument of Popular Government* (Princeton, 1938).

SELECTED BIBLIOGRAPHY

——, *The Doctrine of Judicial Review* (Princeton, 1914).
Coxe, Brinton, *An Essay on Judicial Power and Unconstitutional Legislation; being a commentary on parts of the Constitution of the United States* (Philadelphia, 1893).
Cushman, Robert E., *Leading Constitutional Decisions*, 8th Edition (New York, 1946).
Davis, Horace A., *The Judicial Veto* (Boston and New York, 1914).
Dictionary of American Biography, edited by Allen Johnson and Dumas Malone (New York, 1928-1936).
Dougherty, John Hampden, *Constitutional History of the State of New York*, 2nd edition (New York, 1915).
——, *Power of Federal Judiciary over Legislation: its origin; the power to set aside laws; boundaries of the power; judicial independence; existing evils and remedies* (New York and London, 1912).
Field, Oliver P., *The Effect of an Unconstitutional Statute* (Minneapolis, 1935).
——, *Judicial Review of Legislation in Ten Selected States* (Bloomington, Indiana, 1943).
Flick, Alexander C., *History of the State of New York*, Volumes VII to X (New York, 1935).
Freund, Ernst, *The Police Power, Public Policy and Constitutional Rights* (Chicago, 1904).
Haines, Charles G., *The American Doctrine of Judicial Supremacy* (Berkeley, 1932).
Haynes, Evan, *The Selection and Tenure of Judges* (The National Conference of Judicial Councils, 1944).
Hixson, Joseph H., *The Judicial Veto in Ohio*, Unpublished M. A. thesis, (Ohio State University, 1922).
Lincoln, Charles Z., *Constitutional History of New York*, Volumes I to V (New York, 1906).
MacDonald, Austin F., *American State Government and Administration*, 3rd Edition (New York, 1946).
McBain, Howard L., *The Law and the Practice of Municipal Home Rule* (New York, 1916).
McGoldrick, Joseph D., *Law and Practice of Municipal Home Rule, 1916-1930* (New York, 1933).
McLaughlin, Andrew C., *The Courts, the Constitution and Parties; studies in constitutional history and politics* (Chicago, 1912).
Meigs, William M., *The Relation of the Judiciary to the Constitution* (New York, 1919).
Mott, Rodney L., *Due Process of Law, A Historical Analytical Treatise of the Principles and Methods Followed by the Courts in the Application of the Concept of the "Law of the Land"* (Indianapolis, 1926).
National Cyclopedia of American Biography (New York, 1892 to 1938).
National Industrial Conference Board, *Industrial Progress and Regulatory Legislation in New York State* (New York, 1927).

Nelson, Margaret V., *A Study of Judicial Review in Virginia* (New York, 1947).
New York State Bar Association Reports 1913, 1914, 1915 (Albany, 1914, 1915, 1916).
New York State Constitutional Convention Committee, Volume I, *New York State Constitution Annotated* (Albany, 1938).
——, Volume II, *Amendments Proposed to New York Constitution, 1895 to 1937* (Albany, 1938).
——, Volume IV, *State and Local Government in New York* (Albany, 1938).
——, Volume VI, *Problems Relating to the Bill of Rights and General Welfare* (Albany, 1938).
——, Volume VII, *Problems Relating to Legislative Organization and Powers* (Albany, 1938).
——, Volume IX, *Problems Relating to Judicial Administration and Organization* (Albany, 1938).
——, Volume XI, *Problems Relating to Home Rule and Local Government* (Albany, 1938).
Ralston, Jackson H., *Study and Report for American Federation of Labor upon Judicial Control over Legislatures as to Constitutional Questions* (Washington, 1919).
Ransom, William L., *Majority Rule and the Judiciary; an examination of current proposals for constitutional change affecting the relation of the courts to legislation* (New York, 1912).
Roe, Gilbert E., *Our Judicial Oligarchy* (New York, 1912).
Spooner, Walter W. and Smith, Roy B., *History of the State of New York, political and governmental*, edited by Roy B. Smith, Volume IV, 1896-1920, by Roscoe C. E. Brown (New York, 1922).
Twiss, Benjamin R., *Lawyers and the Constitution, How Laissez Faire Came to the Supreme Court* (Princeton, 1942).
Warren, Charles, *The Supreme Court in United States History*, Volumes I to III (Boston, 1922).
White's Conspectus of American Biography, A Tabulated Record of American History and Biography (New York, 1937).
World Almanac and Book of Facts 1941 (New York, 1941).
Wright, Benjamin F., *The Contract Clause of the Constitution* (Cambridge, 1938).
——, *The Growth of American Constitutional Law* (Boston, 1942).

ARTICLES

Beard, Charles A., "*The Supreme Court; Usurper or Grantee?*" Political Science Quarterly, 27: 1-35 (March, 1912).
Boudin, Louis B., "*Government by Judiciary*," Political Science Quarterly, 26: 238-270 (June, 1911).
Corwin, Edward S., "*The Basic Doctrine of American Constitutional Law*," Michigan Law Review, 12: 247-276 (February, 1914).

——, "*The Doctrine of Due Process of Law before the Civil War*," Harvard Law Review, 24: 366-385, 460-479 (March and April, 1911).

——, "*The Establishment of Judicial Review*," Michigan Law Review, 9: 102-125, 283-316 (December, 1910) and February, 1911).

——, "*The Establishment of Judicial Review in New York*," Michigan Law Review, 15: 281-306 (February, 1917).

Edgerton, Henry W., "*The Incidence of Judicial Control over Congress*," Cornell Law Quarterly, 22: 299-348 (April, 1937).

Meigs, William M., "*The Relation of the Judiciary to the Constitution*," American Law Review, 19: 174-203 (March-April, 1885).

INDEX

Ahearn, John F., 42
Anderson, William, 13
Andrews, John B., 155

Bancroft, George, 8
Baumes Law, 71
Beard, Charles, 8
Benedict, Russell, 30
Bliss, F. Walter, 210
Bonynge, Paul, 43
Booth cases, 8
Borah, William E., 36
Boudin, Louis B., 8, 29, 44, 155
Brandeis, Louis D., 61, 154

Cardozo, Benjamin N., 31, 32, 61, 131, 132
Carr, Robert K., 8, 9
Cohen, Henry, 32
Commons, John R., 155
Cooley, Thomas M, 146
Corwin, Edward S., 8, 9, 10, 87, 101, 145, 150, 194
Cotillo, Salvatore, 47, 48
Coxe, Brinton, 8
Crane, Frederick E., 131, 213
Cullen, Edgar M., 153
Cushman, Robert Eugene, 14
Cuvillier, Louis A., 36, 37

Davis, Horace A., 8
Dewey, Thomas E., 10
Duncan Company, 109
Dougherty, John Hampden, 8

Edgerton, Henry W., 7, 14

Field, Oliver P., 7, 8, 9, 13
Flick, Alexander C., 15
Foley, James A., 209
Fowler, Robert Ludlow, 29, 203
Freund, Ernst, 154

Haines, Charles Grove, 7, 8, 9
Hamilton, Alexander, 10
Harding, Warren G., 12
Hastings, John A., 34, 37
Haynes, Evan, 155
Hearst, William Randolph, 41
Hixson, Joseph H., 9
Hoadly, George H., 151
Holmes, Oliver W., 14, 61, 78, 152, 155, 173
Hudson River Water-Power and Paper Company, 109

Hughes, Charles E., 12

Kelby, Charles H., 104
Kent, James, 10, 40
Ku Klux Klan, 62, 77

Lehman, Herbert H., 12
Lehman, Irving, 32, 44, 125, 132
Lincoln, Charles Z., 10, 52, 54, 65, 107

MacDonald, Austin F., 35, 159 '
Marshall, John, 28, 86
McBain, Howard L., 115, 116, 117
McClellan, George B., 41
McGoldrick, Joseph D., 120, 121
McLaughlin, Andrew C., 8, 9
Meigs, William M., 8
Merwin, James H., 160
Miller, Nathan L., 12
Mott, Rodney L., 145, 146

Nelson, Margaret V., 9

O'Brien, John F., 125, 132

Pound, Cuthbert, 61, 131
Pound, Roscoe, 154

Ralston, Jackson H., 154
Ransom, William L., 8
Roberts, Owen J., 159, 166, 214
Roe, Gilbert E., 8
Roosevelt, Franklin D., 12
Roosevelt, Theodore, 36, 105, 147, 154

Seabury, Samuel, 44
Smith, Alfred E., 12
Smith, Ray B., 146
Smyth, George W., 47
Spencer, Herbert, 152
Spooner, Walter W., 146
Sulzer, William, 25

Taney, Roger B., 86
Thompson, Smith, 31
Twiss, Benjamin R., 146

Warren, Charles, 8
Werner, William, 39, 153
Whitehorn, Joseph A., 38
Whitman, Charles S., 12
Wilson, town of, 109
Wright, Benjamin F., 8, 9, 86, 87

251